W9-BNI-848

INSIDERS' GUIDE® TO

PORTLAND, MAINE

SARA DONNELLY AND MEREDITH GOAD

INSIDERS' GUIDE®

GUILFORD, CONNECTICUT

AN IMPRINT OF THE GLOBE PEQUOT PRESS

The prices and rates in this guidebook were
confirmed at press time. We recommend, however, that you call establishments before traveling to obtain current information.

INSIDERS' GUIDE®

Text design by Nancy Freeborn
Maps by XNR Productions, Inc. © Morris Book
Publishing, LLC

ISSN 1935-1003
ISBN 978-0-7627-3562-4

Manufactured in the United States of America
First Edition/First Printing

CONTENTS

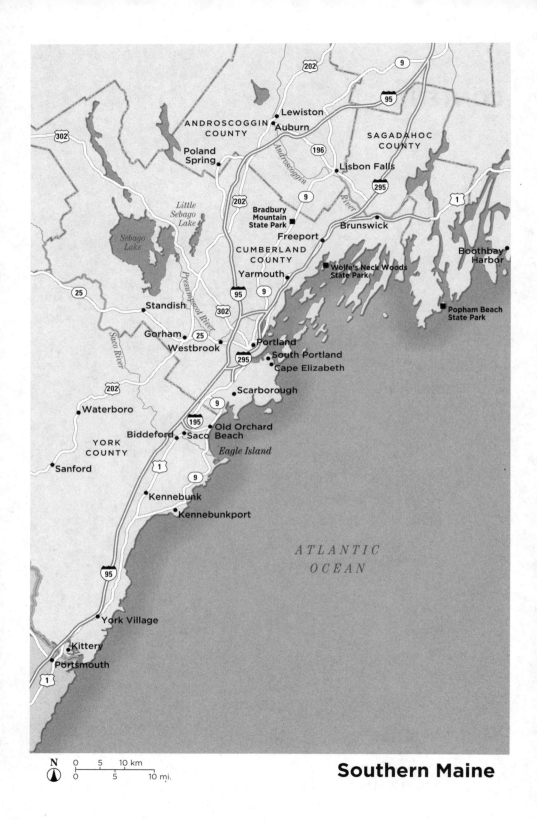

Southern Maine

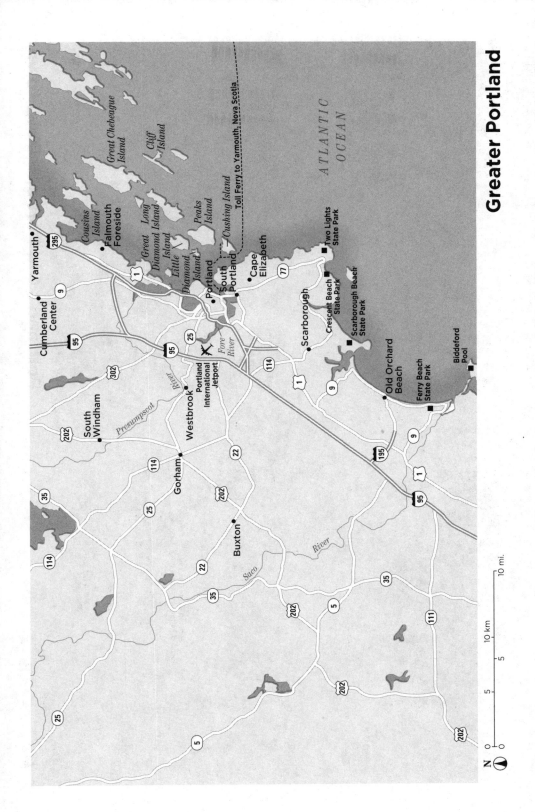

Greater Portland

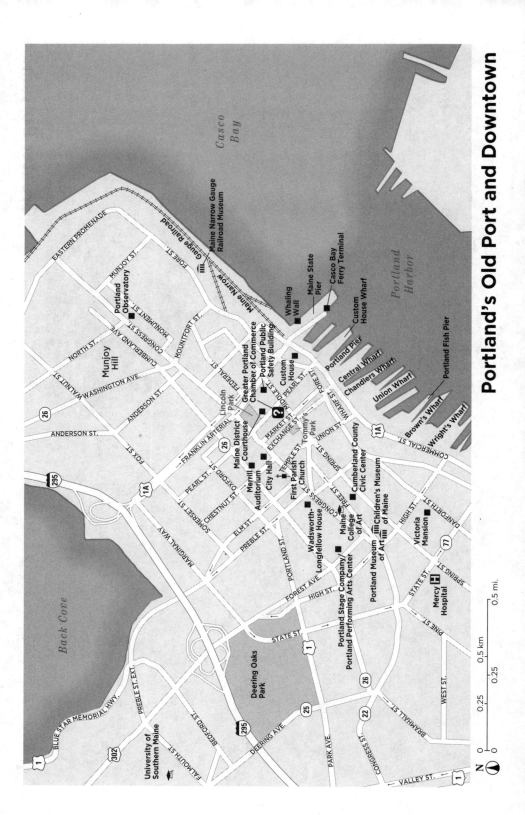

Portland's Old Port and Downtown

PREFACE

Portland, Maine, has it all—a beautiful coast-line, friendly people, an eclectic cosmopolitan flair. I've spent most of my life here, and even when I left to travel the world, I always compared each city to Portland, each street to the street I grew up on, each quaint downtown to our Old Port. Nothing quite measured up to what our 19th-century poet Henry Wadsworth Longfellow called the "city by the sea." Sure, I'm biased, but once you've spent a couple of days here, you may be too. Portland is small enough to foster our unique Maine character, hip enough to infuse some big-city flavor, conscientious enough to protect our parks and environment with an iron fist, and weird enough to keep things interesting even when the weather freezes us in for months on end.

Lately, more and more people must be telling what used to be the best-kept secret in the country. Portland is growing rapidly—there are new, multimillion-dollar luxury developments planned for the Old Port (which only two decades ago was a rowdy ghost town), area real estate prices have skyrocketed, and there are now plenty of shoestring theaters, eclectic secondhand clothing stores, and mixed-media art galleries (when I was growing up here more than a decade ago, the local joke was Portland has only one of everything—but at least it has that one). Portland is a small town growing rapidly into a hip, happening metropolitan hub. But, like Mainers themselves, Portland has never abandoned its humble roots. Evidence of our sense of place is everywhere—it's in the historical landmarks lovingly maintained by hundreds of volunteers, it's in the fierce debates within the city's leadership about maintaining the character of the city in the face of large development opportunities, and it's in the way many Portlanders, every day, value each other. Welcome to the City by the Sea. Enjoy it. We all do.

—Sara Donnelly

ACKNOWLEDGMENTS

Thanks first to my family and friends for helping me pick out the best parts of Portland to detail in this book. Extra appreciation is due my grandparents, whose stories of a lifetime in Portland have given this place such color for me.

There were many Portlanders who helped this project along, either by providing additional information, proofreading chapters for content, or pointing me in the right direction. Among them, I'd like to thank the Maine Historical Society (chiefly its librarian Bill Barry), the Portland Room at the Portland Public Library, Linda Fish of the Greater Portland Convention and Visitors' Bureau, the Portland Planning Department, Portland's Downtown District, the Portland Public Works Department, Portland's city clerk's office, Joe Conforti at the University of Southern Maine, Martha Davoli at Maine Medical Center, the Center for Grieving Children, Greater Portland Landmarks, and the local architecture buffs who helped me.

Finally, I'd like to thank this city. You rock, Portland. Keep it up.

—Sara Donnelly

HOW TO USE THIS BOOK ?

Portland is a community rich in history and the arts, a place where one can bask in the beauty of the natural world during the day and then relax in the evening at a concert or dine at a fine restaurant. This guide is intended to help you navigate your way through this vibrant city by the sea so that you don't miss any of its hidden treasures.

The book begins with the region's historical background, starting with its Native American roots and moving through colonial unrest, devastating fires, wartime, its shipbuilding years, and its development as a booming trading port and maritime center. Throughout these pages, there is ample evidence of Portland's close ties with Casco Bay, a relationship that is reflected in everything from the character of the working waterfront to the city's artistic sensibilities and its social scene. You'll also learn about Portland's emergence as a city steeped in Maine tradition, yet open to the social and economic changes of the 21st century.

Whether you are just visiting Portland or eyeing a permanent move, this book will provide a road map to what's available in transportation, accommodations, and leisure-time activities. To get the lay of the land, read the Area Overview chapter to learn more about specific neighborhoods and vital statistics of the region. Included in this chapter is a chart outlining everything from the weather to major schools and employers. Portland is a fairly easy town to get around in, but if you want to know whether it's more practical to take a cab or the local bus line to your destination, flip to the Getting Here, Getting Around chapter. This chapter, along with the detailed lists of boat cruises in the Beaches and Ocean Activities chapter, also provides extensive information on the best ways to get out on the water. A visit to Portland is not complete without seeing the city from Casco Bay, whether it's aboard a ferryboat making a routine run to one of the islands or a whale-watching cruise steaming out to sea.

The Nightlife, Shopping, and Attractions chapters are clearly organized and offer specific suggestions for how to enjoy the fun side of the city. The Nightlife chapter is organized by type of activity and contains entries on wine bars; lounges; comedy and live music; and movie theaters. Portland has an extensive array of bars and brewpubs, as well as coffeehouses where locals pass long afternoons sipping joe while they work on their laptops or gaze out the window. You'll find a large selection of them listed here. Portland is known as a gay-friendly town, so in this chapter you'll also find listings for the gay bar and club scene. The Shopping chapter will take you to some of the city's hippest specialty shops in the Old Port shopping district and Portland's downtown area and will also point you in the right direction for the bargain-basement outlet stores southern Maine is known for among tourists. This chapter is also for antiques hounds looking for shops to scout for hidden finds.

The Restaurants chapter is by no means intended to be a complete guide to what's available here. Portland is a huge restaurant town, where new places open up practically every week and old favorites quietly close or transform themselves into something new, so it would be impossible to include every dining establishment in the city. View this cross section of restaurants as merely a sampling, although a tasty one, of what the city has to offer. If you don't find what you're looking for in these pages, just ask some locals, and chances are they will be able to point you in the right direction. This is a town that loves food.

The Architecture chapter is more than just a listing of interesting buildings and historical facts. It also offers an actual walking tour of the city that will teach you about the stately mansions and Victorian charm that can be seen in neighborhoods throughout Portland. If you're considering a move here, the Neighborhoods and Real Estate chapter is one that you will want to read. It provides details about family-friendly areas of the city and scopes out the hot real estate market here.

For outdoor fun, consult both the Beaches and Ocean Activities chapter and the Parks and Recreation chapter. The Beaches and Ocean Activities chapter is more than just a listing of local spots to get a tan or take a dip in the chilly (even in August) North Atlantic. It also contains advice on where to go for water sports action, such as kayaking, and fishing. The Parks and Recreation chapter features information on everything from birding to biking. Here, you'll learn about Portland's extensive park system as well as how to get a hunting or fishing license. And if you're dying to see a few of the lighthouses for which Maine is so well known, consult the Attractions chapter. Detailed directions are included.

Finally, although Maine is known as "Vacationland," this guide is intended to help visitors find something to do in Portland year-round. Mainers love their festivals, whether they are held over the winter to get them through the long, cold months, or in summer, when the entire population comes out of hibernation to celebrate the return of warmth and sunshine. You'll find references to these events sprinkled throughout the book, but especially in the Festivals and Annual Events chapter, where they are organized by month.

No matter what time of year you visit Portland, there is plenty to do and see. This guide, through extensive listings and cross-references, will help you find attractions and activities to suit every taste.

AREA OVERVIEW

Be careful when you visit Portland. You might just end up moving here.

It was just a matter of time before people "from away" began discovering all that this small, eclectic city just two hours north of Boston has to offer. In recent years Portland has made any number of "best of" lists created by national magazines or other organizations. In 2005 *Outside* magazine dubbed Portland one of the "New American Dream Towns," a place where lawyers mingle with lobstermen, the White Mountains are only a short drive away, and a "reassuringly high" number of cars have sea kayaks strapped to their roofs. The magazine cited the area's low crime rate, growing demographic diversity, large network of green space, and environmental sensibilities.

Portland has garnered other honors as well: *TravelSmart*, a consumer travel newsletter, called it one of the "10 Safest and Most Culturally Fascinating Cities" in the United States; fineliving.com said it is one of the "10 Perfect Places to Live in America"; and the National Historic Trust deemed Portland one of a "Dozen Distinctive Destinations." The city is often hailed as a great place to raise kids because of good schools and excellent quality of life. It has been called one of the 10 best "art towns" in America because of its distinctive downtown Arts District, its excellent art museum and large number of local galleries, the presence of a fine local art school, and its long tradition of harboring artists who move here for inspiration.

Portland is Maine's largest city, with a population of more than 64,000—more if you count the "Greater Portland area" of surrounding suburbs. The heart of the city is known by locals simply as "the peninsula," the finger of land that points into Casco Bay and contains the Downtown District, city hall, office buildings, restaurants, the Old Port shopping district, and, of course, the waterfront. The city's footprint covers an area of just over 26 square miles and is changing rapidly, even as its red brick character—a reflection of a city in survival mode after suffering a few devastating fires in the past—and its Victorian charm remain intact. Two multimillion-dollar redevelopment projects are in the works downtown, projects that will bring new commercial and residential opportunities to the area.

Portland's climate is illustrative of that old saying, "If you don't like the weather, just wait a minute." Yes, winters can be long and cold, sometimes dipping well below zero, but it's nothing that an old-fashioned "January thaw," with the mercury soaring into the 30s and 40s, can't cure. The city normally gets about 71 inches of snow, with the inch count rising as you move inland. (The warmer ocean air provides a bit of a buffer along the coast during snowstorms.) When the snow melt comes, along with spring rains, the transition to summer can be muddy some years, hence Mainers' fondness for calling it "mud season." But late spring brings flowers and trees popping out all over town. Summer makes everything worth it; as Mainers like to say, if you can't take the winters here, you don't deserve the summers. Summer temperatures average in the high 70s, though some days easily reach the 80s and occasionally even the 90s. But when it's sweltering 30 miles inland, the sea

> **i** Portland is the county seat of Cumberland County, which was incorporated in 1760. The county was named after William, Duke of Cumberland, who was the son of King George II.

breeze along the coast helps to keep things cool in Portland. Sometime around Labor Day, the weather gods seem to flip an invisible switch, and all of a sudden there's a crisp little nip in the air. A deep breath becomes a form of refreshment. No matter how glorious the days of summer, the approach of autumn brings a new energy and excitement to the community. Memory of the previous winter is safely tucked away, and the crunch of colorful leaves underfoot heralds the approach of the first snowfall.

Although Maine is, overall, a conservative place, Portland is more socially liberal than the more rural parts of the state. And it is more racially diverse, as well. About 14 percent of all of Maine's people of color live in Portland. The city is also a refugee resettlement area where refugees from unsettled parts of the world—Sudan, Somalia, Cambodia, Vietnam, and elsewhere—come to start a new life. More than 40 languages are spoken in the public schools here.

As in the rest of Maine, jobs, taxes, and the overall economy are always an issue here. Portland experiences some of the "brain drain" that affects the rest of the state when young people move elsewhere for better, higher-paying jobs. But other folks move here and stay here because of the quality of life and proximity to the outdoors. Portland has all of the advantages of a big city—theater, arts, a symphony orchestra—without the crime, gridlock, and pollution of more populated areas.

Part of Portland's charm is its waterfront atmosphere. Trawlers and other fishing boats dock right alongside sightseeing vessels and within sight of the huge tankers that regularly churn into port to unload their cargo. The harbor is a working port that, in terms of tonnage, is the largest in New England. In 2005, just under 30 million tons of cargo landed here, including more than 191 million barrels of

crude oil and other fuels. The port of Portland is the largest oil port on the East Coast, and the 25th largest port in the United States.

The city is also one of the largest fishing ports in New England. And it is fast becoming a coveted destination for cruise ships. In 2006 about 28 cruise ships carrying more than 46,000 passengers and crew made a stop in Portland. A high-speed ferry known as *The Cat* runs between Portland and Nova Scotia from late May through mid-October, departing Portland at 2:30 P.M. and reaching Yarmouth, Nova Scotia, at 9:00 A.M. the next day. *The Cat* can carry 900 passengers and 240 vehicles.

The Greater Portland area has a number of neighborhoods and districts. Here we provide a brief overview of each of them.

OLD PORT/DOWNTOWN DISTRICT

Most of Portland's residents live in "off-peninsula" neighborhoods. But some people wouldn't live anywhere else than right in the heart of downtown. The Old Port and Downtown District are bounded by the Franklin Arterial–India Street corridor, Congress Street, High Street, and Commercial Street. This is the area where the original settlers made their home in 1633. Today, it is a mix of offices, restaurants, boutiques, apartments, hotels, condos, and other business and residential quarters on streets lined with brick sidewalks. Many of the more historic buildings are built on the same characteristic cobblestone streets where the city rose from the ashes after the Great Fire of 1866.

EAST END/EASTERN PROMENADE

If you travel east from downtown and Franklin Arterial, you'll come to the East End, which ends abruptly at Casco Bay. It's also known as Munjoy Hill, after its first settler, George Munjoy. Cattle grazed here in the 1700s, and when a flood of immigrants began arriving on

Portland ranked 20th in *Inc.* magazine's 2006 list of "Hottest Midsize Cities for Entrepreneurs."

i Portland had an important role to play in the Underground Railroad and the antislavery movement. The city plans to install permanent markers showing the steps along the Portland Underground Railroad Freedom Trail from the waterfront to points on the East End, where some antislavery activists are buried in Eastern Cemetery.

these shores, this is where many of them settled. This working-class neighborhood is characterized by lots of single-family homes and multi-unit apartment buildings, and until recent years it was one of the most affordable parts of the city. But as Portland has gained in popularity, so has the East End, with its access to East End Beach, a popular walking trail that follows the shoreline, and an increasingly hip atmosphere. Along the Eastern Promenade are stately Victorian homes with stunning views of Casco Bay. Portlanders gather here every Fourth of July for the city's extraordinary fireworks display. If you're in town on July 4, don't miss this spectacular event.

BACK COVE

Back Cove is Portland's own version of Boston's Back Bay area. This neighborhood has always been desirable because of its proximity to one of the more popular walking paths in the city and the fantastic views of the Portland skyline. Middle-class homes fill this section of the city, which is bounded by Baxter Boulevard, Washington Avenue, and Forest Avenue.

BAYSIDE

Bayside is a longtime industrial and commercial neighborhood that was created in part by the filling in of parts of Back Cove in 1823. Bounded by Cumberland Avenue, Franklin Arterial, Forest Avenue, and Marginal Way, Bayside is also home to many of the city's social service agencies. It is currently undergoing a $100 million redevelopment that will bring more commercial and residential construction to the area.

PARKSIDE

Parkside is located directly across from Deering Oaks Park, the largest park in the city (see the Parks and Recreation chapter). Over the years, it has developed something of a reputation for rowdiness, but as real estate in Portland gets scarcer and more expensive, this neighborhood is undergoing gentrification, as are other parts of the city.

THE WEST END/WESTERN PROMENADE

The West End, bounded by High Street, Congress Street, Commercial Street, and the Western Prom, has gained a reputation as the hippest part of the city. Portland's two hospitals, as well as both public and private schools, are located here. The West End is home to Portlanders of every stripe—students, families, retirees. It's always been one of the more expensive parts of the city to live in, but in recent years property values and rents have skyrocketed as transplants from Boston and New York have bought up investment properties and second homes. Some of the older apartment buildings have been converted to condos. It's here that you'll also find some of the most impressive Victorian architecture and grand mansions in the city, since much of this neighborhood was built up after the 1866 fire. The Western Prom, 175 feet above sea level, is one of the best places in Portland to see a sunset.

DEERING

Deering was once its own town, until Portland took it over at the turn of the 20th century. Today, it is a quiet family neighborhood in the

i When Portland annexed the town of Deering in 1899, the city grew from 1,600 acres to 11,000 acres.

Close-up

Public Restrooms

If you walk around any tourist town, you're likely to see signs in all the stores that say sorry, no public restrooms or restrooms are for customers only. Portland is no exception. So here is perhaps one the most valuable things you'll find in this guidebook: a list of public restrooms sanctioned by the city.

Casco Bay Lines Ferry Terminal
Commercial Street and Franklin Arterial
Hours: Monday through Thursday, 4:45 A.M. to 11:45 P.M.; Friday, 5:00 A.M. to 12:30 A.M.; Saturday and Sunday, 7:00 A.M. to 11:45 P.M.

Fore Street Garage
419 Fore Street
Hours: Monday through Thursday, 6:00 A.M. to midnight; Friday, 6:00 A.M. to 1:30 A.M.; Saturday, 8:00 A.M. to 1:30 A.M.; Sunday noon to 9:00 P.M.

Portland City Hall
389 Congress Street
Hours: Monday through Friday, 8:00 A.M. to 4:30 P.M.; closed holidays

Portland Public Library
5 Monument Square
Hours: Monday, Wednesday, and Friday, 9:00 A.M. to 6:00 P.M.; Tuesday and Thursday, noon to 6:00 P.M.; Saturday, 9:00 A.M. to 5:00 P.M.

Spring Street Garage
45 Spring Street
Hours: Monday through Saturday, 6:00 A.M. to midnight; Sunday, 8:00 A.M. to midnight

Visitor Information Center
245 Commercial Street
Hours: (May 15 through October 15) Monday through Friday, 8:00 A.M. to 5:00 P.M.; Saturday and holidays, 10:00 A.M. to 5:00 P.M.; closed on Sunday
Hours: (October 16 through May 14) Monday through Friday, 8:00 A.M. to 5:00 P.M.; Saturday and holidays, 10:00 A.M. to 3:00 P.M.; closed on Sunday

northeastern part of the city that's divided into three sections—Deering Center, East Deering, and North Deering. North Deering and East Deering are dominated by mid-century suburban housing and border the town of Falmouth. The Deering Center area includes Baxter Woods, between Stevens and Forest Avenues, and Evergreen Cemetery, on

Portland Vital Statistics

Here's a quick overview of some interesting facts about our City by the Sea. Some of these tidbits, especially the historical highlights, are covered in more detail later in the book.

Maine governor: John Baldacci (Democrat)

Population: Portland: 64,249; Greater Portland area: 270,000

Area (square miles): 26.2

Nickname (Maine): The Pine Tree State

Motto: Portland: *Resurgam* ("I will rise again"); Maine: *Dirigo* ("I lead")

Average temperatures (degrees Fahrenheit): July (high/low) 79/59; January (high/low) 34/17

Normal annual rainfall: 44 inches

Normal annual snowfall: 71.3 inches. In any given year, Portland has an 83 percent chance of having a white Christmas.

City founded: Settled by the British in 1632; incorporated as a town in 1786

Maine's major colleges/universities: University of Maine system, Bates College, Bowdoin College, Colby College, College of the Atlantic, University of New England, Husson College, Maine College of Art, Maine Maritime Academy, Unity College, St. Joseph's College, Thomas College

Important dates in history:

1632	English settlers arrive on the Portland peninsula, calling it by its Indian name, Machigonne.
1637	George Cleeve was granted a 2,000-year lease from Britain's King James for land encompassing all of modern-day Portland.
1652	Portland and Casco Bay become part of the Massachusetts Bay Colony.
1775	Portland bombarded by the British Royal Navy during the Revolutionary War.
1786	The city is called Portland for the first time by settlers living here.
1820	Maine becomes a state, with Portland as its capital until 1832.
1823	Steamships begin traveling back and forth from Boston to Portland.
1852	Construction of Portland's Commercial Street is completed.
1866	July 4 Great Fire destroys Portland, leaving 10,000 homeless.
1920	Maine women, in a September state election, become the first women in the nation to exercise their voting rights under the 19th amendment.
1941	Portland is the home port of the U.S. North American Fleet during World War II.
1970s	After falling into seedy disrepair, the Old Port begins its transformation into the modern shopping district that it is today.
1996	On September 27 the oil tanker Julie N strikes the Million Dollar Bridge (predecessor of the Casco Bay Bridge) and spills 179,634 gallons of No. 2 fuel oil into Portland harbor. It is the largest oil spill in Portland's history.
1997	The new Casco Bay Bridge opens. The 4,748-foot drawbridge is built with "fenders" to help prevent another incident like the *Julie N* oil spill.
1998	An ice storm paralyzes Maine, leaving 690,000 people without electricity.

Major area employers: Maine Medical Center, UnumProvident, Idexx Laboratories, Hannaford Bros., Wal-Mart, L.L. Bean, Banknorth, Fairchild Semiconductor, National Semiconductor, Wright Express, state of Maine, municipality of Portland

Median household income (2000): $35,650

Famous sons and daughters of Maine: Henry Wadsworth Longfellow, poet; Joshua Chamberlain, Civil War hero; Hannibal Hamlin, vice president under Abraham Lincoln; Harriet Beecher Stowe, author of *Uncle Tom's Cabin;* Edna St. Vincent Millay, poet; Chester Greenwood, inventor of the earmuff; Margaret Chase Smith, first woman in U.S. history elected to both houses of Congress and known for her early stand against McCarthyism; Leon Leonwood Bean, founder of L.L. Bean; E. B. White, author of *Charlotte's Web* and other children's classics; Andrew Wyeth, artist; Edmund S. Muskie, 1968 vice-presidential candidate and secretary of state under President Jimmy Carter; John Ford, film director; George Mitchell, Senate majority leader from 1988 to 1994; Samantha Smith, 10-year-old girl who wrote to Soviet president Yuri Andropov and became an ambassador for peace; George H. W. Bush, 41st U.S. president; Stephen King, author

Major airport: Portland International Jetport

Major interstates: Interstates 295 and 95 (Maine Turnpike)

Public transportation: Metro (bus system); Portland International Jetport; Casco Bay Ferry; Amtrak/Downeaster

Driving laws: Right turn on red permitted; headlights must be on when wipers are in constant use; seat belt must be worn at all times.

Alcohol laws: Legal drinking age is 21 years; blood alcohol content of .08 percent or higher is considered operating under the influence in Maine.

Daily newspaper: *Portland Press Herald/Maine Sunday Telegram*

Sales tax: 5 percent

Stevens. Both green spaces include popular trails used by locals for exercising, bird watching, and other activities.

STROUDWATER

Stroudwater is one of the older neighborhoods in the city and was once the site of mills that made masts for the British Royal Navy. It's located on outer Congress Street, near the Portland Jetport, but the neighborhood is surprisingly quiet, and the tidy homes are among the most desirable in the area.

THE ISLANDS

There are hundreds of islands dotting Casco Bay, and for hundreds of years people have tried to live on them. Some island communities took root, blossoming from colonial farming and fishing communities into full-fledged towns with year-round homes, summer cottages, and elegant hotels. Today, five islands are considered part of the city of Portland: Peaks, Cliff, Little Diamond, Great Diamond, and Cushing. Long Island seceded from Portland in 1993.

THE SUBURBS

The Greater Portland area includes several suburbs that offer alternatives to the city of Portland scene. If you cross the Casco Bay Bridge, you'll come to South Portland and Cape Elizabeth, where property values can be higher—depending on the part of town—but neighborhoods are extremely family oriented, and homes are closer to many of the southern Maine beaches and parks. The Maine Mall and many of the area's big-box stores and strip malls are concentrated in one particular area of South Portland. To the north you'll find Falmouth and Cumberland, both tony communities with higher property values. Until a few years ago, Cumberland was a farming community with a more rural character, but it is

i The 2000 U.S. Census found that Portland is among the top 10 metropolitan areas for its percentage of gay and lesbian couples.

increasingly becoming more gentrified, with soaring housing prices to show for it. To the west is Westbrook, an old paper mill town that is now one of the more affordable of Portland's suburbs.

GETTING HERE, GETTING AROUND

Once you arrive in Portland, you'll soon discover why it's known as a very walkable city, particularly on the Portland peninsula. On the peninsula, you can walk or bike just about anywhere. Even folks who live in some of the closer outlying areas, especially South Portland, find it convenient—not to mention good exercise—to walk or bike across the Casco Bay Bridge every day to work.

GETTING HERE

By Car

The Maine Turnpike (Interstate 95) is a toll road and the main artery coming into Portland from both the north and the south. Travelers coming from Portsmouth, N.H., Boston, and other points south can reach the city from exits 44 through 48. Take exit 44 or exit 45 to connect to Interstate 295, which will lead you right into the heart of downtown Portland. From the north, take the Maine Turnpike right into Portland. If driving from more than an hour away, take the Gardiner exit near Augusta and cut over to toll-free I–295 South, which leads directly into downtown Portland.

U.S. Route 1 more or less parallels the Maine Turnpike and follows the coastline in southern Maine before heading north to the Canadian border. Travelers who aren't in a hurry may enjoy passing through some coastal towns and taking scenic detours, but they'll also deal with traffic lights, suburban development, and stop-and-go traffic, especially during tourist season. For the fastest route to Portland, stick with the Maine Turnpike.

From the west, take U.S. Route 302 from the White Mountains of New Hampshire or Route 25. Both roads end in the city of Portland.

By Plane

But first, you have to get here. If you are flying, there are three basic ways to get to Portland: Boston's Logan International Airport, the Manchester-Boston Regional Airport in New Hampshire (100 miles away), and, of course, the Portland International Jetport. It's a good idea to compare fares flying into these three locations because flying into the Portland Jetport historically has been more expensive, particularly for families. If you're single or flying alone, it's often not worth the inconvenience to fly into Boston or Manchester. But if you're a couple or a family, flying into Boston or Manchester can mean saving a couple of hundred dollars or more. In 2004 an estimated 400,000 Maine passengers chose the Manchester airport, where the presence of low-cost carrier Southwest Airlines has helped to keep fares down. If you choose to fly into Manchester, you still have to pay to get to Portland somehow. Only you can decide how much your wallet can handle. The good news is that as of May 2006 low-cost carrier JetBlue now flies into Portland, offering four daily nonstop flights from New York City starting at $54 each way, a less expensive option for those who want to fly directly into Portland.

i If you're coming into town from the south on the Maine Turnpike, the signs will tell you to get off at exit 44 for I–295 and downtown Portland. But if you wait until exit 45, you can get off the turnpike and onto I–295 without paying a toll.

When in Portland, chances are you'll hear the word *Downeast* in reference to parts of coastal Maine. It's an old sailing term from the days when ships sailed downwind from Boston to ports that lay to the east in Maine.

By Bus

If you decide to fly into Boston, there are three options for getting into Portland. You can rent a car or shuttle service and drive, following Interstate 95 straight up through New Hampshire into Maine. You can also take the bus or train. Concord Trailways' (800–639–3317) "Way2Logan" program offers 10 nonstop express buses from Logan Airport to Portland daily. The trip takes about two hours, and the bus driver will help you pass the time by showing a movie; by the time it's over, you will have arrived in Portland. The bus drops you off at the Portland Transportation Center on Thompson's Point, a building that houses both Concord Trailways and the Amtrak Downeaster (see entry below). From there, just go outside to an awaiting taxi or (May through September) catch a Metro bus or Portland Explorer bus to your downtown destination. There are many other scheduled trips from Logan to Portland on Concord's schedule that are not express service but make, say, one stop at Boston's South Station. For a complete schedule, go to www.concord trailways.com.

You do not need reservations for Trailways tickets, which cost $24 one way or $39 for a round-trip from Logan to Portland. There is no Trailways counter at Logan. You buy the tickets directly from your driver on a first-come, first-served basis. (You can pay cash, but the driver will accept MasterCard or Visa.) Tickets can also be purchased in advance, but that does not guarantee a seat. The buses pick up passengers at Terminals A, B, C, and E at designated pickup areas marked by a bus sign. For more detailed directions for each terminal, check the Concord Trailways Web site.

Vermont Transit Lines also has several buses traveling between Boston's South Station and Portland each day. You'll need to take a cab or a shuttle from Logan Airport to South Station. For schedules and current fares, call (800) 552–8737 or visit www.vermonttransit.com.

By Train

If the romance of rail entrances you, travel from Boston to Portland via the Amtrak Downeaster (www.AmtrakDowneaster.com or 800–USA–RAIL). Five trains daily leave from Boston's North Station. At two and a half hours, it's a longer trip than the bus, and the train makes several stops before arriving in Portland. But you can ride in comfort and relax. The train has outlets for your laptop, or you can watch the landscape roll by as the train heads north into New Hampshire and Maine. There's a cafe car that serves microbrews, snacks, and light meals, such as soups, sandwiches, salads, hot dogs, burgers, and pizza. Reservations are recommended for the Downeaster. Tickets from Boston to Portland are $22 one way or $44 round-trip.

Transportation Facilities

Portland Transportation Center
100 Thompson's Point Road
Hours: daily, 4:30 A.M. to 10:45 P.M. and 2:45 to 3:15 A.M.

This is the local transportation hub for Concord Trailways and Amtrak—the place where your bus or train will pull in to drop you off in Portland. It's located just minutes from downtown Portland and Casco Bay. From here, you can catch a city Metro bus or a Portland Explorer bus that will take you where you need to go in the city. There are also taxis waiting outside. Should you need it during your stay, parking is available here for $3.00 per day for the first 14 days, and $4.00 per day for every day thereafter.

The Portland Explorer is a shuttle bus that drops passengers off at the Portland International Jetport, the Maine Mall, the International Marine Terminal, the Old Port shopping district, and three local hotels: the Eastland Park Hotel, the Hilton Garden Inn at

i Looking for accommodations on the Portland Jetport campus? Try the Embassy Suites Hotel at (207) 775–2200 or the Hilton Garden Inn at the Jetport at (207) 828–1117.

the Jetport, and the Marriott Hotel at Sable Oaks. The fare is $2.00. Children 12 and under ride free.

If you are leaving from the Portland Transportation Center—to take a day trip to Boston, for example—the center is easily accessible off Interstate 295. Heading north on I–295, take exit 5, then take a right off the ramp to Route 22W, and the terminal will be straight ahead. From I–295 South, take exit 5A.

Mermaid Transportation Co.

P.O. Box 10676
Portland, ME 04104
(207) 885–5630, (800) 696–2463
www.gomermaid.com

Mermaid Transportation is a shuttle service that travels between Portland and both the Boston and Manchester airports. It takes about two hours to reach Portland from either airport. The Mermaid vans will drop you off at the jetport, the parking area at the Portland Transportation Center, local hotels, and the Casco Bay Ferry Line terminal on Commercial Street. They also provide private charter services. For a quote on rates, enter your flight information on the Web site or call Mermaid directly.

Portland International Jetport
1001 Westbrook Street

The Portland International Jetport had its beginnings in the late 1920s and early 1930s. It was originally a private airfield, owned by Dr. Clifford "Kip" Strange, who flew a Curtiss Jenny. Much of the airport's history can be seen today on the walls of the terminal, where old photographs of its early days help passengers pass the time before their flights. Today's modern facility, just off I–95 exit 46, is situated on 700 acres about 5 miles from downtown Portland and services more than 1.4 million travelers per year.

Six airlines currently fly into Portland: Continental (800–525–0280), Delta (800–221–1212), Northwest (800–225–2525), United Express (800–241–6522), U.S. Airways (800–428–4322), and newcomer JetBlue (800–JETBLUE). In recent years, as the major carriers have struggled financially, many have switched to flying smaller, commuter jets in and out of Portland for most of the year. But when summer tourist season arrives, full-size aircraft reappear on the tarmac. Nonstop flights are available to Atlanta, New York, Chicago, Washington, D.C., Charlotte, Cincinnati, Cleveland, Detroit, Minneapolis, and Philadelphia. Direct flights to Cleveland and Minneapolis run only during the summer.

To keep an eye on a departing or arriving flight from home or your hotel, visit www.portlandjetport.org and click on the arrivals and departures page. The information there is refreshed every five minutes by the airlines.

The airport is small—it has just 11 gates—and we have found that arriving an hour and a half before a scheduled departure usually leaves plenty of time to make a flight. But during the busiest periods, especially early mornings when the security line grows longer than usual, it's best to give yourself two hours. The airport's "rush hours" are 6:00 to 8:00 A.M., 10:00 A.M. to 2:00 P.M. and 5:00 to 7:00 P.M. All of the airlines' counters are open by 5:00 A.M. daily, except for one or two that don't open until 6:00 A.M. on Sunday. There is no curbside check-in, but it's not really necessary at this community airport.

Parking at the jetport can be a problem sometimes, especially during busy periods such as the Christmas holidays. It's a good

i Swing by the Greater Portland Convention and Visitors' Bureau at 245 Commercial Street in Portland for an extensive collection of brochures on area accommodations, restaurants, and attractions. You can also call the GPCVB at (207) 772–5800 for referrals to area businesses.

idea to call ahead (207–772–7028) to see how busy it is in the garage and at the surface lots. Parking rates in the garage and all lots are $1.00 per half hour. In short-term parking, there's an $8.00 daily maximum; in the long-term garage, the daily maximum is $9.00; and at the long-term surface lot, the daily maximum is $7.00.

Inside the terminal you'll find a gift shop and newsstand, restaurant, ATM, visitor information booth, and Starbucks to help you keep your eyes open while waiting for those early-morning flights. If you need to page someone, you can do so at the visitor information booth.

Car rental booths are located near the baggage claim area. Other transportation—taxis, limousines—can be arranged through the ground transportation booth just outside the door at baggage claim. Twenty hotels in the Greater Portland area offer free shuttle service to and from the airport. For a complete list, with phone numbers, go to www.portlandjetport.org/Shuttles.asp.

As we mentioned earlier in this chapter, transportation to downtown Portland is also available at the jetport through the city's Metro bus service and the Portland Explorer.

Maine Aviation
1025 Westbrook Street
(207) 780–1811
Located at the Portland International Jetport, Maine Aviation offers charter flights on private aircraft. Its fleet includes large luxury jets, light jets, and turboprops.

TAXIS

Metered fares in Portland are $1.90 for the first 1/10th mile, and $0.25 for each additional 1/10th mile. For waiting, the rate is $0.30 a minute. For a list of fares to towns outside the Greater Portland area, check the Portland Jetport Web site at www.portlandjetport.org/transportation.asp.

ABC Taxi
(207) 772–8685

A Maine Taxi and Livery Service
(207) 712–4850

Airport Limo Taxi and Livery
(207) 773–3433

All Star Taxi
(207) 318–6477

AM & PM Taxi
(207) 772–7800

American Taxi
(207) 749–1600

Cal's Taxi Service
(207) 854–9495

Elite Taxi
(207) 871–7274

Friendly Taxi
(207) 772–4240

Jetport Taxi
(207) 775–6990

Kleen Taxi Ko
(207) 773–0055

Lucky Express Taxi & Delivery
(207) 807–4877

Maniac Taxi
(207) 318–2222

Old Port Taxi
(207) 772–8294

Portland Airport Taxi Cab
(207) 774–5666

Silver House Taxi & Discount Limo
(888) 264–4411

South Portland Taxi
(207) 767–5200

Trust Taxi
(207) 450–4392

Where To Taxi
(207) 772–4240

Whitmore's Taxi
(207) 871–0206

Wings Cab Co.
(207) 871–8800

Within Ten
(207) 347–5168

Wolf's Taxi
(207) 772–8500

Zou's Taxi Service
(207) 807–4040

LIMOUSINES

For a complete list of ground transportation companies that service the Portland International Jetport, go to www.portlandjetport.org/limo.asp. Here we have listed only a few in the Greater Portland area.

Bay Limo and Livery Co.
(207) 878–2292

Excalibur Limo Service Inc.
(207) 878–0900

Landmark Limousine
(207) 774–3137

Lilley's Limousine
(207) 741–2121

Portland Limousine
(207) 797–2478

RENTAL CARS

A C Rent-A-Ride
(207) 773–3367

Alamo
(207) 775–0855 (Portland International Jetport)
(877) 603–0615

Avis Rent a Car
(207) 674–7500 (Portland International Jetport)
(800) 831–2847

Auto Europe
(207) 828–2525

Budget Car Rental
(207) 774–8663 (Portland)
(800) 527–0700

Dollar Rent A Car
(800) 800–4000

Enterprise Rent-A-Car
(207) 772–0030 (Portland downtown)
(207) 822–9990 (South Portland)
(800) 736–8222

Hertz
(800) 704–4473 (local)
(800) 654–3131

National Car Rental
(207) 773–0036 (Portland International Jetport)
(888) 868–6207

Thrifty Car Rental
(207) 772–4628

LOCAL BUSES

Metro Greater Portland Transit District
127 St. John Street www.gpmetrobus.com
Metro is the Greater Portland area's bus service. It's a clean and convenient way to get around town and is probably one of the city's most underutilized resources, although ridership averages 1.3 million annually. In addition to Portland routes, Metro buses travel to the Maine Mall area in South Portland and also to Westbrook and Falmouth. In May 2006 Metro added buses powered by compressed natural gas to the fleet, making for a quieter ride that's better for the environment.

The bus schedules, though, are probably better suited to working, shopping, and sightseeing than to nightlife. Most schedules end before midnight. If you're going out on the town late at night and think you won't want to drive home, a taxi might be the best bet.

Color-coded route maps and bus schedules can be picked up at Portland City Hall or the Metro downtown transportation center on Elm Street, or they can be downloaded at www.gpmetrobus.com. They are also available at most Shaw's and Hannaford's super-

ℹ️ For just $20, students 18 and under can buy a Metro summer youth pass and ride the Portland and South Portland bus lines anywhere they go from June through August.

markets on the bus routes, at Westbrook City Hall, and on buses.

Here are a few tips for visitors looking for a scenic ride, or the fastest way to popular local destinations.

- The #1 Metro bus goes up Munjoy Hill, past the Portland Observatory, and offers a great view of the Eastern Prom and Casco Bay.
- The #8 Metro bus travels along the Portland peninsula and provides a good overview of Portland for a first-time visitor or resident. A few highlights along the route include Congress Street, the Old Port, Casco Bay Lines, the Portland Museum of Art, Longfellow House, Victoria Mansion, Mercy Hospital, and Maine Medical Center.
- The #5 Metro bus takes riders to the Maine Mall, the Portland Jetport, and the Portland Transportation Center (Amtrak and Concord Trailways).

Music is allowed on buses (as long as you use headphones), as are skateboards. The buses also have bike racks, so you can take your ride with you. All buses are wheelchair accessible.

Fares are $1.25 one way, and exact change is required. You can also purchase what is called a "Ten Ride Ticket" for $11. Just show it to the bus driver, and he'll punch it for you. Ten Ride Tickets do not have an expiration date. A monthly pass is $37.50, and a day pass is $5.00. Seniors and people with disabilities can show their Medicare cards and pay half price: 60 cents for a regular fare and $5.50 for a Ten Ride Ticket.

Metro accepts transfers from South Portland City Bus, ZOOM bus, and Concord Trailways. On weekdays, from 11:00 A.M. to 1:00 P.M., there is a free "Lunch Hop" on Congress Street between Monument Square and Congress Square.

Shaw's, Hannaford, and Goodwill stores offer "Bus and Buy" stamps, which reward customers with a free ride home. Ask the bus driver for a transfer when you get to the store and then get a stamp at the store for the return trip.

FERRIES, CRUISES, AND WATER TRANSPORTATION

Casco Bay Lines
56 Commercial Street (at Franklin Street)
(207) 774–7871
www.cascobaylines.com

If you're looking to visit the islands, or just get out on the water for the day, one of the ferries run by Casco Bay Lines can take you there. The ferry line is the oldest ferry service in America, serving as a critical connection to the mainland for the people who make the Casco Bay islands their home. The island residents actually own and operate the service, which is governed by a 12-person board of directors made up of residents, a representative of the city of Portland, and a member appointed by the Maine Department of Transportation. The fleet is used to deliver mail, bring kids to the mainland for school, and carry groceries. Islanders deliver lumber and other freight, even cars, via the ferries, too. Each year, the ferries—anointed with fanciful names like *Island Romance* and *Machigonne* (the Indian name for the Portland peninsula)—transport more than 977,000 passengers and 25,000 vehicles.

You can piggyback on these trips. Cruising the bay is one of the best ways to get to know the islands and gain a new perspective on the mainland. You'll cruise past island forests and rocky cliffs and watch harbor seals at play in the water as you pass by. It's also fun to view homes and summer cottages on the islands and imagine what it would be like to live there yourself! Make sure to bring a sweater or light jacket because it can be significantly cooler out on the water. Even on a sweltering summer day, the weather can change quickly. If you get too chilly, you can always retreat inside, but all the real fun is up on deck. Binoculars are a good idea, too, both for bird watching and for getting a closer look at the islands. You can bring lunch or snacks on board, as there are no snack bars except for the summer Bailey Island cruise. You can buy sodas on board, however. Working Portlanders have been known to brown-bag it on the short, 20-minute ferry ride to Peaks just to get outside for a bit when the weather warms up.

In addition to Peaks, the ferries make regular daily runs to Great Diamond Island, Little Diamond Island, Long Island, Chebeague Island, and Cliff Island. In the summer there's also the daily run to Bailey Island. Rates and schedules vary by season, and there are discounts for seniors and children (no charge for children under five). Full spring and summer round-trip fares typically range from $6.25 for a ride over to Peaks Island to $9.50 for a journey out to Cliff Island. You can bring your bike or dog along, but it will cost you. A ticket for a bike costs $5.25 (unless it is taken as freight); dogs, which must be leashed at all times, can travel with you for $3.25. No reservations are necessary, unless you're part of a large group of 20 or more. Tickets can be purchased in advance and are good for 60 days. They are collected when you board the boat in Portland.

To get the most out of your trip, consider one of the scenic cruises, such as the three-hour Mailboat Run ($13 adults), which combines the business of the ferry line with informative narration for passengers. View the bay at sunset on the two-and-a-half-hour Sunset Run ($13 adults), or by the light of the moon on the Moonlight Run ($11.50 adults), which takes one hour and 45 minutes. The summertime Bailey Island cruise ($18.50 adults) lasts almost six hours, including a layover of about two hours on Bailey Island for passengers who want to try the fare at Cook's Lobster House or just explore the area. This cruise will take you right by 17-acre Eagle Island, the former home of famous Arctic explorer Admiral Robert Peary; the island is located about 3 miles off the coast. But the long cruise may be too much for some visitors, especially children.

Captain Gene Willard, a senior captain for Casco Bay Lines, calls the three-hour Sunrise on the Bay cruise ($13 adults) a "hidden little jewel in Casco Bay." The cruise lasts three hours and starts at 5:05 A.M. Pay attention to the expected time of sunrise because, depending on the time of year, some of the trips will offer better sunrises than others. "It's an absolutely beautiful ride," Willard says. "The water's usually the calmest of the day, and it's just gorgeous. You get to see the harbor seals, and there are loons on Casco Bay. It's the best boat ride of the day."

Casco Bay Ferry Lines also offers three-hour music cruises with a cash bar, and tickets are usually well under $20, especially if you buy them in advance. The ferries can be chartered for private cruises or lobster bakes for larger groups.

The ferry terminal is easy to find. If you're coming from either the south or north on I–295, take exit 7 (Franklin Street). Follow Franklin Street all the way to the end at Commercial Street, and you'll drive right into Casco Bay Lines. Next door to the ferry terminal is a city parking garage (207–761–9591) where you can park your car for $1.00 an hour or $14.00 for 24 hours. This garage is obviously the most convenient, but it fills up fast on the weekends, so you can't always count on its being available. There are several other parking options in the vicinity, including a city garage on the corner of Pearl and Fore Streets (Custom House Square Garage; 207–774–2748), where the rates are $1.00 an hour or $12.00 for 24 hours. In addition, a number of businesses in the area have surface lots that allow parking for a fee, and with permission. For a current list of those lots, visit www.portlandmaine.gov/misc/news/parking.pdf.

Portland Express Water Taxi
(207) 415–8493
www.portlandexpresswatertaxi.com

If the ferry just doesn't seem fast enough, or you want to reach an island the ferry doesn't go to, call a water taxi. It's more expensive than a ferry ride because it is an on-demand service, but it offers more flexibility since a ride is just a phone call away. Captain Gene Willard, descended from the same family of Willard Beach fame, works full time for Casco Bay Lines but started this business on the side about three years ago. He is the eighth generation in his family to make a living on Casco Bay. Willard runs his taxi service year-round and in three years has missed only one day of operation.

His quoted prices are steep compared with the ferry ($40 to $65 one way for most islands), but prices are often lower than that, especially if you don't mind sharing a ride with others headed in the same direction. Most of his business in the wintertime comes from locals, especially people such as builders and contractors on their way to meet with island home owners, who don't like the idea of time ticking by while their by-the-hour contractor is cruising on a ferry. Willard also shuttles campers and picnickers from the mainland to the unimproved state parks on the islands, such as Jewel Island, and does a lot of interisland transport. And if you're just one of those people who like to arrive in style, you can catch a water taxi from Portland to the Saltwater Grille Restaurant across the harbor in South Portland for $30 round-trip.

PARKING GARAGES

Parking can be difficult on the Portland peninsula. In the Old Port district, finding a parking space on the street on a weekend night can be like trying to find a single fish in the ocean. Parking restrictions apply in residential neighborhoods—pay attention to signage outlining alternate-side parking rules—and no parking is allowed on city streets at all during major snowstorms. (During overnight snow bans, you can park in city garages after 5:00 P.M. and stay until 8:00 A.M., and you will only be charged $3.00.)

In addition to the parking options listed under Casco Bay Lines, this list of other city parking garages will come in handy.

Casco Bay Garage (city owned; independently operated)
54 Commercial Street,
next to Casco Bay Lines
(207) 774–8653
Hours: Monday through Thursday, 4:45 A.M. to 11:45 P.M.; Friday, 5:00 A.M. to 12:30 A.M.; Saturday and Sunday, 7:00 A.M. to 11:45 P.M.
Rates: $1.00 per hour; $14.00 per day

Custom House Square Garage
Corner of Pearl and Fore Streets
(207) 774–2748
Hours: Monday through Wednesday, 7:00 A.M. to 10:00 P.M., Thursday, 7:00 A.M. to 11:00 P.M.; Friday, 7:00 A.M. to midnight; Saturday, 9:30 A.M. to midnight; Sunday 8:30 A.M. to 9:30 P.M.
Rates: $1.25 per hour; $14.00 per day

Elm Street Garage (city owned)
21 Elm Street, between Portland High School and the Portland Public Library
(207) 871–1106
Hours: Monday through Friday, 6:00 A.M. to 10:00 P.M.; Saturday, 8:00 A.M. to 10:00 P.M.
Rates: First half hour free; $1.00 per hour thereafter

Fore Street Garage
Fore Street between Exchange and Union
(207) 772–7738

i If you're in downtown Portland and your parking meter expires, you'll get a green ticket. If it's your first, you're in luck: The city has a parking forgiveness program that automatically forgives the first violation every six months.

Casco Bay Bridge

For centuries people have been crossing the Fore River, in one way or another, from the Portland peninsula to what is now South Portland. They've traveled by boat, by foot, by bicycle, and by car.

In 1820 a wooden structure known simply as the Portland Bridge was built across the river. The wooden bridge rose just 4 feet above the water and had a leaf that drew up so ships could pass through. That bridge was replaced in 1916 by a new structure that was 24 feet above the water at high tide. It became known simply as the "Million Dollar Bridge" because that's about how much it cost to build. In its later years, it carried 32,000 vehicles each day over the Fore River.

By 1994 the Million Dollar Bridge was almost 80 years old, and its concrete was beginning to crumble. It was time for a replacement. Construction began on a new $130 million drawbridge.

But what to call it? The $130 Million Bridge? Everyone had their own idea of a good name for the new structure. The Maine Department of Transportation referred to it simply as the Portland–South Portland Bridge, but other suggestions poured in from the public. Some people thought it made the most sense to call it the Fore River Bridge, since it spans the Fore River. A local historian suggested naming it after Civil War hero Joshua Chamberlain. And schoolchildren campaigned for the bridge to be named after Henry Wadsworth Longfellow. The poet had crossed the river so many times to visit the lighthouse keeper at Portland Head Light, the kids reasoned, that he deserved to have the structure named after him.

So divisive was the issue that officials decided to create a bridge-naming committee. The committee considered 137 names before settling on Casco Bay Bridge. Rejected were the other four finalists: Harbor Bridge, Citizens' Memorial Bridge, Mariners Bridge, and Mariners' Memorial Bridge. The bridge doesn't cross Casco Bay, but the committee noted that travelers would be able to see it from the bridge. The Maine legislature made the name official.

Today, the modern Casco Bay Bridge is still a focal point for people living in the Greater Portland area. It's one of the largest drawbridges in the country. The bridge has four bascule leaves, two on each side, that work together as the bridge opens

Hours: Monday through Thursday, 6:00 A.M. to midnight; Friday, 6:00 A.M. to 1:30 A.M.; Saturday, 8:00 A.M. to 1:30 A.M.; Sunday noon to 9:00 P.M.
Rates: $2.00 for the first hour; $1.25 for every hour thereafter; $14.00 overnight

Spring Street Garage (city owned)
45 Spring Street, next to the
Cumberland County Civic Center
(207) 874–2842
Hours: Monday through Saturday, 6:00 A.M. to midnight; Sunday, 8:00 A.M. to midnight
Rates: First half hour free; $1.00 per hour thereafter

Casco Bay Bridge. MEREDITH GOAD

and closes for passing ships. Each leaf weighs 920,000 pounds and is 180 feet long, 40 feet wide, and 24 feet high. The bridge contains more than 20 million pounds of structural steel and 300 million pounds of concrete.

The new bridge opened on Labor Day weekend in 1997 to much pomp and circumstance. There were fireworks, a 5K road race, and a boat parade to celebrate, and a raffle was held to see who would be the first to cross it. (Half of the money raised was earmarked to pay for the $100,000 opening celebrations.) The winner of a new car—and the right to be the first one to drive across the new bridge—was a 71-year-old woman from Cape Elizabeth.

Temple Street Garage
(city owned; independently operated)
11 Temple Street, next to the Nickelodeon Cinema
(207) 772–5762

Hours: Monday through Friday, 6:30 A.M. to midnight; Saturday 7:30 A.M. to midnight; closed on Sunday
Rates: $1.00 per hour; $12.00 per day

HISTORY

The history of Portland is a tale of a phoenix, the mythological bird that rose from the ashes. It is a story punctuated with devastating destruction, remarkable resilience, and persistent optimism. The city's seal, bearing the Latin motto *Resurgam* (meaning "I will rise again") and the phoenix, was adopted in 1786 after a devastating attack by the British Royal Navy forced residents to rebuild the city from the ground up. The seal is imprinted on the wrought-iron doors of Portland's city hall as a reminder of this and other tragedies that Portland has survived since the area's first settlers came here nearly four centuries ago. From bloody colonial battles with neighboring Native Americans and the British, to the Great Fire of 1866, to offshore threats from German submarines during World War II, the City by the Sea has suffered and endured enough to fill volumes.

Through all of its troubles, Portland's citizens have remained dedicated to the land along Casco Bay. They have returned time after time to rebuild the ruins of the city and have altered the personality of the area with each rebirth. Portland has been home to residents willing to risk life and limb to protect their city. It has been home to brazen Revolutionaries, hundreds of lascivious, drunken sailors, a famous prohibitionist who made Portland the first "dry" city in the nation, and countless generations of immigrants from all over the nation and the world who continue to move here in droves, changing the culture of the city and helping to make it one of the most socially liberal, tolerant, and unique spots in the nation.

The Portland Room in the Portland Public Library at 5 Monument Square is a unique resource for books, periodicals, and photographs about Portland past and present. One interesting title is *Changing Portland* (2005), edited by University of Southern Maine professor Joseph Conforti. You can also learn more about Maine's history at the Maine Historical Society's Research Library at 489 Congress Street, behind the Longfellow House. For more information, call (207) 774–1822.

THE COLONIAL YEARS

In the beginning it seemed as though the land along Casco Bay might never be colonized. The first few English settlers to move to the area avoided the mainland altogether and instead set up camp on the Casco Bay islands, where the fishing and fur trade with the Native Americans was bountiful. The first such settler to arrive was wayward former servant Walter Bagnell, who in 1628 established a trading post on Richmond Island off the coast of modern-day Cape Elizabeth. Bagnell had been cast out of Massachusetts by Puritans annoyed by his partying ways, and, on Richmond Island, he proved he had not learned a thing from his troubles. In 1631 local Native American chiefs angry with "Great Walt" and his shady business practices burned his home, with Walt inside.

Soon after, John Winter, an agent for merchants in Plymouth, settled Richmond Island and established a lucrative, and amicable, fish and fur trade with local Native Americans. Luckily for Portland, he was deeply protective of his island, and when English settlers George Cleeve and Richard Tucker tried to move there, he refused to allow them. Instead, Winter pointed them in the direction of the overgrown forests along the mainland. Cleeve and Tucker reluctantly obliged and in 1633 built the first house erected by English settlers on what the Native peoples called

Machigonne or "the Neck"—the long thin peninsula stretching from the modern-day West End to Munjoy Hill. Cleeve and Tucker called the new settlement Falmouth. It was the beginning of the colony that would one day become the city of Portland.

By the late 17th century, about 400 settlers had carved out a rustic life on the Neck. But this was soon disrupted when the tiny colony found itself in the center of two bloody wars that threatened to destroy the settlement forever. Located north of Massachusetts Colony, Falmouth's allegiance to Britain made it an easy target for French-Canadian fighters and their Indian allies to the north during King Phillip's War. The colony was leveled by Native Americans and enemies of Britain in 1675 and managed to rebuild only to be attacked again by Native Americans in 1689 during the French and Indian War. During this last brutal exchange, Falmouth colonists fought for six straight hours before forcing their enemies back into the forest. Unfortunately, several months later the Indians returned and successfully burned the settlement to the ground. The attackers left no white settlers alive in Maine east of present-day Wells. For more than a decade after this battle, no English settler set foot on the Neck.

Finally, around 1700, settlers slowly returned to Falmouth, and the colony began to build some measure of security and prosperity. Sawmills were established at the mouths of the local rivers to transform trees into lumber that was then loaded onto ships in the Falmouth port. The first three streets were built in the town during this period (Fore, Middle, and Back, later renamed Congress), and a meetinghouse was erected on the site of the present-day First Parish Church on Congress Street (see the Architecture chapter for more information). This wooden church was the center of the social, religious, and political life of the tiny town and was affectionately dubbed "Old Jerusalem."

In addition to the lumber trade, fishing and shipbuilding also became staple industries for Falmouth. In fact, the market for these items was so strong that the settlement often neglected farming and traded for all necessary food supplies.

REVOLUTIONARY WAR

But, once again, peace was short-lived. Portland found itself awkwardly torn between the British and the colonists during the American Revolution. Residents of the town supported the Revolution, but the town's lumber merchants enjoyed a lucrative trade supplying masts to the British navy. In 1775 Revolutionary fervor took over, and Portland refused to deliver the masts to Britain, prompting Captain Henry Mowatt of the British navy to punish the town by blasting it with his cannons and burning it to the ground. The bombardment lasted 12 hours, and, at the end of it, 414 of the town's 500 buildings were destroyed. Falmouth lay smoldering. Cannonballs were lodged in the damaged facade of "Old Jerusalem" (for more on viewing these cannonballs today, see the Architecture chapter). Many colonists left forever after their homes were destroyed. Those who stayed dug in their heels and vowed to send as many men as possible to support the Revolutionary effort against the British. After America finally became independent, residents of the Neck decided to separate from Falmouth and create the town of Portland on July 4, 1786.

i The masts meant for the Royal Navy that triggered Mowatt's attack on Portland were never delivered. They were hidden for years up the Fore River as a snub to the British and later were used to build Sawyer's Wharf at the foot of High Street.

19TH-CENTURY PORTLAND

During the first half of the 19th century, Portland grew into one of the most important trading ports in the country. Artistry and culture flourished, a library was built, and several newspapers were published. Tax-supported

 Close-up

Neal Dow, Father of Prohibition

One of Portland's most famous, or infamous, residents was Neal Dow—a two-time mayor, a dedicated Quaker, and a nationally renowned prohibition enthusiast who helped make Portland the first "dry" city in the country. Dow drafted, and helped pass, the first state bill in the nation banning alcohol and spearheaded the prohibition movement that resulted in the National Prohibition Act of 1920.

According to city lore, Portland's romance with drink prior to Dow's influence was long and fiery. During the American Revolution, Alice Greene's Tavern was a popular gathering spot where British military captain John Burgoyne's surrender was said to have been celebrated so fervently that one celebrant was accidentally shot to death with a cannon. By Dow's time, chronic drinking was rampant in Portland. Grocery stores featured free samples of spiked punch. Alcohol flowed freely at nearly every kind of communal gathering, including town meetings, funerals, and Fourth of July celebrations. Workers would even take townwide rum breaks twice a day, once in the morning and again in the afternoon.

Through it all, Dow watched from his house on the corner of modern-day Congress and Dow Streets (see the Attractions chapter for information on tours of the Dow Memorial). He believed Mainers consumed more alcohol per capita than any other state in the union, and he was convinced that the preoccupation with drink was at the root of poverty and the destruction of the family. Dow devoted his life to abolishing drinking and was instrumental in the Maine legislature's passage in 1851 of "An Act for the Suppression of Drinking Houses and Tippling Shops," which prohibited the manufacture and sale of alcohol. Dubbed "the Maine Law" by the rest of the country, it was the first of its kind and became a model for prohibition laws across the nation.

Dow became an instant prohibition hero after the Maine Law was passed, and he traveled around the country lecturing on the evils of alcohol. He even ran for president on the Prohibition ticket in 1880. Although he lost his bid for the presidency, the so-called "prophet of prohibition" did serve as mayor of Portland from 1851 to 1859. Under his watch, prohibition was strictly enforced in the city—the mayor threw any found liquor into the sewer and searched shipments of any new merchandise arriving in Portland.

Dow's temperance convictions made him an unpopular character locally—according to the 1940 history book *Portland City Guide* by William Willis, he was

public education was created, and famous men such as Henry Wadsworth Longfellow and the writer and arts patron John Neal called Portland home.

During the 19th century, coastal towns throughout New England began to grow their maritime economies. Part of this growth was geographic—sand and rock were used to push back the shoreline and create more developable land. During the middle of the 19th century, Portland planners dumped tons of fill into the waters along the Neck to build

Neal Dow. NEAL DOW GOVERNING BOARD/MAINE WCTU

"subjected to all manner of humiliating affronts." In a particularly noteworthy display of public discontent under Dow's rule, one man was shot when an angry mob tried unsuccessfully to break into a supply of medicinal liquor stored in the basement of a municipal building. Desperate times? You be the judge. All told, Portland, along with the rest of Maine, was "dry" for nearly 82 years (from 1851 to 1933), thanks largely to Dow.

more roads and commercial and industrial neighborhoods. In 1857 the city added fill to the waters in Back Cove on the north side of the peninsula. Roughly half of the cove was filled in to create the neighborhood now called Bayside.

Since Cleeve and Tucker first set foot on the Neck, only two streets, Cumberland and Oxford, had been added to the original three, Fore, Middle, and Back (later Congress) Streets. In 1852 Portland completed construction on what would become the artery of its

In 2002 a local businessman erected a statue memorializing George Cleeve on his property near the East End walking path after the city council refused to accept the memorial to the early Portland settler because activists were concerned, among other things, that he may have owned a slave.

burgeoning maritime economy, Commercial Street. Expansive, bustling Commercial Street, which today is easily one of the craziest modern traffic anomalies on the East Coast, was of course built before two-lane automobile traffic was ever a consideration. The 100-foot-wide, mile-long street that runs along the water in Portland Harbor was built to link the Grand Trunk railway line on the east end of the peninsula and trains south to Boston on the west end of Portland and to create more space for the construction of the huge warehouses and wharves that now crowded the burgeoning port. Commercial Street allowed Portland, which was quickly solidifying its status as the busiest port in the Northeast during the late 19th century, to handle more goods at greater volumes. Sugar refineries, canning factories, shipyards, coal yards, grain elevators, and distilleries lined Commercial Street, which was known for its hectic days (when arriving merchants and sailors were hard at work) and its rowdy nights (when visiting sailors drank and partied until morning).

By the late 19th century, Portland had firmly established herself as a railway and maritime commercial center relying on domestic and international trade, most notably with Canada to the north. The city's downtown and waterfront streets were crowded with commercial and residential buildings, and the majority of the city's population worked and lived in these few blocks. The Portland Observatory on Munjoy Hill, which was built in 1807 at the beginning of Portland's maritime economy boom, became a key signal station for the city. Lookouts posted in the tower's cupola were responsible for running flags to alert merchants that their

ships were returning to port (for more on the observatory see the Architecture chapter). By the summer of 1866, Portland was the largest commercial port in the nation. No one in the city could predict that one of the greatest American disasters of the century was waiting just around the corner.

THE GREAT FIRE

During the evening of July 4, 1866, Portland experienced several horrific hours that changed the city forever.

The Great Fire of 1866 began during the Independence Day celebrations. A spark, perhaps from a discarded cigar or children playing with firecrackers, ignited a small fire in a Commercial Street boatyard. The fire spread to a nearby lumberyard and then to Brown's Sugarhouse, an enormous sugar factory on Maple Street. The building was soon engulfed in flames, and the fire became even stronger. A south wind carried the fire beyond Commercial Street, through the present-day Old Port area, and up Munjoy Hill to the base of the observatory. Portlanders frantically tried to salvage their belongings as the fire swept across the city. In the end only two deaths were confirmed, but the property loss was staggering. Eighteen hundred buildings were destroyed (causing about $12 million in property loss), and 10,000 Portlanders were left homeless. Longfellow, after visiting the scorched city, compared it to the ash-covered ancient city of Pompeii.

Where fate had forsaken them, weather saved them. During the summer months immediately following the Great Fire, thousands of homeless Portlanders lived in "tent cities" while rebuilding their property. The weather that summer was mercifully mild, and the reconstruction effort moved quickly. At the time, the Great Fire was the most

After the Great Fire, a city ordinance was passed requiring all new buildings in the downtown to be constructed of stone or brick.

destructive fire the country had ever seen. Relief supplies and workers poured in from all over the country to help rebuild the city. The business and financial buildings of Portland along the water in the Old Port were the hardest hit by the fire and had to be completely rebuilt. Middle Street, which before the fire had been partially residential, was rebuilt as a strictly commercial area. The Old Port that we see today was the result of the rebuilding efforts immediately following the fire of 1866. Ironically, we have the Great Fire to thank for the sturdy brick and stone buildings that make the Old Port one of the best examples of Victorian-era commercial architecture in the country (see the Architecture chapter for more on Portland's famous buildings).

CHALLENGES OF THE 20TH CENTURY

The start of the 20th century in Portland heralded a new beginning for the City by the Sea. During the latter half of the 19th century, Portland attracted a diverse crop of new immigrants to the city. Whereas previously Portland's British descendants had shared neighborhoods only with Irish and Canadian transplants, the dawn of the 20th century brought more immigrants from countries like Italy, Greece, Poland, and Armenia. These new citizens were attracted to the intimate community of the port city and the bustling promise of its rebuilt waterfront. They clustered in neighborhoods, largely divided ethnically, in the West End and Munjoy Hill.

The new wave of immigrants changed the face of Portland's politics forever. Prior to 1923 the city was divided into nine wards, each ruled by an elected representative. City politics were governed by an elected mayor, a board of ward aldermen, and a common council of 21 men. The ruling party majority had for decades been fiscally conservative, but the new wave of immigrants demanded expanded social services and a more accessible government. In 1923, after a bitter debate, a Progressive reform to convert Port-

land's leadership won in a voter referendum. Portland's new city government was run by a city manager and a board of five councilmen, each elected by an at-large vote. The change stirred up animosity between wealthy native-born residents, who under the previous system had held a vise grip on city politics for decades, and the working class on Munjoy Hill and elsewhere, who viewed the new system as more accessible and responsive to the needs of the poor. The current city government remains largely true to this groundbreaking Progressive reform—a city manager and a city council of eight, five members who are elected from city districts, and three who are elected for at-large seats.

PORTLAND AND THE WAR EFFORT

As Portland approached 1929 and the dark days of the Great Depression, the Canadian government named St. John, New Brunswick, and Halifax, Nova Scotia, as its primary southern ports, leaving Portland's Canadian trade in ruin. The Depression hurried the area's economic decline, and the once bustling stretch of Commercial Street grew silent. Portland's Harbor would not be busy again until 1941, when the phoenix city would rally once again to transform itself into one of busiest port cities in the country—this time as a builder of World War II ships.

Portland's involvement with World War II is still talked about today, and the record of its contribution is scattered around the city in former forts now turned into tourist attractions (see Fort Williams Park and the Portland Head Light in the Attractions chapter).

In 1941, when the country entered the

war against the Axis Powers, Casco Bay was the closest deepwater port to Europe. As a result, the waters off Portland were used to create convoys that would accompany cargo ships to Europe. Hundreds of minefields and underwater detection devices were planted in the bay's waters. Outposts were erected on Great Diamond, Peaks, Cushings, and Long Islands. Fort Williams on the mainland, Fort Leavitt on Cushings, and the Peaks Island Military Reservation on Peaks all had guns aimed at the oceans around the city. Other base stations were disguised as beach cottages or boats. The lighthouse at Two Lights was even co-opted to protect the bay from what was then considered a very likely attack by German submarines. Luckily, Portlanders managed to work doggedly for the war effort in the city's shipyards and ports from 1941 to 1945 without ever suffering a confirmed attack by the enemy.

During America's four-year campaign in World War II, Portland played a vital role by supplying the navy with thousands of 10,000-ton capacity cargo ships built in two emergency shipyards in South Portland. A company called the Todd-Bath Iron Shipbuilding Corporation won a war contract for the naval ships. The company built its first shipyard on the east side of Cushing Point in South Portland. Several months later the company built a second shipyard, under a subsidiary called the South Portland Shipbuilding Corporation, on the west side of the Point. Thirty thousand skilled and unskilled men and women flocked to fill the jobs at the two shipyards. Villages, housing projects, and homes were hastily erected in South Portland to house the flow of workers from outside the city. These neighborhoods, like Redbank Village, Sagamore Village, and Elizabeth Park, remain some of the most densely populated suburban neighborhoods in Greater Portland.

PORTLAND TODAY AND TOMORROW

The Old Port Reborn

By the 1960s the Old Port had degenerated into one of the seamiest neighborhoods in town. Abandoned warehouses and dilapidated buildings lined the narrow streets of the once bustling port, which had fallen into disrepair when demobilization after World War II slowed the maritime and manufacturing economy. Many old buildings that had stood for over a century were leveled by city planners desperate to find a way to salvage the area. In 1970 real estate investors and commercial and residential renters in the Old Port joined forces to create the Old Port Association, which lobbied to renovate the old warehouses and revive the Old Port as a commercial district. Block by block, the Old Port Association worked to repair sidewalks, plant trees, and remodel old buildings to accommodate bars and restaurants. By the mid-1980s the Old Port was well on its way to a phoenixlike rebirth as the cultural heart of the city—home to a working waterfront reminiscent of the city's economic roots as well as dozens of trendy shops, restaurants, galleries, and nightspots. The Old Port now attracts a bustling tourist industry and is home to close to 200 boutiques and restaurants.

A Diverse City

Portland has a history of change that continues to be distinctly dynamic. The area is unique to the region—in a state whose population is nearly 97 percent white, according to 2000 U.S. Census statistics, Portland's population is relatively ethnically diverse. Munjoy Hill's residents, for example, are 71 percent white, 12 percent Asian, and 11 percent black. Over the past decade Portland has attracted thousands of immigrants from Africa, Central America, and Southeast Asia, who join the descendants of European immigrants from the turn of the last century. The

i In 1862 the U.S. government hanged the infamous slave trader Nathanial Gordon of Portland. He was the only American ever executed for the crime of slavery.

city is also home to a large gay and lesbian population. In fact, Portland passed one of the first gay-rights ordinances in the country in 1992. According to the 2000 census, Portland has the third-largest population of lesbian couples in the country after Santa Fe, New Mexico, and Burlington, Vermont, and the 10th-largest concentration of gay male couples in the nation. The city is home to a number of gay-friendly churches, gay nightspots, and the Rainbow Business and Professional Alliance (a gay business association).

Today, Portland is defined by its eclectic arts community, its relatively affluent, diverse, and well-educated population, and its distinctly liberal politics. The city's inhabitants and elected officials are nearly all Democratic, and many lean to the progressive wing of the party. In 2002 Portland elected Green Party candidate John Eder to the state House of Representatives. Eder was the only Green state representative in the country.

As Portland continues to grow and diversify into the new millennium, the City by the Sea will no doubt face complicated economic, social, and planning challenges that come with expansion. Already, debates related to suburban sprawl, a shortage of affordable housing, and efforts to preserve the working waterfront occupy the local headlines. As the city progresses toward a future decidedly more metropolitan than any the state has ever known, it will certainly be fascinating to witness what form the phoenix assumes this time.

ACCOMMODATIONS

If you're at all familiar with what Portland has to offer, you probably know that you'll need much more than one day to soak it all in. Luckily, whether you're looking for family-friendly accommodations, seaside retreats, or historic hotels in the heart of the downtown, Portland has what you need to get a good night's rest. This chapter lists the best hotel and motel accommodations the city has to offer. Here, you'll find chain establishments as well as independently owned facilities, many within walking distance of the downtown and Old Port districts. Amenities particular to each facility are noted, as are any major attractions in the immediate vicinity. Depending on the location, this can include easy access to the Maine Mall, Portland's city center, or the International Jetport. The listings indicate which hotels and motels are pet friendly. If you are traveling with a furry friend, it's best to call ahead to notify the lodging's proprietor and to check on any added charges—many facilities in Portland charge an extra "sanitation fee" to accommodate your pet.

This chapter covers hotels and motels on the peninsula and beyond, including notable accommodations in Portland's suburbs— Cape Elizabeth, Scarborough, and South Portland. Lodgings in Portland have been divided into four categories—the Downtown/Old Port, the West End, Munjoy Hill, and Portland beyond the Peninsula. The last category includes listings located in a largely commercial district a few miles west of the downtown. The Deering neighborhood is conspicuously absent, as Deering is largely residential and does not have any hotels or motels. Listings closest to the downtown tend to have the highest rates and are the most popular, because of the quality of the facilities as well as their convenient location within walking

distance of the Old Port. But other accommodations off the peninsula have their own distinctive appeal, including the Inn By the Sea in Cape Elizabeth, famous for its lavish wedding receptions, and the numerous hotels and motels at the Maine Mall, where you can shop till you drop right onto your pillow at a hotel within walking distance of the stores.

The inns listed in this chapter are limited to those that do not offer complimentary breakfast. If you yearn for the intimacy of a hot meal around the breakfast table at a small guesthouse or inn, check out the Bed-and-Breakfast Inns chapter.

Portland is a popular place for visitors year-round but particularly during the summer, when the population of the city proper (roughly 64,000) is said to double because of tourists. Rooms during the peak season from Memorial Day through Labor Day, therefore, tend to fill up fast, and for many popular hotels it is advisable to book as early as possible.

Accommodations abound not only in Portland but also throughout the entire southern Maine region, which is always a popular destination for travelers. Only those facilities that are within a 20-minute drive from the city center are listed in this chapter. This means that accommodations in nearby Freeport (of L.L. Bean fame) and Old Orchard Beach (or OOB, a popular seaside resort town) are not listed here.

For more information or advice on accommodations, including those in Freeport, contact the Greater Portland Convention and Visitors Bureau at 245 Commercial Street (207–772–5800; www.visitportland.com). For those of you set on beachfront lodging, call the OOB Chamber of Commerce at (207) 934–2500 or visit their Web site at www.oobme.com.

For the most part, the chapter doesn't list lodgings that are part of national chains, except those that are distinctive because of location, affordability, or special amenities. There is no intention to slight national chains, but because many of them are so well known, you pretty much know what to expect.

Nearly all accommodations listed here offer both nonsmoking and smoking rooms, and most hotels and motels in the area accept discounts through groups like AAA or AARP—make sure to inquire when booking your room. All of the establishments listed here accept major credit cards. Although all hotels and motels are required by law to be wheelchair accessible, you should ask detailed questions about facilities for guests with disabilities to make sure the building is truly accessible for you or your travel buddy. Many facilities provide complimentary shuttle service to the airport, train station, and bus stations; be sure to confirm this when making your reservation if you plan to rely on the transport.

Portland is an eclectic city, and its hotels and motels are no different. From an elegant hotel that dates back to the Roaring Twenties to brand-new accommodations by the bay and suites for extended-stay and business travelers, the city and surrounding suburbs offer the most diverse selection of lodgings in the state. Let this chapter guide your search for the best place to hang your hat.

Price Code

Nailing down rates isn't easy in Portland, which enjoys a peak season not only during the summer but also during the winter (thanks to skiers) and briefly during the fall (otherwise known as "leaf-peeper season"). Still, the summer season in Portland is by far the most popular, and so rates listed in this chapter are confined to the weeks between Memorial Day and Labor Day. It is always

i In 1999 Portland was named "One of North America's 10 Dream Towns" by *Outside Magazine*.

important to confirm rates prior to reserving a room, as many hotel and motel managers interviewed for this chapter claim rates fluctuate daily according to the market. Popular holidays like the Fourth of July may also cause room rates to spike higher than expected. You should also note that Maine levies a 7 percent room tax for accommodations, so be sure to factor this into your travel budget. Rates in the price key refer to standard, double-occupancy rooms.

$. . . . . $80 to $130
$$ . . . . $131 to $200
$$$ . . . . $201 to $270
$$$$ . . . . $271 and up

HOTELS AND MOTELS

Downtown/Old Port

The Eastland Park $–$$
157 High Street
(207) 775–5411, (888) 671–8008
www.eastlandparkhotel.com
The Eastland Park offers more than an elegant night's rest with the convenience of a central location downtown. Staying at the Eastland Park is equal to experiencing a piece of Portland's most celebrated past. When construction began on the lavish Eastland Park Hotel in 1925, it was the largest hotel north of New York City. From the beginning it seems that the Eastland had a knack for the dramatic. When the doors of the 200-plus-room hotel swung open in June 1927, Portland radio personality Graham McNamee and then-governor Ralph Brewster flew over Portland harbor and dropped the keys to the hotel's front door into the ocean, supposedly ensuring that the hotel would never close. Though it never did close for good, the Eastland has gone through its share of changes over the past 80 years, including stints under the ownership of both the Sonesta and Radisson hotel chains. But now, after a massive $2.5 million renovation completed in June 2004, the Eastland has reclaimed its original name and its original glory.

The Eastland is located just off Congress Street near the Portland Museum of Art. Each of the simple, elegant guest rooms includes a coffeemaker, a hair dryer, dataports, cable TV, an office desk, and complimentary wireless Internet access. The hotel business center also offers secure remote printing.

The Eastland Park still retains much of the original elegance it had during its days of pomp and circumstance in the early part of the last century. Valets and bellmen wear navy blue and gold-trimmed uniforms reminiscent of staff uniforms from the 1930s. An enormous bouquet of flowers greets guests in the elegant hotel lobby, which features high ceilings and the original marble floor and crystal chandelier.

Last but not least, the Eastland is home to easily the classiest cocktail lounge in town—the Top of the East. Located on the 13th (er, "R") floor of the hotel, the Top of the East features wide windows with stunning views of Portland worthy of the Great Gatsby himself. Relax in the city's only rooftop lounge while you look out at Casco Bay, the Portland skyline, and the western mountains. The lounge is open Sunday through Wednesday from 4:00 P.M. to midnight and Thursday through Saturday from 4:00 P.M. to 1:00 A.M.

i The Eastland's guest register has always included rich and famous visitors—does the name Julia Roberts ring a bell? In 1927 legendary pilot Charles Lindbergh became one of the first stars to stay at the Eastland after a lavish banquet was thrown for him in the hotel's ballroom.

Hilton Garden Inn at
the Portland Downtown Waterfront $$$
65 Commercial Street
(207) 780–0780, (800) HILTONS
www.portlanddowntownwaterfront.garden
inn.com
The Hilton Garden Inn at the Portland Downtown Waterfront sits along Commercial Street steps away from Casco Bay in Portland's Old Port. Located right across the street from the Casco Bay Ferry Terminal, the hotel boasts brand-new amenities (it first opened its doors in 2003) blocks away from all of the action in the busiest streets of the Old Port. A room at the Hilton Garden Inn has all of the perks you'd expect from an internationally renowned hotel chain—high-speed wireless Internet access throughout the hotel, electronic door locks, a workspace in each room, 27-inch cable TV with complimentary HBO, and, of course, comfy king and queen beds.

Although you're a stone's throw from the Old Port and all of its entertainment and eateries, you may want to hang out a bit inside the hotel and stare out the window (many of the 120 guest rooms at the Garden Inn have ocean views) or explore the building to check out the fitness center, the business center, the indoor heated pool and whirlpool, or the Pavilion Lounge and Bar. If you need to bring your work with you, no worries—the Hilton Garden Inn also can accommodate large business functions. A complimentary shuttle service is available as well as non-smoking and smoking rooms.

Holiday Inn By the Bay $$
88 Spring Street
(207) 775–2311, (800) 345–5050
www.innbythebay.com
For more than three decades, the Holiday Inn By the Bay has cast its shadow on the downtown from its elevated perch on Spring Street. The hotel sits on the unofficial border between the West End (which, according to conventional wisdom, begins, oh, around High Street) and the downtown and is the area's "Old Reliable" for quality, convenient accommodations.

The Holiday Inn By the Bay boasts 239 guest rooms and executive suites, half of which have a view of Casco Bay. Guest room amenities include dataport Internet access, phones with voice mail, and coffeemakers, and the hotel has a fitness center, a sauna, a 24-hour business center, and Greater Portland's largest indoor hotel swimming pool.

Ample parking is available with valet service, which is handy because with this prime location in the center of town, you'll probably want to leave your car behind and hoof it most days. The hotel is located on Spring Street, which runs along the peninsula from the Evergreen Cemetery deep in the West End to Middle Street in the heart of the Old Port. The theme of the Holiday Inn By the Bay could truly be "location, location, location": A 10-minute walk west on Spring will land you in one of the most architecturally beautiful residential neighborhoods in the country, and a mere five-minute walk east will find you peering into boutiques, sipping locally brewed java, and breathing in the salty air in the Old Port.

Portland Harbor Hotel $$$
468 Fore Street
(207) 775–9090, (888) 798–9090
www.portlandharborhotel.com
The Portland Harbor Hotel is another of the city's newest hotels (it was completed in 2002) and is located along Fore Street (a street known for its nightlife) in the Old Port. But the Portland Harbor Hotel itself is not a party spot. Each deluxe room includes custom-made bedroom furnishings with his-and-her armoires, wireless high-speed Internet access, digital cable, Music Choice digital stereo, and bathrooms to knock your socks off. The hotel's attention to the powder room is decidedly unique. Luxury bathrooms with granite showers, soaking tubs, and a separate bathroom stereo system are standard here. Come to think of it, luxury bathrooms seem like common sense—after a long day exploring Portland, who wouldn't like to relax in a warm bath and then crawl under 250-thread-count sheets to doze off? A complimentary turndown service and a chocolate on your pillow complete the scene.

Rooms at the Portland Harbor Hotel include views of Fore Street and Union Street, or the hotel garden. Light sleepers beware: The Old Port's bars and nightclubs can be extremely noisy over the weekend, especially during the summer and especially on Wharf

Street, which is right next to the hotel. If you mind throngs of loud partiers below your window at 1:00 A.M., request a room facing the interior courtyard. The Portland Harbor Hotel is also home to a top-rated restaurant and a courtyard with fountains and a full bar. Concierge and valet service is also available. Pets are allowed, with an additional pet fee of $35 per night.

The Regency Hotel $$$
20 Milk Street
(207) 774–4200, (800) 727–3436
www.theregency.com
The Regency is located in a 19th-century armory in the center of the Old Port on a cobblestone side street a stone's throw from the water. The hotel features 95 luxury guest rooms, each with complimentary newspaper services, high-speed Internet access, nightly turndown services, and complimentary coffee delivered to the room with a wake-up call in the morning. The Regency is a favorite for locals and visitors alike, and many honeymooning natives have spent the first nights of their marriage here. Guests at the Regency are treated royally and have access to a number of amenities, including valet parking, an in-house spa, a fitness center, and, of course, the shops, restaurants, and entertainment available throughout the Old Port. Ask about the Regency's custom guest packages, which can include lodging, meals, and services from the spa. Pets, we're sorry to say, are not allowed.

Munjoy Hill

Victorian Terrace $$$–$$$$
84 Eastern Promenade
(207) 774–9083, (800) 393–9083
www.victorianterrace.com
The Victorian Terrace is made up of three 19th-century houses that sit side by side along the Eastern Promenade—a popular spot for jogging, sledding, and otherwise hanging out and also the location of the annual July 4 fireworks. At the Victorian Terrace you won't have to make do with one

room. Instead, apartments are the norm. Each apartment is elegantly decorated and includes television with cable, VCR, an iron and ironing board, a full kitchen, free off-street parking, free local calling, a weekly housekeeping service, and a spectacular view of the ocean. The Victorian also features coin-operated laundry rooms. The grounds include a grill on the front lawn, a Zen garden, and a porch for sitting and enjoying one of the most beautiful views in the city. Some of the apartments even have their own private decks. And, as an added comfort, the proprietor of the Victorian Terrace places a teddy bear on every pillow each night. Pets are accepted on a case-by-case basis; ask about the additional pet fee.

i Portland's annual Fourth of July fireworks are launched over the bay from the Eastern Promenade in front of the Victorian Terrace.

Portland beyond the Peninsula

Doubletree Hotel $$
1230 Congress Street
(207) 774–5611, (800) 222–TREE
www.doubletree.com
Located on outer Congress Street, one of busiest streets in the city, the Doubletree is part of a neighborhood loosely called the Ballpark District because of Hadlock Field, a baseball park a few blocks away (for more on Hadlock Field and the Sea Dogs professional baseball team, see the Parks and Recreation chapter). Outer Congress is home to many locally owned and national retail stores that make this neighborhood more commercial than residential. But, despite being in a commercial district, the Doubletree is still only minutes away from Portland's waterfront and the Old Port (however, it's probably best to make the trip by car because traffic on outer Congress can make the walk dangerous). Parking abounds in the hotel's large parking lot, and the Doubletree has the added convenience of being close to both the Portland

Jetport and the city's bus and train stations (the Concord Trailways bus station and the Amtrak/Downeaster train station, in fact, are just around the corner).

The hotel is sleek, clean, and affordably priced. A standard room includes high-speed Internet access, an ironing board, a coffee-maker, and a speakerphone, among other amenities. The hotel offers a heated indoor pool, a fitness center, a cafe, and Pete and Larry's Lounge, which has been known to have karaoke at night (faint of heart, beware!). The hotel is pet friendly and sweets friendly—each guest is greeted with freshly baked chocolate chip cookies.

Fairfield Inn $–$$
340 Park Avenue
(207) 871–0611
www.fairfieldinn.com
The Fairfield Inn is located in the Ballpark District near Hadlock Field, 1 mile from Portland's downtown. It is run by the national Marriott hotel chain, which means this hotel has amenities for both the leisure and business traveler. A state-of-the-art card-key security system keeps each guest room secure. Each room has a well-lit work desk; free HBO, CNN, ESPN, and basic cable; and free local phone service. There is an outdoor pool, which is open during the summer, and a coin-operated laundry room. A complimentary continental breakfast is also provided every morning, and smoking rooms are available.

Holiday Inn–Portland West $$
81 Riverside Street
(207) 774–5601, (800) 695–8284
www.portlandholidayinn.com
The Portland West Holiday Inn is located just off Interstate 95 on Riverside Street, an industrial and commercial road that is packed with restaurants and bars. While it's really not located in a conventional "neighborhood," this hotel offers all of the amenities you've come to expect at a Holiday Inn, like dataport Internet access and room phones with voice mail, as well as extras specific to the Portland

West location, such as a new indoor garden courtyard, two heated pools (one inside, one outside), a fitness room complete with a whirlpool and a sauna, and Zachary's Restaurant and Lounge, which features live bands on Friday and Saturday nights. Meeting and banquet facilities are available for rent at the hotel, and pets are welcome.

Howard Johnson Plaza Hotel $–$$
155 Riverside Street
(207) 774–5861, (800) I–GO–HOJO
www.hojo.com
The Howard Johnson Plaza Hotel is located in the Riverside district of Portland near exit 48 of the Maine Turnpike (I–95). Each room at the HOJO includes a coffeemaker, Internet dataports, and a 25-inch television with cable and HBO, among other amenities. Special "home office rooms" are also available for the business traveler. These rooms have added perks, including a microwave and refrigerator, a desk workstation, a cordless phone, and complimentary snacks and bottled water. The HOJO also features an indoor pool, a hot tub, a fitness center, a lounge, and two in-house restaurants. In addition, the hotel has 10 convention rooms available for booking.

Motel 6 $
1 Riverside Street
(207) 775–0111, (800) 4–MOTEL6
www.motel6.com
The Motel 6 on Riverside Street offers reliable, inexpensive lodging in a commercial district only 3 miles from the city's downtown. Rooms at Motel 6 are simple and clean, albeit relatively small (some rooms seem to barely fit all the furniture). Every room is outfitted with dataports and free HBO and ESPN. Free coffee is available in the motel lobby. Pets are welcome, and kids stay free.

Super 8 Motel $
208 Larrabee Road, Westbrook
(207) 854–1881, (800) 800–8000
www.super8.com
Portland's Super 8 Motel actually lies just over the town line in neighboring Westbrook. The motel is a standard Super 8 offering— amenities include free continental breakfast; television with cable, CNN, HBO, and ESPN; an indoor pool and hot tub; and fax services. Children under 12 years old stay free with their parents, and group rates are available. Downtown Portland is less than 10 miles away.

Greater Portland

Sure, it might be nice to stay in the city, but then you'd miss out on all the wonderful accommodations just minutes away in the Portland suburbs of South Portland, Cape Elizabeth, and Scarborough. Most Portlanders know that the best deals and the best finds aren't in the city proper. In this section you'll find listings for chain motels and hotels perfect for the family on the go, as well as lavish independently owned hotels tucked away by the ocean. And the best part is that each of these facilities is no more than a 20-minute drive from Portland's downtown.

For South Portland and the Maine Mall area, which has the largest cluster of hotels and motels in the city, a few notables are highlighted, but you might also want to call the Greater Portland Convention and Visitors Bureau for more information on chain hotels not listed, including the Days Inn and the Marriott.

Embassy Suites Hotel $$
1050 Westbrook Street
(207) 775–2200, (800) 753–8767
www.embassysuitesportland.com
The Embassy Suites Hotel is located just 500 yards from the Portland Jetport. As the hotel's name implies, suites are the norm here, with 119 spacious two-room accommodations, each with a separate bedroom and living room. Each suite comes equipped with a galley kitchen, a sofa bed and work desk, and two televisions with cable and in-suite movies. Be sure to check out the popular Café Stroudwater restaurant on the first floor, which has received a five-star rating from the

Portland Press Herald for its American-style bistro cuisine. Included with each room is a full breakfast and two-hour happy hour.

The Higgins Beach Inn $$
34 Ocean Avenue, Scarborough
(207) 883–6684, (800) 836–2322
www.higginsbeachinn.com

Owned by proprietors Bob Westburg and Diane Garofalo, the Higgins Beach Inn is a three-story, 19th-century colonial revival hotel a block away from the popular beach for which the inn was named (see the Beaches and Ocean Activities chapter for more on Higgins Beach). The inn has functioned as a guesthouse for nearly 100 years after being converted from a private home by former owners Mr. and Mrs. Edward Samuel Higgins around the turn of the last century. Rooms at the inn are quaint and reminiscent of bed-and-breakfast accommodations, with antique furniture and limited high-tech amenities—guest rooms do not have televisions, and wireless Internet access is available only on the first floor. Some rooms have shared baths; others have private baths. The entire hotel is nonsmoking.

Be sure to stop for a meal at the in-house restaurant, Garofalo's, which is named after co-owner Diane and recently received four out of five stars from the *Portland Press Herald*.

The quiet neighborhood along Higgins Beach where the inn is located is populated largely by locals during the colder months but swells with visitors young and old during the summer. The inn is therefore strictly a seasonal stopover; it is open only from mid-May through mid-October.

> **i** Too many places to go and too many people to see? The staff at the Time Machine, an independent concierge service in South Portland, can complete simple day-to-day tasks for you, such as shopping, laundry, light office work, and pet transportation, so you can kick back and enjoy the finer things. Call (207) 741–5000 for more information.

Inn By the Sea $$$$
40 Bowery Beach Road, Cape Elizabeth
(207) 799–3134, (800) 888–4287
www.innbythesea.com

The Inn By the Sea is a sprawling, luxury hotel that overlooks Crescent Beach, one of the most popular stretches of shoreline in southern Maine. Here, you have your choice of guest room suites, one-bedroom lofts and garden cottages, and two-bedroom beach house units, each immaculately decorated with provincial country flair. The inn is a popular spot for locals and visitors alike and is often booked for wedding ceremonies and receptions and small corporate meetings. A stay at the inn could be both relaxing (take a leisurely stroll along the beach or order gourmet lobster dishes at the inn's Audubon Room Restaurant) and active (outdoor activities at the inn include tennis, cross-country skiing, and swimming in the outdoor heated pool). Golfers can also fit in a game or two at the nearby Purpoodock Golf Club.

Pets are welcome in certain "pet-friendly" suites that come with special pet amenities. The inn also offers a "doggie menu" and a dog-walking service. To reserve with your pet, you must give the inn advance notification, including your pet's name.

The Marriott at Sable Oaks $$–$$$
200 Sable Oaks Drive, South Portland
(207) 871–8000, (800) 752–8810
www.mariotthotels.com

Tucked away on a quiet hill near the Maine Mall, the Marriott at Sable Oaks features an 18-hole golf course in its backyard for the golfing enthusiast. The hotel has 227 guest rooms, including five suites, and each room includes a large work desk, cable TV, wireless Internet access, two telephones with voice mail, and an in-room coffeemaker. If you're not interested in hitting the greens, check out the in-house fitness center (with a whirlpool and sauna) or take a swim in the indoor heated pool.

> **i** If you find yourself in a pinch for accommodations at the last minute, take Interstate 295 south from Portland and get off at exit 2 to Scarborough. The stretch of Route 1 West that winds through town is lined with several discount motels, many of which often have peak-season vacancies.

The Sheraton $$$–$$$$
363 Maine Mall Road, South Portland
(207) 775–6161, (800) 325–3535
www.sheraton.com/southportland

The cylindrical Sheraton Hotel has remained a visual landmark at the Maine Mall since it opened its doors in the 1970s, which is saying quite a bit, given that the current competition includes too many neon signs and sprawling box stores to count. The Sheraton is located in the center of the Maine Mall area—its immediate neighbors include Macy's department store—and this makes it a favorite for visiting shoppers. But the Sheraton doesn't appeal just to consumers; this hotel, which is owned by Starwood Hotels and Resorts Worldwide, Inc., is also a favorite for all types of leisure and business travelers. Sure, the curvy design of the building is a gaudy reminder of kitschy modern architecture, but inside, each of the 219 guest rooms and suites is sleek and contemporary. Each room features floor-to-ceiling windows that overlook the bright lights of the mall and beyond, and kids are sure to love the heated indoor pool and the glass ceiling on the building's roof.

EXTENDED-STAY AND TEMPORARY ACCOMMODATIONS

Extended Stay America
Portland-Scarborough
2 Ashley Drive, Scarborough
(207) 883–0554, (800) EXT–STAY
www.extendedstayhotels.com

The Extended Stay facility is located in Scarborough near the Maine Mall. The single-room Extended Stay studios include a fully appointed kitchen, a workspace with WiFi Internet access, free local phone calls with personalized voice mail, laundry facilities, an ironing board and iron, and kitchen and dining utensils. Housekeeping services are also included for both overnight and extended-stay visitors. And, for those of you who wouldn't consider a home away from home without your favorite pet, Extended Stay allows pets for an additional sanitation fee of $25 per day with a maximum total charge, per stay, of $75. Suites during peak season cost $99.00 per night, or $64.99 a night for seven or more nights.

The Percy Inn
15 Pine Street
(207) 871–POET, (888) 41–PERCY
www.percyinn.com

Dale Northrup, the former hotel critic turned innkeeper who owns the Percy Inn in Portland's West End, also owns three apartment-style suites that he rents out strictly for long-term guests. The Park Row apartment is located on Park Street in a gorgeous Federal-style brick row house that dates back to the early 19th century. The apartment includes a living room with a working fireplace, a full kitchen, a bedroom with an ornamental fireplace, and a full bath. Two other studios are also available at different locations in Portland's West End. All three extended-stay accommodations must be rented for at least one week. All long-term accommodations, like the Percy Inn itself, are located in one of Portland's most elegant residential neighborhoods, just blocks away from the city center. Pets are not allowed. Weekly rates run from $400 to $700, depending on the location.

Residence Inn
800 Roundwood Drive, Scarborough
(207) 883–0400, (800) 331–3131
www.residenceinnscarborough.com

Part of the Marriott hotel chain, the Residence Inn in Scarborough is designed for extended stays. Each of the 78 suites includes a separate living and sleeping space, a fully equipped kitchen, and a sofa bed in the living room. High-speed Internet access in every suite is complimentary. A hot breakfast buffet is served daily, and an evening social happens every night Monday through Thursday. Pets are welcome, but owners must pay a $75, nonrefundable "sanitation fee." Suites run on a tiered-rate system starting at $199 per night.

Sable Oaks Suites
303 Sable Oaks Drive, South Portland
(207) 775–3900
Formerly owned by the national AmeriSuites hotel chain, Sable Oaks Suites was purchased by a local owner in early 2005 and offers strictly suite accommodations. Located near the Maine Mall, the hotel has 130 suites, each with separate living and sleeping areas, a refrigerator, a microwave, a wet bar, a coffeemaker and complimentary coffee, and cable TV. Suites can sleep up to six people. Sable Oaks also features a fitness center, a heated indoor pool, laundry services, and valet parking. Complimentary hot breakfast is served every morning. Nightly rates start at $159; for bookings of seven or more nights, the nightly rate drops to $99.

Because Sable Oaks had only recently switched ownership at the time of this book's publication, you should probably call ahead to confirm that the amenities and rates listed here are still valid.

Victorian Terrace
84 Eastern Promenade
(207) 774–9083, (800) 393–9083
www.victorianterrace.com
The Victorian Terrace apartments may be rented for longer stays at a peak-season weekly rate of $900 to $1,800, depending on the size of the apartment. Monthly stays cost between $2,400 and $5,000. For more on the Victorian Terrace, see the listing in the "Hotels and Motels" section of this chapter.

BED-AND-BREAKFAST INNS

Portland is renowned for its historic architecture, so it's no wonder that quality bed-and-breakfast accommodations are plentiful. Many of these bed-and-breakfast inns are clustered in the West End neighborhood, where some of the city's wealthiest residents built their estates in the mid- to late 19th century. Several of these former homes have been restored and redecorated into bed-and-breakfasts, with interior design styles ranging from the modern to the Victorian. Beyond the West End are other B&Bs, including a quaint wood-frame home near Deering Oaks Park, which is one of the best deals in the city, and an oceanside cabin that smells of fresh pine. When you stay in a Portland B&B, you may forgo the amenities of cable television and in-room telephones, but in return you'll gain the experience of sleeping in some of the finest buildings on the East Coast—a pretty reasonable trade.

Despite the emphasis on the simple life, you won't give up all of the outside world if you choose to stay in one of the city's B&Bs. Portland is nothing if not progressive, and many of the innkeepers listed in this chapter have added amenities for the business traveler, including Internet access, fax machines, and, in some cases, free use of a communal office. Where available, these amenities are listed.

Bed-and-breakfast inn accommodations are a breed apart from hotel and motel lodgings. Many of the B&Bs listed in this chapter have no more than 10 guest rooms, and most value peace and quiet—meaning that pets and children are difficult to accommodate in most cases. While the inns are legally required to accept families with children, most request that you call ahead and notify them of the age of your child beforehand to

make sure that the inn (and your reserved room) is appropriate. Smaller inns that are full during peak season (Memorial Day through Labor Day) may have a tougher time accommodating children than larger inns or those with enough empty rooms to afford each guest some privacy. Always call ahead and don't be afraid to negotiate.

Most bed-and-breakfasts listed here do not accept pets, nor do they allow smoking on the premises. Exceptions, however, are noted.

Rates for bed-and-breakfast inns in Portland tend to hover around $20 to $50 a night higher than local hotel and motel accommodations. Because of the small size of the city, the B&B market tends to be incredibly competitive, so each proprietor has attempted to develop a unique angle to attract guests. Many of the inns feature beautiful original artwork and gorgeously maintained antiques. Others cater to the family or the business traveler. Where appropriate, the unique features of each accommodation are noted. Because the amenities offered vary by establishment, it's best to call ahead to make sure that the bed-and-breakfast offers what you need.

Whatever your preference, be it family-style accommodations or the serene decadence of a smaller inn, we hope this chapter helps you find the perfect inn for your needs.

Price Code

The following price code will help you identify the location that best fits your budget. Prices listed in this chapter correspond to average in-season room rates for double occupancy. The peak season in Maine typically runs from Memorial Day through Labor Day.

$. . . . . $45 to $65
$$ . . . . $66 to $90
$$$ . . . . $91 to $135
$$$$ . . . . $136 to $200
$$$$$ . . . . $201 and up

You should note that Maine adds a 7 per-cent room tax for accommodations. Some establishments offer discounts through AAA, AARP, or their own frequent-guest programs. Most also take payment in at least one major credit card, but you should call ahead to confirm.

WEST END

The Chadwick $$$–$$$$
140 Chadwick Street
(207) 774–5141
www.thechadwick.com
This small inn's proximity to the largest hospital in the state (it's just a block away from Maine Medical Center) makes it a popular spot for relatives of hospital employees or patients who are in town for a couple of nights. For this reason, owner Sarah DeDoes offers a special rate for Maine Med–related guests.

Finding the Right B&B

Bed-and-breakfasts often can't afford extensive advertising, so finding the right B&B for your family can be a bit challenging. Luckily, you can get information on many of the accommodations in Portland and beyond from the Maine Innkeepers' Association, an industry trade group that represents 650 lodging properties of all types throughout the state. To get more information on a member bed-and-breakfast, visit the association's Web site at www.maine inns.com or call the association at (207) 865–6100.

But you don't have to be headed to the hospital to enjoy the Chadwick. DeDoes is a former public transportation employee who has done her share of traveling, and her globe-trotting flair touches every part of the interior design of this Queen Anne–style home. The inn is cozy, there are only four rooms, and each room has an ethnic theme. For example, the African Room boasts bright yellow and brown trim around a queen-size bed. The Irish Room includes a full-size bed, white walls, and bold hunter-green accents. Each room comes with complimentary liqueur matched (loosely) to its exotic theme, and afternoon tea and sweets are served every day in the lounge. The rooms do not have television, but TV is available in the guest lounge. All of the rooms have private baths, although most are not attached to the rooms. DeDoes supplies thick terrycloth bathrobes for those guests with satellite bathrooms.

An office with a fax machine, Internet access, and a paper shredder is available free of charge. DeDoes is also a notary public. Due to the size of the inn, DeDoes refers families with children or pets to more appropriate lodgings elsewhere. The Chadwick is non-smoking. Off-street parking is available.

The Inn at Park Spring $$$$
153 Spring Street
(207) 774–1059, (800) 437–8511
www.innatparkspring.com
Owned by husband-and-wife team John and Nancy Gonsalves, the Inn at Park Spring has both Victorian ambience and a great location to its credit. The inn is located on Spring Street, near High Street. It is the West End Victorian inn closest to the downtown (the Portland Museum of Art is right around the corner). Situated in an 1835 brick town house, the inn features six guest rooms (all of which were decorated by Nancy), each with a private bath. The rooms on the first floor are located in the back of the house; one is decorated with a cottage flair and the other in traditional European style. The second floor features classic Victorian interiors. The third-floor rooms

are more modern, with wall-to-wall carpeting. Lodging at the inn includes a complete gourmet breakfast as well as coffee, tea, and snacks. Rooms do not have TVs, although the sitting room on the first floor has a small set (as well as complimentary port and brandy). Children over 10 years old are welcome, but pets are not. Off-street parking is available.

The Inn on Carleton $$$$
46 Carleton Street
(207) 775–1910, (800) 639–1779
www.innoncarleton.com
Owned by southern natives Sue and Phil Cox, this impeccably preserved town house dates back to 1869, when it was owned by merchant and shopkeeper Gilbert Bailey. The Coxes have owned this six-room inn for 12 years and have outfitted the entire interior with ornate Victorian-era furniture—and we're not talking about just a few vases and a chair or two. Either Sue or Phil has carefully selected each piece—from the dew-drop crystal chandelier in the sitting room to the antique wooden birdhouse in the dining room—to recreate the Victorian elegance enjoyed by Bailey. And luckily for weary travelers, the most memorable antiques are the beds.

The Inn on Carleton is famous among travelers for its beds. Each room in this inn features an elegant, Victorian-era bed that will take your breath away. Nearly all of the beds are tester beds, meaning four posters capped with a velvet or satin-lined wooden canopy. The oldest bed in the inn is located in the Lord Brian Room. According to the Coxes, this queen-size half-tester bed decorated with hand-carved cherubs dates back to the royal court of France circa 1830.

A fax machine is available for guests, and some rooms have phone jacks for modem hookups. Each room has a private bath. Both pets and smoking are prohibited at the inn, although Ben and Jerry, the Coxes' two Maine coon cats, lounge in the inn's common areas. Accordingly, those with severe fur allergies might want to stay elsewhere. The Coxes accommodate families with children age nine and older. Full breakfasts are served family-style in the dining room. Parking is available.

Morrill Mansion $$$–$$$$
249 Vaughn Street
(207) 774–6900
Opened in August 2006, the Morrill Mansion is Portland's newest B&B. The mansion is located a couple of blocks from the Maine Medical Center hospital in Portland's West End and was the home of Charles Morrill, who owned B&M Baked Beans on the north side of Portland. This brick, Italianate-style mansion has seven guest rooms, with private bathrooms, as well as a guest living room and a dining room with a fireplace. Owners David and Chris Parker foster a friendly, quiet atmosphere. The Parkers' pug dog, Moby, calls the mansion home, but no guest pets are allowed. Rooms have modern amenities, and rates include a continental breakfast.

The Percy Inn $$$–$$$$$
15 Pine Street
(207) 871–POET, (888) 41–PERCY
www.percyinn.com
Dale Northrup, owner of the Percy Inn, worked as a hotel reviewer for 20 years before opening his own home away from home here on Pine Street. Northrup applied his decades of experience in the business to his inn, adding unusual amenities to each room that he found particularly useful while traveling (for example, each nightstand is equipped with a weather radio). The inn is located in an 1830s-era brick town house, not far from Congress Street and the downtown. A small sitting room featuring an oft-utilized player piano is located just to the right of the entrance. Northrup cooks the buffet-style breakfast every morning in the kitchen on the first floor and keeps extra scones and cakes in the second-floor breakfast room all day for snacking. Each room is decorated simply and elegantly and named after a famous poet in honor of Longfellow Square (of Henry Wadsworth Longfellow fame), which is just around the corner from the Percy.

Each room has its own TV/VCR, phone, fax machine, CD player, weather radio, and wet bar. During the summer Northrup offers guests heading to the beach a complimentary packed cooler, beach blanket, and towels. Satellite suites and extended-stay accommodations can also be booked through the Percy Inn.

Light sleepers take note: This inn is located across the street from one of the most popular bars in town—Blackstones. In our experience, Blackstones' clientele is one of the nicest around, but on weekends the sidewalk across the street can be noisy with people outside smoking cigarettes.

Speaking of smoking, it's not allowed at the Percy. Pets aren't either. Call ahead if you have children. Parking is available. If you enjoy lots of sunlight, be sure to ask for a sunny room, as some rooms can be dim.

Pomegranate Inn $$$$–$$$$$
49 Neal Street
(207) 772–1006, (800) 356–0408
www.pomegranateinn.com

If you like ornate decadence shaken with a twist, the Pomegranate Inn is unmatched. Owned and operated for 16 years by interior designer Isabel Smiles, each room in this spacious mansion has been painstakingly decorated from top to bottom with bold colors, modern art, and fantastical furniture. Be sure to check out the two enormous papier-mâché pomegranates in the dining room window. According to the inn manager, Chris Monahan, Smiles wanted the Pomegranate Inn to be a place that is distinctively different from the homes of most visitors. And we think she succeeded.

Smiles commissioned renowned interior designer and artist Heidi Gerquist to hand-paint designs on the walls of all but one of the eight guest rooms. Gerquist used bright colors like navy blue leaf designs over teal in one room and large, impressionistic orange flowers over warm red walls in another. All of the rooms have their own baths, and one, in the carriage house out back, has its own private entrance through the garden. Each room is uniquely stunning and comes equipped with a telephone and television. Five of the rooms have fireplaces.

Breakfast includes a fruit course, a hot entree like poached eggs and salmon, and fresh baked goods. Guests are greeted between 4:00 and 6:00 P.M. each evening with wine and tea in the main room. Children over 16 are welcome at the Pomegranate, but pets are prohibited. The Pomegranate is a non-smoking inn.

The West End Inn $$$$
146 Pine Street
(207) 772–1377
www.westendbb.com

The West End Inn is situated in a 19th-century brick row house in the heart of its namesake neighborhood. If you're looking for a nice, quiet retreat in a traditionally decorated Victorian-style home, the West End Inn is your place. Its current owners, Dan and Michele Brown, purchased the inn in 2003. The B&B has six rooms, all named after islands on Casco Bay; each one has a private bath and elegant four-poster or canopy bed. A hearty breakfast of homemade granola, homemade baked goods, and hot entrees like lemon pancakes with blueberry compote is served in the bright dining room on the first floor. The original Norman Rockwell prints hanging on the downstairs walls under chandeliers suspended from ornately carved ceilings evoke the elegance of times gone by.

The inn cannot accommodate pets and, according to the assistant manager, is not equipped for infants or toddlers. Smoking is not allowed within the building. Each room has cable television, but if you want to hook up your modem or use the fax machine, these complimentary amenities are available in the lounge. The inn may also be booked for small private events. Off-street parking is available.

OTHER PORTLAND NEIGHBORHOODS

The Inn at St. John $–$$$$
939 Congress Street
(207) 773–6481, (800) 636–9127
www.innatstjohn.com

The Inn at St. John is the oldest continuously operated inn in the city. Originally dubbed the Hotel Victoria, the inn was built in 1897 by railroad baron John Deering to house passengers arriving by train from the nearby Union Station. The Union Station train depot has long since been demolished, but this Portland staple continues to greet guests more than a century after its creation. These days, the 39-room inn is the perennial favorite for visitors looking for hotel prices with a Victorian inn flourish.

The inn is essentially a mix of hotel and bed-and-breakfast influences. Each room is decorated with a fairly traditional Victorian flare, except the three newly renovated first-floor rooms, which have whirlpool tubs and a Holiday Inn–style simplicity. Most of the rooms have private baths, and all have television with cable and HBO. The lobby is large and not as inviting as most (it functions mostly as a through-way for traffic to and from guest rooms), and the morning meal is a simple continental breakfast with baked goods brought in from off-site. While pets are off-limits, smokers will be happy to learn that this is one of the few inns in Portland that allows a lighted cigarette. Perhaps because of this option, the inn's lobby can have a slight musty odor to it, although all the guest rooms are kept fresh and clean.

The inn's location near busy St. John street is not ideal: The Greyhound bus station is across the street, and a small strip mall and chain restaurants are around the corner. While parking is available, occasionally guests must park on the street or in adjacent restaurant lots when the inn's lot is full. Despite these drawbacks, the inn is still a reliable favorite for inexpensive, comfy accommodations. If you want to feel like you're in a Victorian B&B when you're in your room, and you don't mind feeling like you're in a hotel in the hallway, the Inn at St. John is the place for you.

Wild Iris Inn $$$–$$$$
273 State Street
(207) 775–0224, (800) 600–1557
www.wildirisinn.com

Located about a 10-minute walk from Monument Square, this inn near Deering Oaks Park is blocks away from the snarl of Victorian-era locales in the West End. If you stay at the Wild Iris, you'll have to trek uphill to get to the downtown area, but this quaint, affordable inn makes the extra five-minute walk worth it. Owned by innkeeper Diane Edwards, this wood-frame house was built in 1892 and has functioned as an inn for the past seven years. Edwards lives at the inn with her teenage daughter and takes care of its upkeep herself, which makes staying at the Wild Iris kind of like visiting the immaculately tidy home of your favorite sister.

The Wild Iris features seven guest rooms, each named after a flower. The largest is the Iris Room on the third floor, with sunny blue walls and a dramatic Palladian window. Five of the guest rooms have private baths.

In an attempt to attract business travelers to the inn, Edwards recently installed an office exclusively for guest use that includes high-speed Internet access, a computer, a printer, and a fax machine. Wireless Internet is also available throughout the inn. The rooms do not have televisions, but there is a set in the common room. There is a small garden behind the building.

Traffic advisory: State Street, where the inn is located, is one of the busiest through-ways in Portland. Light sleepers may want to request a room at the back of the house.

Breakfast is described as an "expanded continental" and is served buffet-style in the dining room. A few rooms are conducive to small children, but Edwards asks that those bringing babies or toddlers call ahead to confirm that an appropriate room has been reserved. Pets and smoking are not allowed.

SCARBOROUGH

The Holiday House
Bed and Breakfast and Motor Inn $$$$
106 East Grand Avenue, Scarborough
(207) 883–4417
www.holidayhouseinn.com
Located along Pine Point Beach in Scarborough, this seasonal B&B and motor lodge is open mid-May through mid-October. The country-style accommodations at the Holiday House are perfect for large families looking for a place to put the kids (the motor lodge) and the grandparents (the adjacent B&B). The Holiday House B&B features eight rooms and is located in a 100-year-old house that has been in the same family for three generations. The motel unit has 16 rooms and does not include breakfast.

The Holiday House was originally opened more than 40 years ago by the Boutet family. Today, Mary and Steven Boutet carry on the tradition begun by Steven's grandparents a half century ago. All eight rooms in the Holiday House are cozy, and each has a view of the ocean. The private beach that makes up the Holiday House backyard is open only to guests. Rooms are decorated with a quaint rustic flavor, and the exposed wood paneling running throughout the house gives the air in the home the crisp aroma of a log cabin. Each room has a TV, basic cable, and a phone with local access. A fax machine is available in the lounge, but there are no modem connections here. In the morning, a continental-style breakfast is served in a simple dining room with panoramic views of the beach. Pets are not accepted at the Holiday House.

THE ISLANDS

Chebeague Island Inn $$$$–$$$$$
Rural Route 1, Great Chebeague Island
(207) 846–5155
www.chebeagueislandinn.com
This island inn is located in a restored 1920s-era hotel on one of the largest islands in Casco Bay. Accessible by ferry from Portland or Yarmouth, the Chebeague Island Inn features 21 guest rooms, each with views of the ocean or gardens. The inn, which was restored in 2004, is within walking distance of the historic Stone Wharf. Some rooms have private baths. None have televisions or telephones. Full breakfast is included with the room. The inn is open June through Columbus Day.

Sunset House Bed and Breakfast $$–$$$
74 South Road, Great Chebeague Island
(207) 846–6568
The Sunset House Bed and Breakfast is an intimate, family-run B&B with four guest rooms, each with private bath. Open year-round, the Sunset House is within walking distance of the beach and the ferry and across the street from a nine-hole golf course. There are bike trails around the building, and bike rentals are available through the B&B. During the winter, cross-country skiing is available on the grounds around the guesthouse. The Sunset House does not accept credit cards.

RESTAURANTS

If you've done any research at all before your arrival, chances are you've heard that Portland has more restaurants per capita than any other city except San Francisco.

There's just one problem: No one has ever been able to prove it. That little tidbit gets thrown around so much in this town that many people have tried to track down the source and some statistics to back it up. They always come up empty. The fact that such a rumor persists from year to year, however, illustrates Portland's identity as a restaurant town. This is a city that loves food and loves to dine out.

Portland's identity is, of course, closely tied to the sea, and it is seafood that most visitors want to focus on when they come here. Lobster in all its forms will always be tops with tourists—succulent steamed lobster with drawn butter, toasted rolls packed with lobster meat and fixings, rich lobster stew, and other various forms of this classic Maine food. And don't forget the steamers. Top it off with a thick slice of juicy blueberry pie, made with freshly raked blueberries harvested from the barrens in August.

Maine is maple syrup in March, fiddleheads and rhubarb in spring, apple pies at autumn agricultural fairs, and winter chowders chock-full of sweet corn or fresh clams. But it is so much more than that. Portland, especially, has a growing and evolving food scene that has captured the attention of publications such as the *New York Times*, *Gourmet*, and *Food and Wine*. Maine chefs have been nominated for, and won, James Beard "Best Chef: Northeast" awards and have hosted Maine-themed dinners at the James Beard House in New York City. And it's no wonder—chefs are no more immune to the beauty and quality of life here than anyone else, so Maine attracts some of the best culinary talent from around the country.

The "Slow Food" movement is particularly active in Maine. Slow Food is philosophically the opposite of fast food or overprocessed food. It uses fresh, regional ingredients obtained from local farmers and is presented simply, seasonally, and creatively. Many of Portland's best restaurants boast about their reliance on regional farms and farmers' markets, artisanal producers, and local fish purveyors in creating their menus.

Wine pairings, caviar tastings, truffle dinners—it seems as if Portland restaurants have special events happening every week. Lots of food-related fund-raisers take place year-round as well, from the Great Chili and Chowder Challenge in February, which benefits a local foster grandparents' program, to the Chocolate Lovers' Fling in March, which benefits the Sexual Assault Response Services of Southern Maine. To find out if any of these events are happening while you're in town, check restaurant Web sites or pick up the "Food and Health" section in the Wednesday edition of the *Portland Press Herald*.

Portland has many excellent brewpubs that also serve good food. A small selection is included here, and you'll find more in the Nightlife chapter.

As you explore Portland's restaurant scene, you'll soon discover that, whether it can be proved or not, the Portland–San Francisco rumor at least seems to be true. There are so many excellent restaurants to choose from that you can only hope to sample a few during a short visit to the city. In this chapter you'll find a good selection of restaurants that are among locals' favorites, but this is by no means a comprehensive list. We have tried to include something in every price range. The listings are organized alphabetically by name. Many of Portland's restaurants are closed on Sunday (although more are beginning to open their doors), so it's a good idea to call ahead on weekends.

NOTE: No smoking is allowed in any of Maine's restaurants.

Price Code

The price code represents the average price of dinner entrees for two people, without cocktails, wine, appetizers, tax, or gratuity. Virtually all of these restaurants accept major credit cards, so we've noted only the rare occasion when the policy is cash only. Prices, hours, and menus can change often in Portland, so it's usually best to call ahead.

$. . . . . Under $15
$$ . . . . $16 to $25
$$$ . . . . $26 to $45
$$$$ . . . . $46 and up

Anthony's Italian Kitchen $$
151 Middle Street
(207) 774–8668
www.anthonysitaliankitchen.com

Anthony's is a little hard to find, but if you ask just about any Portlander, they'll be able to point you in the right direction. It's hidden downstairs, sandwiched between Videoport, one of the city's best-known video stores, and Bull Moose Music, a popular music store. Anthony's serves reliably tasty pizza, pasta, and sandwiches, along with beer and wine, in a casual, intimate atmosphere and at a reasonable price. Virtually everything other than a large pizza is priced under $10, making it a good spot for families. You might also see some Portland Pirates fans here after a game, digging into a plate of lasagna or chicken marsala. Here you'll learn the difference between a Boston Italian and a Maine Italian—the sandwich, that is.

If you'd like some entertainment with your Chicken Anthony (chicken, broccoli, and ziti in a garlic butter sauce), visit on a Friday or Saturday night, when Anthony's hosts "World of Broadway" cabaret-style dinner theater from 7:00 to 9:00 P.M. For $55 per couple, your server will bring you a six-course meal and then get up on stage to sing "Luck Be a Lady" from *Guys and Dolls*. You may even catch the proprietor, Anthony Barrasso, belting out "Wonderful World." Barrasso is an active player in community theater and began "World of Broadway" nights to showcase local talent, especially younger singers who don't get a lot of other opportunities to show what they can do. You'll find free parking in the back of the building on weekday evenings and weekends. Anthony's is closed on Sunday.

Back Bay Grill $$$–$$$$
65 Portland Street
(207) 772–8833
www.backbaygrill.com

Back Bay Grill is an intimate restaurant that is a longtime favorite of locals. The chef changes the menu seasonally so that he can offer the freshest ingredients from local farmers and artisans. He's known for his Duck Two Ways, a dish whose name speaks for itself. Other typical preparations may center around filet mignon, rack of lamb, Scottish salmon, or Gulf of Maine halibut. The bar features specialty cocktails, such as the Back Bay Grill Bourbon Cider Manhattan, and the wine list has been winning Wine Spectator Awards since 1998. Back Bay Grill is open for dinner only, and reservations are recommended. Parking is on-street only, but it's usually not difficult to find a spot.

Becky's Diner $$
390 Commercial Street
(207) 773–7070
www.beckysdiner.com

Becky's is the best-known diner in Portland, a place that started out as a kind of fueling station for fishermen on their way out to sea and is now a veritable tourist attraction after being written up in such tony publications as *Esquire* and *Gourmet*. The business was started by Becky Rand when she was a newly single mother of six and needed to find some way to support her kids and put them through college. The diner, located on Hobson's Wharf on Portland's waterfront, still opens at 4:00 A.M. for the fishermen and doesn't close until 9:00 P.M. It's open seven days a week and closes only on Thanksgiving, half of Christmas eve, and Christmas day. The food is typical diner fare—meat loaf, ham steak, roast turkey, and, of course, lobster rolls and other seafood. Breakfast items range from fruit bowls and pancakes to five different kinds of home fries. Sit at one of the red stools at the counter or slide into a booth, but if it's the smells and sizzles of diner food you're looking for, you won't be disappointed by Becky's.

Bintliff's American Café $$$
98 Portland Street
(207) 774–0005

Bintliff's has been a favorite of locals since it opened in 1990. The restaurant serves dinner Wednesday through Saturday, but it is the daily brunch that has made it so popular with Portlanders. Brunch is served from 7:00 A.M. to 2:00 P.M., and there is something on the menu for just about anyone's taste. There are seven different kinds of eggs Benedict, including the Downeast Benedict, made with lobster, crab, or salmon. You can make your own omelet, or go for the Oyster and Smoked Bacon Frittata. Try the Georgia Pecan Caramel Waffles, the Classic Tuscan French Toast, or a plate of the specialty pancakes, such as the Banana Pecan Pancakes or the Gingerbread Pancakes with Lemon Syrup. There's local Grandy Oats granola, and homemade corned beef hash, too. Bintliff's has a full bar that serves classic brunch cocktails, such as Bloody Marys and mimosas. Brunch reservations are accepted Monday through Friday only. Dinner is served from 5:00 to 9:00 P.M., and reservations are accepted.

Cinque Terre Cucina Italiana $$$$
36 Wharf Street
(207) 347–6154
www.cinqueterremaine.com

The name Cinque Terre refers to five ancient fishing villages in the Italian Riviera. This ele-gant restaurant with an "upscale casual" atmosphere is tucked away down a cobblestone street in the Old Port. Cinque Terre serves authentic Northern Italian cuisine using fresh seafood from local purveyors, handcrafted pasta, and specialty ravioli. Gnocchi, branzino, house-made gelati, panna cotta, and the chocolate fondant torte are just some of the preferred selections on the menu. The owners of Cinque Terre have their own farm where, six months out of the year, they grow vegetables—including many interesting Italian varietals—for use in the restaurant's kitchen. The wine list, winner of a Wine Spectator Award, is all Italian, and there is a full bar. Cinque Terre is open seven nights a week for dinner, and reservations are recommended.

David's Restaurant $$$
22 Monument Square
(207) 773–4340
www.davidsrestaurant.com

If you're going to the theater or a concert at the Merrill Auditorium or the Cumberland County Civic Center, David's is a good spot to stop in for a bite before the curtain goes up. David's serves creative American dishes and has an extensive wine list, including lots of half bottles and wine by the glass. Some dishes that are customer favorites include pepper-crusted, sushi rare tuna with sesame peanut soba noodles, Szechuan citrus sauce, and sesame asparagus; a mixed grill of Portland sirloin and skewers of jumbo Gulf shrimp and sea scallops; and lobster, scallop, and sweet potato cakes with red pepper and lobster sauce. Scotch connoisseurs take note: David's is known for having Maine's largest selection of single malt scotches. The restaurant is open for lunch Monday through Friday from 11:30 A.M. to 4:00 P.M. Dinner is served seven nights a week, starting at 5:00 P.M. There is live entertainment, featuring jazz or folk music, on Thursday and Sunday from 6:00 to 9:00 P.M. Parking is available on the street and in several nearby garages.

DiMillo's Floating Restaurant $$$
25 Long Wharf
(207) 772–2216
www.dimillos.com

If you want to soak in the ambience of Portland Harbor, this is the place to go. DiMillo's is a popular tourist spot, and for good reason. Lobster is the restaurant's specialty, and you can't beat the view. DiMillo's is a casual place located in a converted car ferry that goes up and down with the tides. Two outside decks open in the summertime, so you can sit in the sun and enjoy a bowl of clam or haddock chowder, or a cocktail, and watch boats as they enter and leave the harbor. In addition to its lobster offerings, DiMillo's also serves other types of seafood, steak, chicken, and several Italian dishes. The restaurant is open from 11:00 A.M. to 10:00 P.M. every day except Thanksgiving and Christmas. Reservations are accepted for parties of five or more. DiMillo's has a phone-ahead policy in which small parties can call 20 to 30 minutes ahead of their visit to get on a wait list. The restaurant has its own parking lot; take a ticket, and it will be validated when you leave.

The Dogfish Café $$–$$$
953 Congress Street
(207) 253–5400

This is a true insider's restaurant because there's no way tourists would wander into this eatery on their own. It's in a tiny, tired-looking building on a busy corner, across the street from a bus station and surrounded by strip malls and fast-food joints. Not exactly what most people envision when they think of fine dining. But this cozy cafe is a favorite neighborhood hangout for Portlanders, and for good reason. Once you open the front door, you'll find a warm and inviting dining space and a full bar. The restaurant has an all-day menu with lots of casual, pub-style fare that you can order from anytime, although during dinner hours you may have to ask your server to bring the menu to you. Standard offerings include sandwiches with homemade chips, quesadillas, crab cakes, and a huge Caesar salad that is more than enough for a meal. Most nights the restaurant has dinner specials that arrive at your table on a small chalkboard. The Dogfish Café is open Monday through Saturday from 11:30 A.M. to 10:00 P.M. Parking is difficult here—the lot is tiny—and the restaurant is so small that the wait times may require some patience.

Duckfat $$$
43 Middle Street
(207) 774–8080
www.duckfat.com

The cheeky name says it all. Duckfat is known for its duck confit and Belgian fries that are cooked in, well, duck fat. This small, casual restaurant sells Portland's own version of European street food, which can be taken away or eaten at one of the bistro-style tables inside. The restaurant is owned by the same people who own Hugo's, a fine dining restaurant just down the street, and the chef in charge of the kitchen is the former sous chef at Hugo's. This is high-end takeout made from scratch. The ever-changing menu consists of an eclectic assortment of paninis, soups, salads, and homemade sodas (ginger brew, cherry-lime, cream soda) on tap. The crisp fries, a customer favorite, come in a paper cone with your choice of creative dipping sauces, including truffle ketchup, horseradish mayo, curry mayo, and duck gravy.

In the mood for something sweet? Try the beignets with cinnamon sugar or chocolate sauce, or the Sweet Panini, with your choice of jam and mascarpone, grilled on brioche and dusted with powdered sugar. The ultra-thick Five Dollar Milk Shake actually costs $4.00 (the name is a reference to a scene in the movie Pulp Fiction) and comes in flavors such as real Tahitian vanilla bean, coffee, mocha, and Belgian dark chocolate. On Friday and Saturday from 5:00 to 9:00 P.M., Duckfat posts blackboard dinner specials. The restaurant is open seven days a week and serves beer and wine. You can walk in, or call in an order for takeout, but Duckfat does not take reservations.

Eve's at the Garden $$$$
Portland Harbor Hotel
468 Fore Street
(207) 775–9090, (888) 798–9090
www.portlandharborhotel.com
Located in the heart of the Old Port, Eve's specializes in Mediterranean cuisine with a strong emphasis on French and Italian cooking. The restaurant is in a hotel, so it's open year-round and serves a diverse clientele, from shoppers in the Old Port and families on vacation to local businesspeople looking to seal a deal over lunch and a martini from the restaurant's martini bar and lounge. During the summer, al fresco dining is available on Eve's Patio. Entrees for two can run an average of $50, but the food is more sophisticated than typical hotel fare. Just try to resist the grilled filet mignon Oscar-style, served with roasted asparagus, fresh Maine crab meat, rich pureed potatoes, and béarnaise sauce. Or try the seared jumbo sea scallops with porcini–foie gras sauce, squash risotto, and spinach.

Eve's has a full bar and offers more than a dozen variations on the martini, including "local martinis" concocted by customers. The Bertini martini, for example, is a blend of Three Olives Vodka, cranberry and pineapple juices, and a splash of lime juice. If you're visiting in February, check out the restaurant's ice bar—the only one in Portland—where you can get your drink served through a martini luge. Eve's accepts reservations. Complimentary valet parking is available directly under the hotel.

Federal Spice $
225 Federal Street
(207) 774–6404
This little place is located in the Old Port under a parking garage across from the post office and just around the corner from a movie theater. It doesn't look like much from the outside, but it's a favorite walk-in spot for people who work in the Old Port. Federal Spice is all about fusion-style wraps, Mex-Mediterranean-Asian-Caribbean combos that are satisfying and a bargain to boot. Ingredients run the gamut and

include curried coconut chicken, jerk chicken, catfish, sweet potatoes, and mango pork. Wraps are served with fresh tortilla chips. Want fries with that instead? Try an order of yam fries, one of the house specialties. Quesadillas, salads, and an ever-popular Thai peanut black bean chili are also on the menu. Daily specials are posted on a blackboard behind the counter. Federal Spice has beer on tap and sodas in a fridge and makes its own iced tea, kicked up a notch in flavor. This is a small restaurant with seating upstairs and downstairs. In the summer a few tables and chairs appear outside on a small sidewalk patio. Federal Spice is open Monday through Friday from 11:00 A.M. to 9:00 P.M., and to 6:00 P.M. on Saturday. Credit cards are not accepted.

five fifty-five $$$$
555 Congress Street
(207) 761–0551
www.fivefifty-five.com
This restaurant offers American food with attentive, upscale service in a warm atmosphere. Balcony seating overlooks the open kitchen on the first floor. The chef here tries to offer something for everyone, from a fire-grilled burger and onion rings ($13.95) to a "lobstah" risotto made with butter-poached Maine lobster, saffron-infused arborio rice, crispy serrano ham, and mascarpone cheese ($27.95). Other customer favorites include pepper-seared diver scallops with organic baby carrot–butter emulsion, caramelized-fennel mashed potatoes, and butter-glazed pearl onions; and grilled—yes, grilled—Caesar salad. The menu is creative and changes often based on whatever local ingredients are available and what is currently inspiring the chef, an alum of Napa Valley's Domaine Chandon. There is a full bar and an award-winning wine list with more than 200 selections, including hard-to-find wines. For $20 the staff will take away the guesswork and pair appropriate wines by the glass with your three-course dinner. The restaurant is open for dinner from 5:00 to 10:00 P.M. Monday through Thursday, 5:00 to 10:30 P.M. Friday

and Saturday, and 5:00 to 9:30 P.M. on Sunday. There is also a Sunday brunch, which is served from 10:30 A.M. to 2:30 P.M. Parking is available on the street or a half block away at a public parking garage on Forest Avenue. Reservations are recommended, especially on weekends and with large parties.

Flatbread Company $$
72 Commercial Street
(207) 772–8777
www.flatbreadcompany.com

Flatbread makes flatbread pizzas with organic ingredients, free-range chicken, and nitrate-free meats. The flatbreads are assembled in an open kitchen and baked in a wood-fired oven that kids flock to while their family's waiting for their order. The organic tomato sauce is made in a wood-fired cauldron, also located right in the dining room. Flatbread is a regional chain, with other restaurants in Massachusetts and New Hampshire, but its location right on Portland's waterfront, across from the Casco Bay ferry, and its fresh flat-breads have made it a local favorite. There's almost always a wait for a table, but you can call ahead and put your name on the list for seating. The flatbreads come in full and half sizes, so you can try more than one kind if you like. Try the one made with homemade maple fennel sausage, sun-dried tomatoes, caramelized onions, mushrooms, cheese, and herbs. The Punctuated Equilibrium flatbread comes with kalamata olives, rosemary, red onions, oven-roasted red peppers, goat cheese, mozzarella, garlic, and herbs. There are also daily specials for both vegetarians and meat lovers. A simple but tasty mesclun salad is available to accompany your meal. Flatbread is open Sunday through Thursday from 11:30 A.M. to 10:00 P.M. and Friday and Saturday from 11:30 A.M. to 11:00 P.M.

Fore Street $$$$
288 Fore Street
(207) 775–2717
www.forestreet.biz

Fore Street is probably the best-known restaurant in Portland because it has been featured in so many national food magazines and, of course, because of its reputation for fine food. The executive chef here, Sam Hayward, was named "Best Chef: Northeast" by the James Beard Foundation in 2004. Located in a former warehouse with exposed brick and large windows, the restaurant celebrated its 10th anniversary in 2006 and continues to impress diners with its fresh, regional cuisine cooked over wood fires and on a turnspit. Hayward is known for his use of local organic ingredients, which he gathers from a stable of at least two dozen farmers and foragers. He buys his lamb, for example, from a Newcastle farmer who raises his animals on offshore islands in Muscongous Bay. His suppliers, Hayward says, provide him with "some of the finest raw materials any chef ever gets to work with anywhere, as far as I'm concerned." The menu changes regularly based on what's available, but there are three dishes that have stayed on the menu since the restaurant opened: turnspit-roasted pork loin; marinated, turnspit-roasted Maine farm chicken; and grilled, marinated hanger steak. An appetizer of mussels roasted in the wood oven with garlic and roasted almond butter is also a customer favorite.

Appetizers and desserts are available in the restaurant's lounge, and the full menu is available at the bar. No reservations are needed to eat at the bar and lounge, but they are recommended for the dining room. Reservations can be made 60 days in advance, and one-third of the tables are held for walk-ins and are awarded on a first-come, first-served basis. It's a good idea to get there early. During busier times of the year, diners start lining up before 5:00 P.M., and the staff starts taking names at 5:00 P.M. Fore Street is open seven days a week for dinner only. Hours are Sunday through Thursday from 5:30 to 10:00 P.M. and Friday and Saturday from 5:30 to 10:30 P.M. In the winter, closing time on Sunday is 9:30 P.M. The bar opens at 5:00 P.M. Parking is available in a lot on the Commercial Street side of the restaurant and in nearby parking lots and garages.

The Front Room $$$
73 Congress Street
(207) 773–3366
www.thefrontroomrestaurant.com

This neighborhood restaurant on Munjoy Hill offers moderately priced "new American comfort food" for brunch and dinner. This is a warm and welcoming space with lots of woodwork and windows. There's a mahogany bar near the entrance, and an open kitchen in back. The brunch menu is filled with breakfast plates, sandwiches, omelets, sweets, soups, and sides, all at affordable prices. Breakfast plates include French toast with whipped butter and maple syrup for $4.50, eggs Benedict for $7.00, and two eggs any style with home fries and choice of meat and toast for $5.50. The chef has an interesting interpretation on biscuits and gravy that people either love or hate. If you're expecting southern-style biscuits, stay away; but if you don't mind trying something new, you'll enjoy these shortcake-like biscuits with seasoned sausage gravy. Dinner entrees include grilled meat loaf with mashed potatoes, vegetables, and gravy; braised beef short rib with horseradish mashed potatoes and roasted cabbage; and Casco Bay scallops with mustard sauce, spinach, and mashed potatoes. Brunch is served Monday through Friday from 8:00 A.M. to 2:30 P.M. and Saturday and Sunday from 9:00 A.M. to 2:30 P.M. Dinner is served nightly from 5:00 to 10:00 P.M.

Gilbert's Chowder House $$
92 Commercial Street
(207) 871–5636

Gilbert's is a place where fishermen and tourists alike come for a steaming cup of thick chowder, lobster rolls, lobster stew, clam strips, and other seafood that is served fast and is friendly on the wallet. This family-style restaurant is on the waterfront, and the decor is decidedly Maine kitsch—with a fisherman's net, a captain's wheel, and a swordfish trophy hanging on the wall. The food is served on paper plates with plastic cutlery. The clam, corn, fish, and seafood chowders come in Styrofoam bowls of different sizes. Other options include a seafood chili and a "super seafood" chowder that contains twice the amount of shrimp, scallops, clams, lobster, and fish. Gilbert's is open daily from 11:00 A.M. to 9:00 P.M.

Granny's Burritos $
420 Fore Street
(207) 761–0751

If you're from the Southwest, let's face it, you're not going to find the kind of south-of-the-border cuisine you're used to here in Portland. But when you get a hankering for a burrito, it doesn't matter if you're at the North Pole—you just need a fix. In Portland Granny's is the place to go for that fix. It's nothing fancy, but the food is satisfying if what you want is a burrito stuffed with simple, non-funky ingredients. Granny's serves both burritos and quesadillas, prepared just the way you want them. You'll be asked what kind of tortilla you'd like—such as white, wheat, chili, or spinach—and whether you want black beans, pinto beans, or a mix of the two. Both the burritos and quesadillas come in a wide variety of options, such as veggie, sweet potato, spinach, chicken pesto, chicken mango, jerk chicken, and, of course, the usual chicken, beef, or chorizo. Most of the burritos start with the basic veggies and fixings. That means cheese, rice, beans, salsa, lettuce, tomatoes, and sour cream. Quesadilla basics include cheese, beans, fresh garlic, tomatoes, and salsa. The menu also features turkey chili, nachos, and salads. Granny's is open daily from 11:00 A.M. to 10:00 P.M., and to midnight on Friday and Saturday. There's a bar upstairs, which is open Monday through Thursday from 5:00 to 10:00 P.M. and on Friday and Saturday from noon to closing.

Gritty McDuff's Brewing Co. $$
396 Fore Street
(207) 772–2739
www.grittys.com

Gritty McDuff's bills itself as "Maine's Original Brewpub." Founded in 1988, the pub has since expanded to locations in Freeport and Auburn. Gritty's brews its own beers on-site and also serves an extensive menu of basic pub fare. Located in the heart of the Old Port, it's a good place to sit down for a bite and a pint after a morning of shopping and sightseeing. Gritty's is an English-style pub that offers traditional pub favorites such as meat loaf, shepherd's pie, and, of course, fish and chips. Gritty's also serves appetizers, including chicken wings, nachos, and pub fries, as well as chilis and chowders, a variety of filling sandwiches, and big, meaty burgers. Wash it all down with some Black Fly Stout. Gritty's is open seven days a week for lunch and dinner.

The Great Lost Bear $$
540 Forest Avenue
(207) 772–0300
www.greatlostbear.com

If it's burgers and beer you're hankering for, look no further. The Great Lost Bear is known for its hamburgers, which come in varieties such as the chili-and-cheese burger and a barbecue burger that comes with a choice of sweet or Tex-Mex barbecue sauce. But it's even better known for its huge selection of beers and for showcasing regional microbrews. More than 50 taps are always flowing with beers from more than 30 breweries, including 15 Maine microbreweries. This huge selection has earned the Great Lost Bear lots of recognition from national publications read by beer aficionados. Among the dizzying array of options are Allagash White, Geary's London Style Porter, Gritty McDuff's Black Fly Stout, Casco Bay Riptide Red Ale, and Atlantic Bar Harbor Blueberry Ale. The atmosphere is vintage college pub, with lots of kitsch adorning the walls, and the food is described as "gourmet junk food." There are, for example, about a half-dozen different styles of chicken wings on the menu, and even more varieties of nachos. The Bear is open seven days a week for breakfast, lunch, and dinner. Reservations are accepted, except for Thursday, Friday, and Saturday nights.

Haggarty's $$
849 Forest Avenue
(207) 761–8222

This small storefront on Forest Avenue serves a small selection of Brit-Indi cuisine. It's takeout and delivery only, but if you're hungry for Indian food in a hurry, this is a nice solution. You can choose from five appetizers, such as chicken chaat (chicken wings marinated in spiced yogurt, then char-grilled) and various kinds of pakora. The rest of the menu consists of eight entrees, including basmati rice and your choice of chicken, beef, shrimp, lamb, vegetables, or paneer. Sides include plain or garlic naan, and salted or spiced fries. Haggarty's is open Monday through Friday from 11:00 A.M. to 9:00 P.M., Saturday from 1:00 to 10:00 P.M., and Sunday from 1:00 to 9:00 P.M.

Hugo's Restaurant $$$$
88 Middle Street
(207) 774–8538
www.hugos.net

One of Portland's best-known restaurants, Hugo's offers a fine dining experience that is sure to enchant. Hugo's chef, one of the most creative in the city, is a native New Englander who has worked in the kitchens of the French Laundry in California's Napa Valley and Virginia's Inn at Little Washington. In 2004 he was selected as one of "America's Best New Chefs" by *Food and Wine* magazine. The kitchen at Hugo's prepares innovative New England cuisine made from fresh, local ingredients and presents it in multicourse menus. The four-course prix fixe dinner includes plenty of seafood but also offers Verjus Glazed Pork Belly served with artisan corn grits, pepper jelly, spiced pecans, and fennel juice, as well as duck prepared multiple ways. There's also a seven-course tasting menu and a four-course vegetable menu. Or try the new four-course potato menu, a creative homage to the organic Maine potato; it includes such original offerings as Butte Potato Consommé and Sweet Potato Spiced Crème Brûlée. The truly adventurous can let the chef choose their courses in an 8- to 12-course chef's menu that is available with advance reservations only. More casual diners can settle in at the bar or a nearby bistro table to sample the wide-ranging bar menu, which includes abridged versions of the regular menu along with such creative stand-alones as Maine Lobster Pierogi and Beet Risotto. Hugo's is a favorite of local foodies, couples looking for a romantic night out, and tourists who have heard about the restaurant from publications such as the *New York Times, Gourmet*, and *Travel and Leisure*. Hugo's serves dinner only and is closed on Sunday and Monday. Reservations are recommended.

Ladle $
58 Exchange Street
(207) 874–SOUP

Mainers love their soup. It's a byproduct of spending half the year hibernating while the thermometer plunges and the snow flies. When this little place opened on Exchange Street, the reaction from locals was "What took so long?" Ladle is a casual spot that features artisanal soups and breads, and not much else unless you count the fabulous chocolate chip cookie that is offered for dessert. No liquor is served here, so if that's what you want, this is not the place for you. Here, it's all about the soup. Usually about a half-dozen varieties are available, in 8-ounce and 12-ounce pours that range in price from $4.00 to $7.00, depending on whether they contain meat or organic ingredients. Try the Rockland clam chowder, the slow-braised beef stew, or the Soupe au Pistou, made with white beans and pesto in a tomato base. The soups change often and are created by a chef known for the French-inspired cooking at his higher-end restaurant, Bandol. The bread is homemade, too. Ladle opens at 11:00 A.M. and closes between 5:30 and 7:00 P.M., depending on business.

The Lobster Shack $$–$$$
225 Two Lights Road, Cape Elizabeth
(207) 799–1677
http://lobstershack-twolights.com/index.htm

This little "shack" just across the bridge from Portland is both a local favorite and a tourist hot spot, mostly for one reason—the spectacular view. Located at the entrance to Portland harbor and just below a lighthouse, the Lobster Shack sits atop the classic craggy Maine cliffs overlooking the Atlantic Ocean. It's just down the road from Two Lights State Park, a must-see for visitors to the Portland area. After hanging out at the park for a while, just head to the end of Two Lights Road, and that's where you'll find the Lobster Shack. There is indoor seating, but most people (in good weather, anyway) prefer to sit at the picnic tables outside and listen to the crashing surf as they crack into their lobster dinners. The food is typical of what you'd find at any Maine lobster pound—lobster and crabmeat rolls, clam cakes, fried clams, lobster stew, clam chowder, as well as hamburgers and hot dogs, french fries and onion rings, and coleslaw. The Lobster Shack is closed in winter.

Maria's Ristorante $$$
337 Cumberland Avenue
(207) 772–9232
www.mariasrestaurant.com

Maria's is practically a Portland institution. The restaurant, which specializes in "authentic Italian cuisine," is still owned and operated by the same family that opened the place in 1960. At dinner, served Tuesday through Saturday, you will pay $11 to $25 for classic Italian entrees, many of which feature Maria's homemade meatballs and sausages. The extensive menu includes customer favorites such as Veal Maria, Eggplant Parmigiana, Zuppa de Pesce, and Haddock Milanese. A popular dinner-for-two special ($59) includes a choice of appetizers, soup or salad, bread, entree, dessert, and wine. The restaurant also serves lunch Tuesday through Friday, at very reasonable prices. The atmosphere is charming and leaves you feeling as if you'd walked into an Old World Italian place in New York City. Maria's has a full bar and an extensive wine list and does special events, catering, and to-go orders. Reservations are recommended. The front entrance is wheelchair accessible. Parking is at the rear entrance, with access from Portland Street.

Mim's $$$
205 Commercial Street
(207) 347–7478

Mim's offers casual fine dining featuring fresh, local ingredients. The menu changes every two to three months, but among the mainstays are a pulled chicken sandwich, fish chowder, and a niçoise salad. The lobster bouillabaisse, a customer favorite, is a tomato-fennel broth loaded with chunks of lobster meat and a rotation of finfish and shellfish such as mussels and crab. The wine list is entirely French, with a large selection of wines by the glass. During the summer the clientele here is made up almost entirely of tourists since the restaurant is located right on Commercial Street in the heart of the Old Port. In winter it's frequented by businesspeople who work downtown. An upstairs patio has a full-service bar and an ocean view. Mim's is open seven days a week for brunch, lunch, and dinner. Brunch is served on Saturday and Sunday from 9:00 A.M. to 3:00 P.M. Reservations are recommended, especially during the summer.

Newick's Seafood Restaurant $$
740 Broadway, South Portland
(207) 799–3090
www.newicks.com

Newick's is a classic family restaurant that serves a variety of seafood, much of it fried but, thankfully, not greasy. This restaurant is part of a regional chain—there are two other Newick's in New Hampshire—but it's such a part of the local landscape that it must be included here. The restaurant and the menu are huge, featuring everything from clam chowder to large platters of clam strips, whole clams, clam cakes, fried baby and butterfly shrimp, coconut shrimp, fried haddock, and bay scallops. Lobster, too, of course. For the health-conscious, there's broiled salmon,

swordfish, and other options. Pasta dishes—with seafood, of course—are available, and the kids can choose from chicken tenders, haddock nuggets, burgers, and fries. Newick's is open Sunday through Thursday from 11:30 A.M. to 8:00 P.M. and Friday and Saturday to 9:00 P.M.

Norm's East End Grill $$–$$$
47 Middle Street
(207) 253–1700

If you're from barbecue country, no matter what the locals tell you, it's tough to find the real deal in Portland. But Norm's offers some tasty meats that come about as close as you'll get in northern New England. Spare ribs, baby back ribs, "country ribs," and barbecue chicken are all served with baked beans and corn bread. There's also grilled sirloin tips served with mashed potatoes. If you want to try a little of everything, order the BBQ sampler, but be warned—it's a lot of food. Sandwiches and seafood—lobster stew, fish and chips—are on the menu as well, and there's a full bar if you want to wash everything down with a beer. Norm's is open seven days a week. Reservations are taken for large parties only.

Old Port Tavern Restaurant
and Lounge $$$
11 Moulton Street
(207) 774–0444
www.oldporttavern.com

This Portland steak house has been serving steaks, chops, and lobster in the Old Port for more than 30 years. Regulars come here especially for the prime rib, as well as the onion soup and rack of lamb. Established in 1972, Old Port Tavern also includes the Mariner's Church Banquet Center, where events from cocktail parties to wedding receptions can be scheduled, and a billiards hall. The restaurant, which has a full bar, is open seven days a week for lunch and dinner. Parking is on the street, but there are also two public parking garages close by. Reservations are accepted.

Oriental Table $$

106 Exchange Street
(207) 775–3388

There are lots of Chinese restaurants in Portland, but workers in the downtown area like this one because of its daily lunch buffet, served from 11:30 A.M. to 2:00 P.M. For around $7.00 you'll get a choice of soup or soda, egg roll or crab Rangoon, fried rice or noodles, and samplings of two entrees. The regular menu offers a large selection of standard Chinese fare. Oriental Table is convenient to Merrill Auditorium and other downtown venues. It's open Monday through Thursday from 11:30 A.M. to 8:00 P.M. and Friday and Saturday to 9:00 P.M. The restaurant is closed on Sunday.

Ricetta's Brick Oven Pizzeria $$–$$$

29 Western Avenue, South Portland
(207) 775–7400
www.ricettas.com

Ricetta's is consistently the top vote getter in "best pizza" contests around town. This brick-oven pizzeria is in a little strip mall just off Interstate 295. A customer favorite is the Grecian, a pizza layered with homemade tomato sauce, spinach, homemade Italian sausage, feta, and mozzarella. Or try the Bolto, with roasted chicken, pesto sauce, broccoli, and fontina cheese. Ricetta's also serves calzones and traditional Italian dishes such as chicken parmigiana, lasagna, pasta Bolognese, and shrimp scampi. Try the light and delicious linguini scipollo—chicken, prosciutto, and tomato spiced with crushed red pepper and served in a lemon cream sauce. Ricetta's is open Sunday through Thursday from 11:30 A.M. to 10:00 P.M. and Friday and Saturday to 11:00 P.M.

Rí~Rá Irish Pub and Restaurant $$–$$$

72 Commercial Street
(207) 761–4446
www.rira.com

This popular pub on the waterfront, next to the Casco Bay ferry terminal, actually contains salvaged and restored interiors from real Irish pubs. Owned by two Dubliners, Rí~Rá has a traditional pub downstairs and a dining room upstairs. There's more about Rí~Rá in the Nightlife chapter, so here we'll focus on the Irish fare. Don't miss the excellent Irish potato cakes with sour cream sauce, an appetizer that Rí~Rá fans consistently rave over as they down their pint of Guinness. For dinner try the Ballycotton fish pie, which contains haddock, salmon, crab, and shrimp baked in a mashed potato crust. Other entrees include a horseradish-crusted sole and Gaelic steak and chips. From the oyster bar you can order garlicky crab claws, which are Jonah crab claws sautéed with garlic, white wine, and butter. For an Irish take on mussels, order them sautéed with Irish whiskey and garlic butter. Rí~Rá is open for both lunch and dinner. Dinner is served Sunday through Thursday from 4:00 to 10:00 P.M. and Friday and Saturday to 11:00 P.M. There's an Irish-style brunch on Saturday and Sunday from 11:30 A.M. to 3:00 P.M.

Sapporo $$

230 Commercial Street
(207) 772–1233
www.meweb.net/sapporo/

Sapporo is one of the oldest Japanese/sushi restaurants in Portland and is quite good. Named after the Japanese city famed for its seafood, Sapporo sits on the waterfront and is a longtime favorite of sushi lovers in Portland. The menu offers Nigiri sushi—a slice of fish on top of a bed of rice—as well as seafood and vegetable rolls. Combination dinners come with miso soup and 12 to 20 pieces of sushi. For customers who just can't do raw fish, lots of teriyaki, tempura, and noodle dishes are available. Sapporo is open for lunch Monday through Friday from 11:30 A.M. to 2:00 P.M. Dinner is served Monday through Thursday from 5:00 to 9:30 P.M., Friday and Saturday from 5:00 to 10:00 P.M., and Sunday from 4:00 to 9:00 P.M.

Silly's $$

40 Washington Avenue
(207) 772–0360
www.sillys.com

Silly's was a hip place to grab a burger or a

Dining on the Islands

A visit to Portland wouldn't be complete without a trip out on the water or a visit to one of the area's fine restaurants. Why not combine the two by hopping on a ferry and having lunch or dinner in one of Maine's many island communities?

Here are just three suggestions. All three can be reached via Casco Bay Ferry Lines or water taxi.

Chebeague Island Inn
61 South Road, Chebeague Island
(207) 846–5155
www.chebeagueislandinn.com
Hours: Dinner, 5:00 to 9:00 P.M. daily

This 1920s-era grand hotel, restored in fine style in 2004, can be reached via a 15-minute ferry ride from Cousins Island in Yarmouth or a one-and-a-half-hour trip aboard Casco Bay Ferry Lines. The Chebeague Transportation Company Ferry (www.chebeaguetrans.com) shuttles passengers between Cousins and Chebeague 8 to 10 times a day. Passengers are picked up in a parking lot on Route 1 in Yarmouth a half hour before each boat leaves and are taken to the dock. Inn personnel will greet you on the Chebeague Island side.

Here you can sip cocktails on the front porch, have a picnic basket packed for you for the day (but call ahead first), enjoy a leisurely Sunday brunch, or sup on seafood and other locally harvested foods at dinner. Start with Maine lobster and chanterelle mushroom soup or crispy fried native oysters, and then go for a main course of sautéed Maine crab cakes, pan-seared Atlantic halibut filet, or other many other choices.

Diamond's Edge
Great Diamond Island
P.O. Box 7472
Portland, ME 04112
(207) 766–5850
Hours: Lunch, 11:30 A.M. to 2:30 P.M. daily (seasonal—call ahead)
    Dinner, 5:00 to 9:00 P.M. daily

Casco Bay Ferry Lines runs about 8 to 10 ferries a day to Diamond Cove, where this restaurant is located. The ferry ride takes about 30 minutes, and Diamond's Edge is just a short walk from the dock. This island was once home to a fort built to protect Portland during the Spanish-American War. The buildings at Diamond Cove have been restored, and the site is now on the National Register of Historic Places.

Dinner here is more upscale and includes menu items such as grilled filet mignon, lobster and seafood sauté, and roasted rack of lamb. Seating is available inside, on the deck, or on the adjacent lawn overlooking the cove.

The Inn on Peaks Island
33 Island Avenue, Peaks Island
(207) 766–5100
(207) 766–5200 (for dinner reservations)
www.theinnonpeaksisland.com
Hours: 11:30 A.M. to 9:00 P.M., Monday through Thursday; 11:30 A.M. to 10:00 P.M., Friday and Saturday; 1:00 to 9:00 P.M., Sunday

Peaks Island is 3 miles from Portland and can be reached in about 20 minutes by ferry. Casco Bay Ferry Lines operates more than a dozen ferry runs to Peaks daily, depending on the time of year, so it is the easiest of these three islands to visit. You can hop on the 5:35 P.M. ferry, for example, have a leisurely dinner, and be headed back to the mainland by 7:45 P.M. (It can get crowded in summer, though, so consider making reservations.)

The Inn on Peaks Island. © THE INN ON PEAKS ISLAND

Best of all, the view of Portland's skyline from the inn's pub is one of the best. Just a short walk up the hill from the ferry, the inn offers moderately priced pub fare. Stylish seating is available indoors; but if you ask for an outdoor table, you can drink in the view, along with your pint of cask-conditioned Shipyard Ale from the pub's 15-gallon brewing system. Sunsets here are amazing. You can watch local kids in swimming trunks trying to eke the most fun out of the dwindling day by jumping off the pier. Ferries and sailboats glide past as if part of a living postcard.

The brunch menu features soups and salads, as well as pub classics, such as fish and chips, club sandwiches, hamburgers, buffalo wings, and fried onion rings. Dinner fare is similar but also includes more sophisticated offerings, such as lobster ravioli.

slice long before other eclectic eateries started appearing in Portland. Its funky menu includes things like fried pickles and plantains, but there are also items that these days are standard fare, like sweet potato fries and Thai-style noodles. Vegans and vegetarians will find plenty to try here, but meat eaters won't be disappointed, either. You can choose from more than a dozen wraps, and dinner entrees include such offerings as applewood-smoked pulled pork and the Macedonian, which is charbroiled lamb pieces and coleslaw served with fries or red beans and rice. Silly's is well known for its pizzas and milkshakes with, well, silly names. The No Smoochie Tonight is a pizza with sausage, ricotta, cheddar and mozzarella cheeses, onions, and lots of garlic. The milkshakes come in tons of flavors. Try a graham cracker– or jalapeno-flavored milkshake, or choose from one of the specialty shakes such as the Elvis Shake, which is made with peanut butter and banana. Silly's is open Tuesday through Sunday from 11:30 A.M. to 9:00 P.M. It closes on Easter Sunday, Independence Day, Labor Day week, Thanksgiving, and Christmas.

Street & Co. $$$–$$$$
33 Wharf Street
(207) 775–0887

This little bistro, which opened in 1989, has developed a reputation for fine Mediterranean-style seafood in an intimate setting. It has an open kitchen and a full bar, and its seafood-only menu features customer favorites such as Sole Française, Grilled Tuna, Lobster Diavolo, and Whole Fish Grilled. Street & Co. is open for dinner only, Sunday through Thursday from 5:30 to 9:30 P.M. and Friday and Saturday to 10:00 P.M. Reservations are recommended. One-third of the restaurant's tables are reserved for walk-ins. Parking is on-street and in nearby lots and garages.

Susan's Fish and Chips $$
1135 Forest Avenue
(207) 878–3240

Every year local publications run their "Best of" contests in which they ask readers to name their favorite spots in Portland for getting a suntan or cutting a rug. In these contests, Susan's Fish and Chips consistently wins categories such as "Best Meal Under $10" or "Best Fried Clams." Susan's has been serving up fried seafood in Portland for 17 years. Locals literally line up here for the fish and chips, haddock burgers, clam cakes, fried scallops, and other seafood dinners that come with french fries and coleslaw. This is a paper-and-plastic restaurant. The portions are large and inexpensive, so this is a popular family place. Susan's is open Saturday through Thursday from 11:00 A.M. to 8:00 P.M. and Friday to 9:00 P.M.

Tandoor $$
88 Exchange Street
(207) 775–4259

This Indian restaurant in Portland's Old Port offers a large selection of Indian cuisine for both lunch and dinner. The wide-ranging menu includes seafood, chicken and lamb specialties, vegetarian dishes, biryanis, curries, kormas, and more. Tandoor has a respectable selection of Indian breads to accompany your meal, and you can top things off with a traditional lassi or mango milkshake. This restaurant is frequented by locals who work in the Old Port and is also convenient to Merrill Auditorium if you're going to catch a show after dinner. Tandoor is open seven days a week.

Twenty Milk Street $$$$
20 Milk Street
(207) 774–4200
www.theregency.com

Sometimes you just want a good steak. If that's the mood you're in, head for Twenty Milk Street, the restaurant located in the Portland Regency Hotel in the Old Port. This warm and inviting space looks like a private club, with its comfortable chairs, chandeliers, brick fireplace, and lush interior fabrics. Breakfast, lunch, dinner, and Sunday brunch are served here, but it's the pricey USDA prime cuts of midwestern beef served for dinner that bring most diners here. Choose from tender center-cut filet mignon, New York sirloin, porterhouse, and club sirloin; top your steak with sauce or butter for a little extra. Potato and vegetable side dishes are ordered separately and are priced separately. If your dining companion doesn't like red meat, there's also plenty of seafood on the menu, as well as rack of lamb, veal or pork chops, and pan-seared duck breast. Reservations are recommended for this intimate dining experience. Dinner is served from Sunday through Thursday from 5:30 to 9:30 P.M. and Friday and Saturday to 10:00 P.M.

Uffa! $$$–$$$$
190 State Street
(207) 775–3380
This little bistro is in Longfellow Square on the West End. The chef here buys his meats, herbs, produce, artisanal goat cheese, and other products from regional farmers through a local farm-to-chef broker. The menu changes with what's available, but offerings may include Trout Almandine, Pan-Fried Cod, and Beef Wellington. Dinner is served Tuesday through Saturday beginning at 5:00 P.M. Sunday brunch is served from 9:00 A.M. to 1:00 P.M. This is a small space, so reservations are suggested. Parking is on the street and behind Joe's Smoke Shop across the street.

Village Café $$$
112 Newbury Street
(207) 772–5320
www.villagecafemaine.com
This Italian, family-style restaurant started as a neighborhood tavern in 1936 and is still going strong today. The menu offers a little something for everyone, including veal or chicken parmigianas and marsalas and lots of other Italian specialties. You'll find pasta dishes, sandwiches, steaks, seafood, pizza, lobster, and several combination plates with pairings like teriyaki steak and shrimp. In addition to early-bird specials, the Village Café has a senior menu for diners 62 years of age and older, with prices ranging from $6.25 to $7.50, available from 11:00 A.M. to 4:00 P.M.,

Monday through Friday (except holidays). A large children's menu features kid favorites such as hamburgers and hot dogs, mac and cheese, and peanut butter and jelly. The Village Café is open Monday through Thursday from 11:00 A.M. to 10:00 P.M. and Friday and Saturday to 11:00 P.M. Sunday hours are 11:30 A.M. to 8:00 P.M., but those are extended to 9:30 P.M. in July and August.

Yosaku Japanese Restaurant $$$
1 Danforth Street
(207) 780–0880
Yosaku is the most recent addition to Portland's sushi scene. Here you'll find 37 different kinds of fish served at the sushi bar, some of it seasonal. The owner goes out of his way to get fish from Japan, such as cherry blossom trout, so named because they migrate upriver at the same time the cherry blossoms are blooming. Diners can sit with their shoes off at traditional tatami tables in the sushi bar area or choose a regular table in a separate dining room decorated with Japanese art. Outside, off the patio, is a Japanese garden with a waterfall. The menu includes such customer favorites as a spicy scallop roll and a hokkai-yaki appetizer. Customers who are shy about sushi are steered toward the teppan-style dishes—grilled tuna, yellowtail, salmon, shrimp, scallops, chicken, and beef. There's also soba and udon noodle dishes, and lots of tempura vegetables paired with shrimp, chicken, and seafood. Yosaku accepts reservations and is open seven days a week. Lunch is served Monday through Friday from 11:30 A.M. to 2:00 P.M. and Saturday and Sunday from noon to 3:00 P.M. The restaurant is open for dinner Monday through Thursday from 5:00 to 9:30 P.M., Friday and Saturday to 10:30 P.M., and Sunday to 9:00 P.M.

PICNICKING IN PORTLAND

You don't have to make a reservation at a restaurant to appreciate Portland's vibrant food scene. The city has lots of bakeries and small groceries that are popular lunch spots and perfect places to grab all the essentials for a picnic on a beautiful summer day.

Buying Your Provisions

Aurora Provisions
64 Pine Street
(207) 871–9060
For gourmet food to go, you can't beat this little neighborhood grocery/cafe in the West End. Aurora Provisions sells a variety of sandwiches daily, with ingredients such as Mediterranean chicken salad or ham and brie. A great summertime choice is the mozzarella, tomato, and cucumber sandwich on rosemary focaccia. You also might want to pick up a cup of gazpacho or a selection from the case of prepared foods. Items in the case change daily but can include sweet potato salad with chipotle-lime dressing, lemon-parmesan chicken breasts, macaroni and cheese, lasagna, dilled salmon, garlic smashed potatoes, and charred chicken salad. Aurora makes some of the best guacamole in the city. There's also a dessert case filled with brownies, lemon squares, and other confections. Top off your picnic basket with a bottle of wine—this little place has a great selection.

Big Sky Bread Co.
536 Deering Avenue
(207) 761–5623
This bakery is located in an old firehouse, where the staff produces a huge selection of dense, chewy breads with names like Amish White and Black Forest Pumpernickel.

There are more than two dozen different loaves to choose from, including honey whole wheat, sunflower, German rye, English muffin, cheddar garlic, cinnamon walnut raisin, and Deep South corn bread. Fans of Big Sky granola call themselves "granola heads," and you'll understand why after trying the addictive bags of honey-sweetened rolled oats with whole almonds and sunflower, pumpkin, and sesame seeds. If you're in the mood for something sweeter, try one of their huge cinnamon rolls or a giant cookie. Big Sky serves lunch

from 11:00 A.M. to 3:00 P.M. On the menu are sandwiches, grilled paninis, soups, and salads.

Black Tie To Go
188 Middle Street
(207) 756–6230
If you're looking for something a little more upscale than a sandwich to go into your picnic basket, this is the place to go. Oh, they have sandwiches, but they also have items such as lemon tarragon chicken salad, apricot almond chicken salad, quiche, crab cakes with portobello mushrooms, salad niçoise, and—a favorite—mozzarella, asparagus, and cherry tomato salad.

Micucci Grocery Store
45 India Street
(207) 775–1854
Micucci's has been selling traditional Italian specialties at low prices since 1949. This neighborhood store is fun to wander around in, so while you're picking up bread and imported meats and cheeses for sandwiches, peruse the endless varieties of pasta, olives, olive oils, biscotti, tomatoes, wines, and Italian cookies. This place has narrow aisles and can get crowded on the weekends, so plan your visit accordingly.

One Fifty Ate Bakeshop
158 Benjamin Pickett Street, South Portland
(207) 799–8998

One Fifty Ate at Willard Square
416 Preble Street, South Portland
(207) 799–0668
One Fifty Ate is a favorite neighborhood bakery and cafe across the Casco Bay Bridge. Their English muffins, scones, and luscious pastries are all made by hand, but locals especially love their outstandingly good bagels. Meals are served at the location on Benjamin Pickett Street, or you can just drop in at both locations to buy goodies to go.

Rosemont Market and Bakery
559 Brighton Avenue
(207) 774–8129

Picnicking with Portland Head Light in the distance. MAINE OFFICE OF TOURISM.

This market is known for stocking specialty meats and cheeses, fresh produce, and other foods from local farms and artisanal producers. You can get a small selection of ready-made soups and sandwiches here, such as a BLT dressed with the market's homemade pesto. Slices of homemade pizza are available, as well as filled croissants that make a nice substitute for a sandwich. A large variety of bread is made on the premises, including baguettes, herbed focaccia, rustic boules, and lots of rolls. On the weekends you'll find specialty breads—challah on Fridays, cinnamon raisin on Saturdays. Rosemont is also known for its impressive wine selection, which includes more than 200 labels.

Sophia's
81 Market Street
(207) 879–1869
If you're into low-carb diets, this is not the place for you. Artisan baker Stephen Lanzalotta, after losing a lot of business to Atkins and other low-carb regimens, decided to fight back by writing a book about the "Da Vinci diet," a way of eating based on a mathematical principle featured in Dan Brown's best seller *The Da Vinci Code*. It's basically a version of the Mediterranean diet. But don't be turned off by this gimmick—Lanzalotta creates beautiful breads, sandwiches, and pastries, some of which are actually based on ancient recipes. Stop in here, and you truly can eat like Leonardo.

Standard Baking Company
75 Commercial Street
(207) 773–2112
If Maine had a "state bread," it probably would be the Standard Baking baguette. This delicacy is sold everywhere around town, but why not stop in at the bakery so you can also

Close-up

How to Eat a Lobster

It's the moment you've been waiting for ever since you arrived in Maine: The butter is melted, you've put on that silly bib, and there's a red, steaming lobster on the plate in front of you.

Now what?

It's not as difficult as it looks to eat a lobster, and the rewards are plenty. Here's one way to do it.

1. Start by gently twisting the claws and knuckles off the body. If you have a hard-shell lobster, pick up that nutcracker and start cracking. If you have a soft-shell lobster, or shedder, the shells may be soft enough to break with your fingers alone. There are chunky morsels of meat in the knuckles, and the claws contain even more. To get at the claw meat, start by tearing off the loose part of the claw. Sometimes a bit of meat will come out with it; other times you'll have to dig for it. Then crack the large claw and push the meat out with your finger or a lobster pick/small fork.

2. To get at the tail meat, start by holding the tail in one hand and the body of the lobster in the other hand. Gently twist back and forth until the tail breaks off. Set the body aside. Pick up the tail and grab the flippers at the end of the tail. Holding the flippers as one unit, gently push up and back on them until they break off from the tail. Set aside. Insert your finger or a lobster pick into the small end of the tail and gently push the tail meat out of the bigger end of the shell. It should come out in one big piece.

3. You'll see a strip of meat running the length of the lobster tail. If you gently pull this back (this meat is edible, so don't throw it away), you'll uncover a dark vein. Pull it out and discard it. Now you're ready to enjoy your lobster tail!

try their blueberry scones, apricot and raspberry gallettes, buttery croissants, or so-good-they're-sinful sticky buns. Standard Baking is located right next door to the Hilton Garden Inn.

Two Fat Cats
47 India Street
(207) 347–5144
Owned by the same folks behind Standard Baking, Two Fat Cats specializes in "sweets from scratch." Nostalgia reigns supreme here, so you'll find only fresh, seasonal fruit pies, real butter in the chocolate chip cookies, and nothing artificial in the chocolate and vanilla cupcakes. Other treats include old-fashioned icebox cakes, banana pudding, and red velvet cake. If you can try only one thing here, though, go for one of head baker Kristen DuShane's incredible pies. These dense pies—they weigh in at almost three pounds—have a to-die-for crust that is rolled out by hand.

4. Other parts of the lobster contain meat in much smaller amounts. Some people like to go hunting for these delicate morsels, but others think they aren't worth the trouble. If you want to savor every last bite, go looking for more meat in the tail flippers, the walking legs (bite down on each leg and squeeze the meat out with your teeth), and the carapace, or body, of the lobster.

The two most common questions that come up during a lobster dinner are "What's that?" and "Can I eat it?"

If you decide to go exploring inside the lobster, for example, you may come across some green stuff that, to be honest, doesn't look all that appetizing. Yet until recently this material, called tomalley, was considered a delicacy. Some people dipped it in butter and spread it on crackers; others just scarfed it right out of the carapace. But eating the tomalley is no longer recommended. The tomalley serves the same function as a liver, filtering out contaminants the lobster has consumed. Researchers have found dioxin (a toxic substance) in lobster tomalley, and consumers are now advised to stay away from it. So while lobster meat itself is safe and nutritious to eat—as long as you don't over do the butter—it's best to stay away from the green stuff.

What about the red stuff? Some people find a red substance in their lobster when they take out the tail meat. That material is lobster eggs, sometimes called coral, and it is considered a gourmet treat in some circles.

Where to Go

Now that you have your picnic basket filled, here are a few good picnic spots where you can enjoy your treats and have an awesome view for dessert.

Crescent Beach, Cape Elizabeth. Located about 8 miles south of Portland, this park features a mile-long, crescent-shaped beach that is good for sunning, swimming, and searching for sea glass that has washed up on the sand.

There are also nature trails and a view of Richmond Island. This family-friendly beach can get crowded in summer, but there is a bathhouse, a playground, picnic tables with grills, and a snack bar. An entry fee is charged. To get there, follow the directions to Kettle Cove (see below), but instead of turning onto Kettle Cove Road, stay straight. The park will be on the left.

Eastern Promenade, Portland. Located on the eastern side of the Portland peninsula, this is where locals gather every year for the

Fourth of July fireworks celebration. It offers grassy hillsides and some incredible views of Casco Bay. To get there, travel northeast on Congress Street, which dead-ends into the Eastern Prom.

Fort Williams Park, Cape Elizabeth. Nearly 1 million visitors a year come to this park, which is the home of the oldest lighthouse in Maine, Portland Head Light. There's plenty of room in this sweeping park for a picnic, and when you're done eating, you can take a walk along the cliffs, tour the lighthouse, dip your toes in the water, or go fly a kite. There is currently no park entry fee, but town officials are considering changing that. Fort Williams is about 5 miles from downtown Portland. To get there, take Route 77 across the Casco Bay Bridge into South Portland. Follow Broadway to the left until you come to Cottage Road, and take a right. Cottage Road will become Shore Road. After about a mile, you'll see the park on your left.

Kettle Cove, Cape Elizabeth. Located on the northern end of Crescent Beach, this picnic spot has tidal pools for the kids to explore and calm water for wading, as well as a network of trails. This rocky cove, about 20 minutes from downtown Portland, is more of a local hangout than a formal park, so there is no entry fee. To get there, take Route 77 across Casco Bay Bridge. Follow Route 77/Ocean House Road for about 5 miles, and then turn left onto Kettle Cove Road.

Two Lights State Park, Cape Elizabeth. This 40-acre park provides sweeping views of Casco Bay and the North Atlantic. There is an entry fee, but the scenery is worth it. The park is a great place to experience Maine's rocky coast and watch the roiling surf, but you'll want to keep a close eye on your kids here—people walking on the rocks who got too close to the waves have been swept into the sea. Park personnel recommend staying at least 20 feet back from the surf. The park has nice trails that wind along the shoreline and back through the tangles of beach rose. There are bathrooms and plenty of picnic tables, many with grills. Or you can spread a blanket on the ground and watch as oil tankers enter Portland harbor and lobstermen go about their business hauling traps. To get to Two Lights State Park, cross the Casco Bay Bridge and follow Route 77 to Ocean House Road. Take a right onto Ocean House Road, which is still Route 77. Follow Route 77/Ocean House Road for about 4.5 miles, and then take a slight left onto Two Lights Road. Stay straight until you come to Tower Road, which takes you into the park.

Willard Beach, South Portland. This small, crescent-shaped neighborhood beach has a bathhouse, a seasonal snack bar (in case you don't want to gather your own picnic fixings), and a playground. There is a sandy beach and plenty of tidal pools for the kids to explore. You can walk to Spring Point Light from here. To get to Willard Beach, take Route 77 across the Casco Bay Bridge and veer left onto Broadway. Follow Broadway to Preble Street. Take a right onto Preble and then a left onto Beach Street.

NIGHTLIFE

As Portland has grown over the years from a little town to a big town to a little city, the nightlife here on the peninsula has also matured, especially for the over-21 set. This chapter highlights the notable activities for Portlanders looking to see and be seen in the evening hours. Here, you'll find listings of the area's best dance clubs, bars, brewpubs, and music venues as well as more subdued offerings at coffeehouses and wine bars. And, as usual, Portland offers up a few activities unique to the area—including disco bowling, a laser show at the planetarium, and, yes, Portland's one and only strip club. In keeping with this quirkiness, we've listed a few "alternative" hot spots for those of you interested in the flipside of the city's nightlife. Because Portland also has a thriving gay and lesbian community, the listings include Portland's most popular gay nightclubs and bars. Portland is also home to a handful of teen spots, which are also included here.

Since almost all of the city's nightlife is centered in Portland's downtown, the listings are clumped by type of venue, not by location. In fact, much of the city's nightlife is centered on two streets in the Old Port—Wharf Street and Fore Street—which run parallel to each other near Commercial Street. The streets are lined with clubs and bars and are so well known for partying that native Portlanders often will say they're "going to Fore Street" without distinguishing the destination. If you're at a loss about where to go any night of the week, a good place to start is the busiest nighttime block on Fore Street, between Market and Union Streets. During the summer, however, be warned that Fore Street and Wharf Street can get particularly rowdy. Partiers in skimpy clothing crowd the streets, especially after 1:00 A.M., when the

bars have to stop serving booze, and cops are now stationed on Fore Street all night to curb some people's tendency to start drunken fights.

Portland's nightlife has two incarnations. During the winter, snow and subzero temperatures tend to stifle the nightlife spirit here, and late-night venues across the board note drops in attendance from December through February. On summer weekend nights, however, the city transforms, and anyone who's anybody seems to be out on the streets mingling. If you're heading out on a weeknight, be aware that the city is still too small to manage much of a scene—you may need to choose your venue carefully, as many of the nightspots without well-known live music will be empty or close to it. But on the weekends, the city comes alive, and nearly every bar, tavern, club, and lounge is packed, especially when the weather warms.

This chapter includes some of the best late-night spots in town. Some of the brewpubs and taverns (like Rí~Rá and Gritty McDuff's Brewing Co.) may also be listed in the Restaurant chapter with more details about the food served. If you're interested in cutting a rug in a more organized fashion, check out the section on ballroom dancing in the Arts chapter.

For more information about specific offerings, the *Portland Phoenix,* an alternative arts and entertainment weekly, has the most nightlife listings of all of the newspapers in the area. Pick it up for free in red boxes all around the downtown. On Thursdays also check out the "Go" section in the *Portland Press Herald* for movie and some event listings for the upcoming weekend.

A few things to remember if you're planning on a night out in Portland:

- Operating under the influence (OUI) laws are strictly enforced here—the legal blood alcohol limit is .08. If there's any question, take a cab.
- Maine's legal drinking age is 21, and bouncers at many of the bars can be extremely particular about identification. If you're from out of town, try to bring two forms of ID in case you need to convince a jittery bouncer to allow you in—we've had friends with legitimate passports turned away, so consider yourself warned.
- Under Maine law, bars must stop serving alcohol at 1:00 A.M. (this is called "last call"). Many bars in Portland stay open after last call until around 2:00 A.M., but then they tend to hurry everyone out the door and close up shortly thereafter. So, if you're looking for a long night, it's best to start early rather than late.
- If you enjoy a cigarette with your drink, listen up—in 2004 a Maine law banning smoking in bars and other nightspots went into effect, joining an already established ban against smoking in all restaurants. If you need to light up, make sure to do it on the sidewalk, or you'll be kicked out of the establishment. You cannot, under any circumstances, smoke inside a bar, nightclub, restaurant, or any other public place of business in Maine.
- If you're drinking, make sure to designate a sober driver. Parking can be challenging downtown during the summer—try a quick sweep through the side streets and then go to the parking garage on Pearl Street or Fore Street if you come up empty. In Portland you don't need to pay parking meters after 6:00 P.M. If you find you need alternate transportation, we've listed a few of the area's taxicab companies. You can also find taxis at the taxi stand on Fore Street in front of Gritty McDuff's, although if you arrive at 1:00 A.M. when the bars and clubs announce last call, you may have to wait awhile to snag a ride.

- Be ready to pay a cover charge for most venues on Friday and Saturday nights. The cover usually ranges from $3.00 to $5.00 per person, but it varies depending on the venue and the act. Call ahead or check out the latest copy of the *Portland Phoenix,* an alternative free lastest copy of the *Portland Phoenix,* and alternative free weekly, to gauge the cost of an event.
- Since Portland is still essentially a newborn in terms of hip urban nightlife, most clubs don't bother much with a dress code. That being said, some popular locales are trying to swank up their look lately, including clubs like Liquid Blue and the lounge Plush, both of which don't admit people wearing sports jerseys or sneakers.

All right, if all of these parental admonitions haven't made you want to crawl under the covers and watch HBO all night, you should be well prepared to enjoy the night here in the City by the Sea. Despite the relatively small size of the Portland nightlife scene, the city still manages to rock, especially on the weekends. So go out and let the good times roll.

TAXICAB COMPANIES

Here is a short list of some of the area cab companies and their dispatch numbers.

ABC Taxi, (207) 772–8685
Elite Taxi, (207) 871–7274
Friendly Taxi, (207) 772–4240
Old Port Taxi, (207) 874–7872

Fore Street is a popular spot for brides having their bachelorette parties. On most weekends you can spot at least one area bride in a skimpy white dress and a veil collecting drinks at the local bars before taking the plunge.

WINE BARS

Café at Wharf Street and Wine Bar
38 Wharf Street
(207) 773–6667

The Café at Wharf Street and Wine Bar features eclectic, candlelit rooms along Wharf Street, which is packed with some of the Old Port's most popular clubs and bars. Here at the Wine Bar, you can escape all of the noise on the street and recline in their velvet sofas sipping wines from their extensive list of domestic and foreign varietals. The Wine Bar also serves American-style cuisine, including fish, salads, and steaks. This is a favorite spot for a casual group meeting or a romantic date.

Una Wine Bar and Lounge
505 Fore Street
(207) 828–0300
www.unawinebar.com

Una Wine Bar and Lounge is an upscale wine bar as trendy as it is expensive, with all the minimalist decor and track lighting to prove it. Sure, Una bills itself as a wine bar first and foremost, but locals know the place best for its cocktails, which often contain weird ingredients like edible flowers and silver and gold dust. Here, you can sit on a chrome stool under elegant track lighting and agonize over which one of their specialty martinis you'll try tonight. If you like dressing in sleek black clothing and checking out some of the best-looking schmoozers in town, or if you're just wishing you were in Manhattan instead of Portland, Una is your place. Live deejays regularly spin techno over the weekends, and there are occasional live band performances. Needless to say, with the live music here, Una on a weekend is too loud for any deep conversation, but who really cares when you're sipping silver dust?

BARS AND BREWPUBS

Amigo's Bar
9 Dana Street
(207) 772–0772

The Portland city council's efforts to control the Old Port nightlife have resulted in temporary bans on late-night entertainment and requests for liquor licenses, among other restrictions.

Amigo's Bar is located directly below Amigo's Mexican Restaurant and is one of the most popular dive bars in the city. Inside, Amigo's features a pool table, a dartboard, a few booths, and not much else save the bar, which stretches the length of the room. Amigo's is always packed on weekend nights with twenty- and thirtysomethings looking to capitalize on the cheap drink prices, live music, and intangible coolness of the place. During the summer Amigo's opens the back patio, and bands play outside. The result is always a packed house.

Binga's Wingas
795 Congress Street
(207) 772–7333

Binga's Wingas opened near Bramhall Square on Congress Street in 2006 and has already become a popular pub spot for locals. Featuring several televisions and fairly standard pub fare, Binga's itself wouldn't be much to write home about if not for its uncanny popularity—it's sure to be packed for major games and on the weekends. Check out Binga's for a cheap pint, some wings, and good conversation.

Bramhall Pub
769 Congress Street
(207) 773–9873

The Bramhall Pub is the official lounge of the Roma Café, an upscale restaurant in a Victorian-era mansion on Congress Street. In recent years this small, unassuming pub has become a favorite for the local Generation X crowd, and you can often find an eclectic mix of twentysomething artists and fiftysomething pool sharks here. The Bramhall features live music on most weekends and bluegrass on Thursday nights, when the local band Jerks of Grass packs the house.

Brian Boru
57 Center Street
(207) 780–1506
www.bboru.com

The fire-engine-red Brian Boru pub is named after the Irish king who united Ireland in the 11th century. The pub was opened by two Irish brothers in 1993 and continues to be one of Portland's most popular nighttime haunts because of both its prime location in the center of the Old Port and its outdoor decks, which are always crammed during happy hour on warm summer evenings. Brian Boru has an extensive list of beers and Irish whiskeys and in 1998 was given the Perfect Pint Award by Guinness for "high standards of quality dispensing, pouring, and presentation." We can't say that we've ever been overwhelmed by the aesthetics of a pint here at Boru, but we can say that the pub is a reliable stop for casual, fun partying any night of the week. During the summer Brian Boru's second-floor patio is often packed with pubgoers who have no qualms about shouting a hearty hello to friends (or enemies) blocks away.

Bull Feeney's
375 Fore Street
(207) 773–7210
www.bullfeeneys.com

Bull Feeney's is named after one of Portland's most notorious residents—John "Bull" Feeney, who, under the name John Ford, directed most of John Wayne's movies during the early days of Hollywood.

Bull Feeney's, like its namesake, is distinctly Irish. Each of its rooms has been decorated with Irish antiques and faux signs recalling the director Feeney. The pub includes a "smoking room" with plush leather chairs and a working fireplace on the second floor (if you actually want to smoke, though, you'll have to go outside due to the statewide ban on indoor smoking). Bull Feeney's also features a traditional "snug"—a small enclosed room where women would gather to allow men their privacy in the rest of the pub during the 19th and early 20th centuries. Of course, the snug at Bull Feeney's is not limited to women anymore, and it's a prime spot for anyone looking to escape the crowded bar and "snug"gle up. If you like live music and dancing, be sure to check out the second-floor stage, which faces a large dance floor.

Gritty McDuff's Brewing Co.
396 Fore Street
(207) 772–2739
www.grittys.com

Gritty McDuff's is a favorite among natives hankering for some local beer in a rustic pub environment. Gritty's first swung open its doors in 1988 and was the first brewpub to open in the state since Prohibition. The brewpub is responsible for starting a modern microbrew heritage that now includes several Maine breweries like Sebago Brewing Company and Stonecoast Brewery. Here at Gritty's you can sample the microbrew's latest offerings on tap in a casual, pub environment. Sit at one of the long picnic tables that help make the Gritty's experience a communal one. Gritty's occasionally has live music on the weekends; call ahead for more information.

Old Port Tavern Restaurant and Lounge
11 Moulton Street
(207) 774–0444
www.oldporttavern.com

The Old Port Tavern Restaurant and Lounge serves up American cuisine in a laid-back atmosphere. The Old Port Tavern (known around town simply as OPT) is perhaps best known for its karaoke, which is held every Monday through Thursday night on a raised stage in the dining room. As is true of the art form, karaoke here attracts both the talented and the talentless, but the ever-energetic crowd makes the whole experience a great time. OPT is also a steak house, with a full menu of pub, casual, and fine dining fare. Enjoy the free happy hour food platter Monday through Friday from 4:00 to 7:00 P.M.

In recent years karaoke has taken over Portland's bar scene, which is either a blessing or a curse, depending on whom you ask. Nearly every small bar in town has a karaoke night, and some offer two or more a week.

Rí~Rá Irish Pub and Restaurant
72 Commercial Street
(207) 761–4446
www.rira.com

The Portland Rí~Rá Irish Pub and Restaurant is part of a chain of similar pubs in seven cities nationwide that is owned by two natives of Dublin, Ireland. The name Rí~Rá comes from an Irish Gaelic term that translates loosely to "devilment or good fun." The pub features an extensive list of beers and Irish whiskeys as well as a full-service Irish-style restaurant upstairs (bangers and mash, anyone?). The Rí~Rá experience is meant to mimic traditional Irish pubs. To this end, Rí~Rá's owners imported not only pieces of a real Irish pub to decorate the Portland interior but also genuine Irish folk themselves—many of the pub's employees are natives of Ireland who come to the United States on a work exchange program. Rí~Rá hosts live music regularly and an all-day celebration on St. Patrick's Day, starting with a traditional Irish breakfast at 7:00 A.M.

Ruski's Tavern
212 Danforth Street
(207) 774–7604

Ruski's has served up a humble pint to generations of Portland's West End residents. Recently, its appeal has expanded to people who don't happen to live just around the corner, thanks in part to winning as "Best Neighborhood Bar" in a few *Portland Phoenix* surveys. At Ruski's the drink prices are as down-home as the clientele. The pub is small, and interior design here translates to a few wooden stools, a bench or two, and a long wooden bar, which takes up most of the room. Ruski's remains a local favorite and is a great place to hang out and slip into a conversation with someone who grew up in the neighborhood. Also, don't miss Rosie's at 330 Fore Street in the Old Port, the downtown cousin of Ruski's (both share the same owner).

Sebago Brewing Company
164 Middle Street
(207) 775–BEER
www.sebagobrewing.com

Sebago Brewing Company is a restaurant and sports lounge that features a selection of beers from the hometown brewery. Here, you can munch on a quesadilla or a peppercorn burger while watching sports on one of the dining room televisions and washing it all down with one of the many beers brewed here in Maine by Sebago Brewing Company. If you don't feel like a beer, Sebago also has a full bar to choose from. If you're a parent looking for a spot that is tailored for adults watching the game but that also serves good grub for the family, Sebago is a good place to go—since it's half restaurant, half brewpub, the place tends to be clean and friendly to the underage set.

Slainte
24 Preble Street
(207) 828–0900

Formerly the Meritage Wine Bar, Slainte (pronounced slan-cha) opened in the summer of 2005. Slainte's decor has remained the same—dark hues are the rule here, along with comfy seating—but there are telltale signs that having beers on tap has changed things here. There's a plasma TV and a mug club for frequent imbibers, and the menu includes standard bar fare like chicken tenders. Slainte features 15 bottled beers and 5 on tap, along with a lengthy wine list. There's live entertainment on the weekends and $1.00 off on beer and wine during happy hour.

Three Dollar Dewey's
241 Commercial Street
(207) 772–3310
www.3dollardeweys.com

Three Dollar Dewey's bills itself as "Portland's

Original Ale House." Since opening 24 years ago in the Old Port, Dewey's has made a name for itself as a large and lively alehouse with a healthy selection of bottled and draft beers. Dewey's also serves American-style cuisine, including nachos, sandwiches, and burgers. The Dewey's popcorn machine is always churning, and free popcorn is available all the time.

SPORTS BARS

Bleachers Sports Bar and Restaurant
118 Preble Street
(207) 772–9229
Bleachers is located near the University of Southern Maine campus in Portland, directly adjacent to the USM Glickman Library. The bar features six televisions, countless sports memorabilia on the walls, microbrew beers, and a full menu with vegetarian options. Be sure to check out the back deck during the summertime.

Fore Play Sports Pub
436 Fore Street
(207) 780–1111
The brazenly named Fore Play is located smack-dab in the center of the block of Fore Street in the Old Port that is notorious for bars and clubs (right between Market and Union Streets). Fore Play has occupied this coveted spot for many years and is consistently packed during summer and weekend nights with rowdy college kids and anyone else attracted to the huge television screens, the foosball table, air hockey tables, pool tables, and the not-so-subtle double entendre of the establishment's name. What Fore Play may lack in class, it makes up for in energy.

COFFEEHOUSES

Breaking New Grounds
13 Exchange Street
(207) 761–5637
For as long as we can remember, this coffeehouse at the bottom of Exchange Street has

been one of the most popular hangout spots in town. The ownership of the shop has changed over the years, but the clientele remains staunchly loyal to whoever happens to supply the java here. Breaking New Grounds offers a great selection of coffee drinks and a few pastries, but the scene here is what makes most people come back. Despite the simple, somewhat spartan interior, something about the shop makes it easy to chat with new people and catch up with old friends. Needless to say, the spot is also popular for many of the area's teens. The coffeehouse is open Monday through Friday from 7:30 A.M. to 10:00 P.M. and Saturday and Sunday from 8:00 A.M. to 10:00 P.M.

Casco Bay Books
151 Middle Street
(207) 541–3842
www.cascobaybooks.com
Casco Bay Books (CBB) is as much a bookstore as a coffee shop (check out the listing in the Shopping chapter for information on the bookstore half). The coffee shop inside the bookstore is most definitely a place where locals go to see and be seen, especially at night. The trendy scene at the coffee shop benefits from the wide waist-to-ceiling windows looking out into the hallway at 151 Middle Street, which allow people passing by to gaze in while CBB coffee sippers are gazing out. The huge windows coupled with the shop's avant-garde books (which attract avant-garde artists) make the CBB coffee shop a great place to check out the local alternative scene. Casco Bay Books is open daily from 10:00 A.M. to 11:00 P.M.

Coffee By Design
67 India Street
(207) 780–6767

620 Congress Street
(207) 772–5533

43 Washington Avenue
(207) 879–2233
www.coffeebydesign.com

Coffee By Design (CBD) is the behemoth of the local coffee scene. Owned by husband-and-wife team Mary Allen Lindeman and Alan Spear, these coffee shops have flourished in the city despite heated competition from both independently owned and chain java shops. Part of the success of CBD is that the stores sell their own special brand of roasted coffees, which are perfected by Alan at the roastery at their Washington Avenue location. Coffee By Design java is so popular in these parts that it has become the house coffee at several of the area's best restaurants and even a few rival coffeehouses. The coffee is also sold online in small and wholesale shipments.

Each CBD coffee shop is run by an upbeat team of coffee connoisseurs who happily brew up and pour out countless espresso and coffee concoctions. Behind the scenes, CBD's owners pride themselves on their commitment to the local community and the arts as well as to fair-trade practices with coffee purveyors in Latin America. The owners donate a percentage of their annual revenue to local community groups and artists. The India Street store is open Monday through Friday from 6:30 A.M. to 6:00 P.M., Saturday from 7:00 A.M. to 5:00 P.M., and Sunday from 8:00 A.M. to 3:00 P.M. The Congress Street store is open Monday through Saturday from 6:30 A.M. to 9:00 P.M. and Sunday from 6:30 A.M. to 7:00 P.M. The new Washington Avenue store (on Munjoy Hill) is open Monday through Friday from 7:00 A.M. to 6:00 P.M. and is closed on the weekend.

JavaNet Café
37 Exchange Street
(207) 773-2469
As its name implies, JavaNet features not only a great cup of joe but also Internet access at any of its computers. Internet access here is priced reasonably—$2.10 for the first 15 minutes and 13 cents for every quarter hour after that. Be sure to check out the JavaNet window bar facing Exchange Street—it's one of the best people-watching spots in Portland. JavaNet is open Monday through Thursday

i Portland may have an energetic nightlife, but it has only a few after-hours eateries, all of which tend to be packed after last call. If you're hungry in the early-morning hours after 1:00 A.M., check out Denny's Diner at 1091 Congress Street or Bill's Pizza at 177 Commercial Street, both of which are favorites for locals with the munchies.

from 7:00 A.M. to 10:00 P.M., Saturday from 7:00 A.M. to 11:00 P.M., and Sunday from 8:00 A.M. to 7:00 P.M.

LOUNGES, DANCING, AND LIVE MUSIC

Asylum
121 Center Street
(207) 772-8274
Asylum has a dance floor capable of accommodating 600 people and a sports bar at the other end of the building with a couple of humongous TVs. There are always two scenes at Asylum on the weekends—the smaller dance floor in the basement tends to be for fans of classic pop from the 1980s and 1990s, while upstairs, live bands and deejays spinning hip-hop are the norm. Live acts can run the gamut from heavy metal to pop, so be sure to check the area listings or call ahead before swinging by.

The Big Easy Blues Club
55 Market Street
(207) 871-8817
The Big Easy Blues Club, as its name suggests, is best known for the blues bands that grace its stage. However, in recent years, the lineup of musicians playing here has been as diverse as the music on the radio. Depending on the night, you could find country western, jazz, blues, or funk. Sly Chi, a popular local funk jam band, frequently plays here. The crowd depends on the music that night—funk tends to attract a young crowd, while blues and country attract a more mature group. Because of the club's variety, be sure to call

ahead to check out the night's roster before heading down to the Big Easy.

Blue
650A Congress Street
(207) 774–4111

Blue opened in 2005 and has already generated a loyal crowd of bar patrons and music lovers. This small, laid-back blues club features new local musicians and talent from beyond Portland. Everything is acoustic here, and the sound tends to be bluesy or folksy. The owners of Blue wanted to open a bar in town where patrons could go to have a good conversation and enjoy music at the same time. They have succeeded. The place is small, the seating is limited, and you can get only wine or beer here, but already Blue is the destination spot for some of the city's hippest, artsy people. Blue even serves light food—the personal pizzas are popular.

Bubba's Sulky Lounge
92 Portland Street
(207) 828–0549

Bubba's has been known locally as a biker bar for years but recently has enjoyed significant mainstream attention due to a series of successful parties thrown by some enterprising young promoters. So don't judge Bubba's by its dingy exterior and darkened windows— inside, the bar is truly a must-see. On weekend nights Bubba's is consistently packed with twenty- and thirtysomethings who take to the retro lit-up dance floor to party the night away. And if the disco floor isn't your bag, there are countless nooks and crannies in which to hide out and chat the night away. If you run out of discussion topics, just look around—the whole bar interior is decked out with odd antiques, aging furniture, and even a few mannequins. Bubba's has two pool tables and two bars, one on each end of the dance floor.

Iguana
52 Wharf Street
(207) 871–5886

The Iguana bills itself as "a slice of Key West in Portland." The Iguana is located at the center of the rowdiest corner of Wharf Street in the Old Port and is best known for encouraging women to dance on the bar top. If you're not interested in watching girls dance for free, you probably won't find much else to do here, because the part of the Iguana not occupied by the bar is relatively narrow and often crowded with people very interested in everything the bar top has to offer. Needless to say, the atmosphere on weekends tends to be loud and crazy.

The Lava Lounge
416 Fore Street
(207) 879–4007

The Lava Lounge is best described as Portland's version of an East Village bar in Manhattan. The theme here is urban chic: metal stools in a room decorated with rich red hues, shiny silver tabletops, and a bar made of metal. The Lava Lounge is a relatively small bar but often hosts some of the area's best deejays spinning techno music. Because of the size of the place and the type of music played here, the scene can get pretty loud—expect to sip your martini amid some pumping bass.

Liquid Blue
446 Fore Street
(207) 774–9595
www.portlandatnight.net

Liquid Blue is a popular nightclub located on Fore Street between Union Street and Exchange, the block that is the epicenter of the downtown club and bar scene. The space at Liquid Blue is nothing to write home about—there's a fairly basic stage painted black facing a wide dance floor, also painted black. Attached to the club is Digger's Pub, a fairly run-of-the-mill spot with a wraparound bar and a pinball machine or two. On Friday and Saturday you can access the staircase to the Plush Lounge upstairs from Digger's; otherwise, the best reason to go to the pub during a busy weekend is to take a break from the club next door. Liquid Blue doesn't start to really hop on weekends until after 11:00 P.M., and then, like magic, the place is suddenly packed. The music here is usually pop (Saturday is '80s "retro" revival night), and the patrons are in their 20s and early 30s. If you like the music here, you'll have a blast, but don't be surprised if you suddenly find your dance space crowded close to midnight.

Local 188
188 State Street
(207) 761–7909
www.local188.com
Local 188 is a gallery, performance venue, tapas bar, and restaurant. For nightlife, it's a favorite stop to enjoy hip alternative art and performances of local bands and spoken-word artists. The bar stocks a wide selection of wine, beer, and spirits.

The Pavilion
188 Middle Street
(207) 773–6422
The dance floor at the Pavilion has survived a number of owners and names, but the interior of the club has remained virtually unchanged for years. And this is a good thing. The space here is one of the nicest in Portland's nightlife scene. The club is located in a former bank dating to the early 20th century and has a high arched ceiling, pillars, a black and white tiled floor, and an oversize silver disco ball (which, of course, was not part of the bank's original interior). The dance floor is relatively large by Portland's standards, and there are four bars (three on the ground floor and one on the second), so the wait for a drink is never too long. If you don't feel like dancing, there are plenty of seats to lounge in and watch the crowd. If you want more privacy, saunter upstairs to the lounge area, which overlooks the main room. Deejays here are the norm, often spinning pop and hip-hop.

Plush
446 Fore Street
(207) 774–9595
www.portlandatnight.net

Plush is located on the second floor of Digger's Pub, which is attached to the Liquid Blue dance club. Plush was conceived as an upscale, urban lounge, but the fact that you have to weave through the crowds at Digger's to get to the staircase leading to Plush certainly clouds that vision. The entire area is decorated with red velvet and mirrors, and some of the tables are made out of beds. Whether this makes for sophistication or tackiness is up to you to decide. Plush bills itself as "Maine's Only VIP Bed Lounge" and is open only on Friday and Saturday nights.

Portland Sports Complex Dome
521 Warren Avenue
(207) 878–0865
www.portlandsportscenter.com
In 2006, after the State Theatre, a midsize venue, closed because of fire-code violations, Dome owner Jim Gratello decided to welcome comedians and bands to a complex that has long been known for hosting local sports games and conventions. The Dome can hold up to 3,000 people and includes the Gold Room, which rivals the Comedy Connection for comic entertainment in Portland. The Dome is currently being booked by the local agency Live Nation, which is known for recruiting some of the country's best musicians to perform in Portland.

The Station
Union Station Plaza, St. John Street
(207) 773–3466
The Station, a nightclub and billiards club, has recently made a name for itself by putting on all-ages shows and attracting national acts. The Station is located in the basement of a mini-mall that houses a Japanese restaurant and a Goodwill retail outlet, among other stores. Here in the underground Station there are rows of pool tables where locals come to hang out and, in an adjacent room, a wide dance floor with a stage at the end of the room. Station promoters have recently begun booking national-level names to this relatively large venue (the Gza from the Wu-tang Clan

performed here in 2005), and it looks like the club, which was once known more for its 25-cent pool tables than its dance floor, may become an oddly popular player in the local live-music scene. Stay tuned.

Top of the East
157 High Street
(207) 775–5411
www.eastlandpark.com/lounge

The Top of the East lounge is on the top floor of the Eastland Park Hotel in downtown Portland and is the city's only bar with a view of the skyline. The hotel is the oldest in the city and is known for its elegant accommodations (see the Accommodations chapter for more details). Top of the East presents a stunning view of the city to the south, west, and north and has consistently ranked among the most romantic date spots in local newspaper reader polls. The specialties of the house are the unique mixed drinks and martinis, which range from the sweet to the strong. Wine and beer are also available, as are finger foods such as shrimp cocktail and gourmet cheese and crackers.

The White Heart
551 Congress Street
(207) 828–1900
www.thewhiteheart.com

The art deco–inspired White Heart opened in 2006 and quickly became one of the trendiest hangouts in town. Located in a part of Congress Street that is usually quiet after dusk, the White Heart, with its conspicuous neon heart shining in the enormous front window, functions as a magnet for the hip set of Portland's twenty- and thirtysomethings. Inside, the bar is relatively narrow, with high ceilings and a small dance floor at the far end. The lighting here is bright, the seats are lush red, and the drinks range from beer to complicated specialty cocktails. Try the classic champagne cocktail, circa 1935: a sugar cube topped with sparkling wine and a few drops of Angostura bitters. Light fare is also available.

GAY BARS AND CLUBS

Blackstones
6 Pine Street
(207) 775–2885
www.blackstones.com

Blackstones, located on a quiet street in the West End, is Portland's oldest gay neighborhood bar. Its dark windows may seem intimidating, but inside the bar is small, cozy, and clean like the best of neighborhood pubs. Blackstones has a pool table and one long, elegant wooden bar. The third Saturday of every month is dedicated to leather fetish, and other events take place on a rotating schedule. Visit their Web site for a calendar.

Somewhere Else
117 Spring Street
(207) 871–9169

Somewhere Else is a small bar that caters to gay men and women. It offers frequent karaoke nights, dancing, and general schmoozing. This is a popular neighborhood bar with a loyal and friendly clientele and a comfortable, intimate atmosphere.

Styxx
3 Spring Street
(207) 828–0822
www.styxxportland.com

Styxx nightclub opened in 2004 in a space that previously held another gay club called the Underground. It's currently the best place for gays and gay-friendly folk to really cut a rug in Portland, so it tends to attract plenty of loyal followers. At Styxx you can jam out to the latest techno and pop music on the expanded dance floor or chill out and play a game of pool in the adjacent bar area. Styxx also hosts regular "theme" nights, such as classic music video night, karaoke, and Industrial Goth night. The dance floor stays open until 3:00 A.M., although Styxx stops serving

i The new Web site http://gayfunin portlandmaine.com is a locally produced guide to all things gay-friendly in the city.

alcohol at 1:00 A.M. Their Web site includes a listing of upcoming events.

ECLECTIC PORTLAND

Comedy Connection
16 Custom House Wharf
(207) 774–5554
www.mainecomedy.com
The Comedy Connection along Portland's waterfront features local and national comedians. It is located behind the Porthole Restaurant, tucked into a narrow avenue leading to the fish factories. The club has been open for more than 10 years and helped local comedian Bob Marley hone his talent for the national stage. Marley, who frequently returns to perform on his home turf, joins other well-known comedians and locals. If you're interested in finding your own inner comic genius, the Comedy Connection regularly hosts amateur nights, stand-up classes, and contests.

Maplewood Dance Center
383 Warren Avenue
(207) 878–0584
www.maplewooddancecenter.com
The Maplewood Dance Center sponsors singles dances and various types of ballroom and country music dances Wednesday through Saturday nights on their 320-square-foot main ballroom floor. The Singles' Network, a local volunteer-run social club, sponsors regular singles mixers here. Call the Dance Center for more information or check out the Singles' Network Web site at www.the singlesnetworkme.com.

Platinum Plus
200 Riverside Street
(207) 772–8033
www.theplatinumplus.com/portland.html
Platinum Plus is the area's only strip club. Located on the outskirts of town in a commercial district that includes mostly chain restaurants and hotels, Platinum Plus stays open late (until 6:00 A.M. on weekends and until 3:00 A.M. on most weekdays) and features the standard roster of buxom ladies dancing on one of four sleek black stages. On Monday nights Platinum broadcasts WWE wrestling on the big screen and offers 25-cent chicken wings and draft beer.

Space Alternative Arts Venue
538 Congress Street
(207) 828–5600
www.space538.org
Space takes many forms. It is a gallery and performance arts venue (see The Arts chapter for more on this) and also a nightspot that regularly features local and national alternative bands, literary readings, and parties. Alternative entertainment and art is the theme here, and performers range from folk and pop bands to avant-garde artists. Space's young owners are well connected with Portland's arts scene, and it isn't unusual for this venue to showcase up-and-coming regional and national talent. For more on upcoming nighttime events at Space, visit their Web site.

Videoport
151 Middle Street
(207) 773–1999
www.videoport.formovies.com
Yeah, so maybe staying in and watching movies doesn't necessarily qualify as "nightlife," but this locally owned, totally eclectic video store is enough of a local entertainment favorite to warrant mention in this chapter. Videoport, located in the Old Port, stocks the typical range of new releases, dramas, and comedies but also has a variety of movies you can't find anywhere else in Portland, including documentaries, foreign films, classics, original kung-fu movies, and locally produced shorts and features. And Videoport's staff is so knowledgeable about films that they're nearly intimidating sometimes.

i The all-volunteer Singles' Network has organized mixers for area singles for over 20 years. To learn more about their events, call (207) 828–5965.

Every night features a different free rental special from a department in the store. If you're truly at a loss, head to the "Incredibly Strange Films" section here; it never fails to impress and appall.

MOVIE THEATERS

Movies on Exchange
10 Exchange Street
(207) 772–8041
www.moviesonexchange.com

Movies on Exchange shows independent films and foreign films on its one small screen and is the only spot in town where you can regularly view films that don't register on the mainstream radar. You won't find state-of-the-art sound systems or elaborate snack bars here, but patrons don't seem to mind. Movies on Exchange is a place for people who prefer films to blockbuster movies, or people who are accompanying those other people. At any rate, our experience here has been hit-or-miss, which says more about the varying quality of indie films than about the theater itself. To help patrons figure out which obscure film is worth a gander, Movies on Exchange distributes an oversize flyer every couple of months with the theater's screening schedule and detailed descriptions of upcoming movies. General admission tickets are $7.00, and on Wednesday all seats cost $5.00.

i Interested in an old-fashioned drive-in double feature? Check out Prides Corner Drive-In in Westbrook (207–797–3154) or the Saco Drive-In Theatre in Saco (207–284–1016). Both are open only during the summer season.

Nickelodeon Cinema
1 Temple Street
(207) 772–9751
www.patriotcinemas.com

The Nickelodeon, or "the Nick" as it is known to locals, presents first-run movies at cut-rate prices. The cinema charges $7.00 for adults and $5.00 for adult tickets before 6:00 P.M. and on Tuesday nights. The Nick was renovated at the end of 2004, and now each theater has brand-new seats and stereo sound. The cinema is located in the Old Port within walking distance of many of the area's hotels and inns. If you drive, we recommend that you park in the garage adjacent to the entrance on Temple Street, as on-street parking spaces here can be tough to find.

Regal Cinemas Clark's Pond 8
333 Clark's Pond Parkway, South Portland
(207) 879–1511
www.uatc.com

Part of the national chain of Regal Cinema movie theaters, the Clark's Pond Regal Cinemas is one of the sleeker movie theaters around. The multiplex is located in a shopping mall adjacent to the Maine Mall in South Portland. It regularly shows first-run films and features several screens, each with stereo sound. Tickets cost $8.25 for adults ($6.50 for a matinee show) and $6.00 for seniors and children. There is another Regal Cinemas in Falmouth, a suburb about a five-minute drive north of Portland. Visit the Regal Cinemas Web site for more information.

SHOPPING

Portland is known not only as a popular spot for local arts and culture but also as a great place to shop. In this chapter you'll find information on some of the area's most reliable and eclectic retailers, including clothing and accessories stores, shoe stores, jewelry and other specialty shops, consignment stores, music stores, bookstores, and specialty food shops. Fans of used books should note that the stores listed here are primarily retailers of new books, but this is not to slight any of the wonderful used bookstores in and around the city center. A few of the best purveyors of used books are listed in this chapter.

As you begin to look through this chapter, you'll no doubt notice that many of the listings are located in and around the Old Port. That's no mistake—much of Portland's shopping is clustered around this commercial neighborhood, which boasts more than 200 independently owned and operated boutiques and stores. If you love to shop, all you need to do is park your car in the Old Port and wander around—you'll find everything from exotic jewelry to funky shoes to sleek clothing. If you enjoy chain retailers, be sure to check out the Maine Mall, which draws people from all over the state and beyond to shop at such notable retailers as Macy's, Gap, and Victoria's Secret.

And if you're looking for outlet options, we have listed information on the Kittery Outlets (about an hour's drive south), the Tom's of Maine outlet in Kennebunk, and the king of Maine retailers—L.L. Bean in Freeport.

The list here is by no means exhaustive, but we have tried to include some of our favorites and some out-of-the-way places you may want to check out. Consider this an introduction to shopping in Portland. The rest is left for you to discover.

CLOTHING AND SHOE RETAILERS IN THE DOWNTOWN AND OLD PORT

Amaryllis
41 Exchange Street
(207) 772–4439
www.amaryllisclothing.com
One of Exchange Street's staple clothiers, Amaryllis sells everything from the funky to the elegant in their small, one-room shop in the Old Port. The shop is a favorite for the urban chic and the aging hippie alike—here you'll find fabulous embroidered handbags, retro-inspired jewelry, designer shirts and skirts, delicate hats for all seasons, and shoes that manage to be both elegant and kind on your arches. If you're in the market for a special-occasion dress, don't forget to check out Amaryllis's evening wear selection in the back of the store.

Casco Bay Woolworks
10 Moulton Street
(207) 879–9665
www.cascobaywoolworks.com
This recently remodeled factory outlet store is located on a narrow cobblestone street deep in the Old Port. As its name implies, Casco Bay Woolworks features clothing woven in wool. You'll find elegant and colorful shawls, blankets, capes, and scarves to complement your fashion in all seasons—from bitterly cold winter evenings to balmy summer afternoons. Each garment has been handcrafted locally. Check out the new additions for men and children.

> **i** Beware the taxman: Maine levies a 5 percent sales tax on retail sales of nonfood items.

Chantal
195 Middle Street
(207) 347–4427
www.shopchantal.com

Chantal is one of Portland's newest entries to the budding ready-to-wear clothing scene. Opened in 2004, the boutique, named after its owner and buyer, features limited-line clothing for men and women and accessories made by talent in Maine and beyond. Here, you can find casual and classic clothing from dozens of designers, including Chip and Pepper, Rebecca Taylor, and Ella Moss.

Cream
87 Market Street
(207) 699–2940
www.creamapparel.com

Billing itself as "Maine's first and only sneaker boutique," Cream opened with a splash in 2006 when it hosted a party at the White Heart, a hip local haunt, and treated party goers to free Vans sneakers. Cream is owned by thirtysomething couple Shane and Michelle McGarvey, who opened the store to bring some of the urban sneaker culture they saw in places like New York City and San Francisco to Portland. The store caters heavily to the local hip-hop crowd, and "kicks" here are all limited edition. Shopping at Cream ain't cheap; most shoes run between $80 and $130. Be sure to check out the glass case of collectors' sneakers—worth hundreds of dollars a pair.

David Wood Clothiers
75 Market Street
(800) 403–6653
www.davidwood.com

David Wood Clothiers has been outfitting men with quality formal and casual apparel since 1978. Billing itself as a refreshing alternative to chain clothing stores and online retail outlets, David Wood is a favorite stop for Portland's "Dapper Dans." The store prides itself on its elegant DW Signature collection, which features clothing, accessories, and cologne from Europe. In addition, David Wood offers

The block of Congress Street at the base of Munjoy Hill (beginning at the intersection of India Street and heading up the hill on Congress) has been profiled nationally for its quirky snarl of gift shops, antiques shops, and top-notch hair salons.

custom-made shirts and suits, an on-site tailor shop, and custom and ready-to-wear tuxedoes. Personal shopping services, shoe repair and reconditioning, and fabric reweaving are also available.

Joseph's
410 Fore Street
(207) 773–1274
www.josephsofportland.com

Joseph's has provided area men with casual and formal attire and accessories since 1974. Canali Clothing Company, Tommy Bahama sportswear, and Hugo Boss are just a few of the designers they carry. A tailor is available on-site to alter your clothes or make them from scratch—Joseph's makes custom clothing, including suits, sports coats, and pants.

J. L. Coombs
22 Exchange Street
(207) 253–5633

This J. L. Coombs on Exchange Street carries many of the same designers that the corporate store in Freeport does. Here, you'll find trendy footwear that's also comfortable. The store carries a diverse selection of funky shoes for women, including shoes by Ecco, Camper, Naot, Fry Boots, Dansko, and Birkenstock, among others.

Mexicali Blues
9 Moulton Street
(207) 772–4080
www.mexicaliblues.com

Mexicali Blues' slogan—"Clothing that fits your mind"—suits this store's alternative bent. Here, you'll find all sorts of brightly tie-dyed outfits, including skirts, pants, and sundresses for children and adults. Mexicali expanded the store in 2003 to accommodate a new jewelry section, which features practically every type of exotic stone accessory you can imagine. In keeping with its flower-child theme, Mexicali also sells incense, hemp bags and accessories, bongo drums, and natural perfume. The employees are helpful, if predictably laid-back.

Milo
151 Middle Street
(207) 541–3842
www.miloportland.com

Milo is a small boutique that features unique men's and women's clothing made by independent designers. Much of the clothing is locally produced, including plenty of cotton T-shirts from Milo in Maine, a clothing line owned and operated by the owners of Milo boutique and the adjacent Casco Bay Books. Prices at Milo tend to reflect the casual style of clothing offered here—clothing priced above $50 is rare—and most everything is comfortable and designed simply. Plus, chances are pretty good that you'll run into Mark High working the register here. He's the co-owner of the store and co-designer of Milo in Maine—and who better to advise you about his line than the owner himself?

i In summer 2006 more than 200 locally owned businesses launched the Portland "Buy Local Campaign" to encourage consumers to shop at locally owned, independent stores.

Serendipity
34 Exchange Street
(207) 772–0219
www.serendipityportland.com

Serendipity specializes in elegant fashions for special occasions and weddings and has close ties to Europe and its sister store, Serendipity Killarney in Killarney, Ireland. At Serendipity, Portland's designer dolls can find their fix of luxurious sweaters, fine clothing, sportswear, and accessories both domestic and foreign.

You won't find many bargains here, but you might not care once you've laid eyes on the perfect dress for that special event.

Shop!
468–470 Fore Street
(207) 772–9060, (877) 890–0772
www.akarihairspa.com

The emphatically named Shop! is a small boutique popular among locals who yearn for the latest fashions from the big city. Located in one of the city's largest spas—the Akari Day Spa—Shop! features everything from women's clothing and lingerie to kitchenware and candles. You may feel as though you've been magically transported to a New York City chic shop, and that's no mistake—nearly every item at Shop! has been selected by Akari's buyers from suppliers in Manhattan, where the spa's owner maintains strong ties. The boutique's steep prices reflect what no doubt must be an arduous transport from big city to small city.

Spoil Me Rotten
43 Exchange Street
(207) 773–0743

Spoil Me Rotten features colorful, fun ready-to-wear clothing and shoes. If you're looking for a dress with sequins, a set of sexy boots, and a sleek, unique top to tie the outfit together, Spoil Me Rotten should be the first stop on your list. Every time we go in this store, we see something new and fabulous. Prices here can climb into the hundreds, but it's also possible to find a great deal.

Stiletto
97 Exchange Street
(207) 775–3033
www.stilettoshoesonline.com

Stiletto Shoes opened in 2002 and shares its name with the sister store that predated it in Portsmouth, New Hampshire. Stiletto is a high-end shoe boutique for women that features products from many of today's premier shoe designers—including Kate Spade, Donald Pliner, Stuart Weitzman, Taryn Rose, Kors,

Hollywould, Isabella Fiore, and Icon. Stiletto also stocks Kate Spade bags and accessories. This sleek, pricey store with track lighting and minimalist design was recently named one of the best places to shop north of Boston by *New Hampshire Magazine*.

Zane
26 Milk Street
(207) 879–1113
www.shopzane.com

Zane may be hidden away on a small side street in the Old Port, but it should be a must-find on your list. Featuring clothing from French Connection, Anna Sui, Sweet & Toxic, and many more, Zane has the latest in sleek urban clothing and accessories for men and women. Whether you dress it up or dress it down, you can find it here.

SPECIALTY SHOPS
Downtown/Old Port

Casablanca Comics
151 Middle Street
(207) 780–1676
www.casablancacomics.com

Casablanca Comics is located in the Old Port business building that also houses Casco Bay Books, Videoport, and Bull Moose Music, among other shops. This store not only carries a wide selection of comic books but also hosts regular events such as "24-Hour Comic Day," in which two dozen artists complete a 24-page comic book over the course of one full day.

The Clown
123 Middle Street
(207) 756–7399
www.the-clown.com

The Clown is an eclectic shop that doubles as a gallery (see The Arts chapter), gift shop, and wine store. The Clown features a wide range of products, including European antique furniture and accessories, contemporary artwork, gourmet foods, ceramics, olive wood items, glassware, pewter, and more. If you enjoy Italian wines, be sure to check out

i The Porteous-Mitchell department store on Congress Street was known as the "Macy's of Maine" during the 1950s and 1960s before falling into disrepair and closing in 1991. Today, the building is part of the downtown campus of the Maine College of Art.

the selection at The Clown, including the owners' own award-winning Classico Chianti, which is made on their farm in Tuscany.

Condom Sense
424 Fore Street
(207) 871–0356
www.qualitycondoms.com

Condom Sense has supplied condoms, sex gag gifts, dirty birthday cards, and exotic massage oils to the masses in Portland for more than 10 years. Here, inhibition is the only dirty word. The one-room store is brightly lit, the door to the street is often propped open, and the friendly employees are always willing to answer questions. Exotic Kama Sutra massage oils and Japanese condoms share shelf space with strawberry-flavored edible underwear and sex board games. If you're looking to spice up your love life and enjoy a good chuckle, Condom Sense should be on your list.

Country Noel
57 Exchange Street
(207) 773–7217, (800) 357–6635

A one-stop shop for everything related to winter holidays, the Country Noel features an extensive line of elegant Christmas tree ornaments, scented Yankee Candles, decorative lights, figurines, and holiday music CDs. If you can't find your holiday knickknack here, it probably doesn't exist. Country Noel, predictably, is busiest during November and December. It is closed for a "Long Winter's Nap" from February 1 to March 31.

Ferdinand
243 Congress Street
(207) 761–2151
www.ferdinandhomestore.com

Situated on Congress Street at the base of Munjoy Hill, Ferdinand is both home store and studio for artist/owner Diane Toepfl. Here, you can find locally made clothing, jewelry, crafts, and pretty much anything else that fits in with Toepfl's quirky aesthetic. Items at this gift shop are functional artwork—don't miss the wall of pretty gift cards.

Folly 101
101 Exchange Street
(207) 773–5227

Folly 101 features an eclectic array of home accessories, furnishings, and jewelry, all with an elegant 1920s flair. You'll find colorful beaded necklaces and bracelets, silver candleholders, and fine woven throw rugs, all at affordable prices. And if you're in the market for romance, be sure to check out their selection of long-burning candles.

L.L. Bean Factory Store
542 Congress Street
(207) 772–5100

The L.L. Bean Factory Store carries selections of some of L.L. Bean's staple products, including casual and sports attire, shoes, camping gear, and sports accessories. The store adheres to L.L. Bean's famous returns policy: If you buy something here and it lets you down, you can return it for store credit or a refund. For more on the L.L. Bean Flagship Store in Freeport, see the "Outlet Shopping beyond Portland" section below.

From late April through October, don't miss the Portland farmers' market, where local farmers and horticulturists sell fresh produce, plants, flowers, and herbs. The farmers' market is located in Monument Square in downtown Portland on Wednesday from 7:00 A.M. to 2:00 P.M. and in Deering Oaks Park in Portland on Saturday from 7:00 A.M. to noon.

Maine Potters Market
376 Fore Street
(207) 774–1633
www.mainepottersmarket.com

The Maine Potters Market has occupied its store in the Old Port for 25 years. Here, you can find unique and beautiful pottery handmade by any one of 15 member potters. All of the pottery is local, and products include mugs, bowls, clocks, and lamps.

Nomia Boutique
24 Exchange Street, second floor
(207) 773–4774
www.nomiaboutique.com

Nomia Boutique, the city's first women-owned and -operated adult boutique, features sex toys, videos, lingerie, and sex workshops geared toward women and couples. Since opening its doors in February 2004, Nomia has quickly become one of the most popular sex stores in the area because of its knowledgeable staff and unthreatening environment. Nomia is on the second floor at 24 Exchange, and discretion is cherished here (employees keep all conversations with customers confidential). On Thursday Nomia hosts a women-only night from 5:00 to 8:00 P.M.

Porte4
366 Fore Street
(207) 347–7104

Porte4 is an upscale jewelry boutique that specializes in estate, custom-designed, and special-order jewelry. At Porte4 you can find that one-of-a-kind ring or necklace for your special someone, but you may have to save up for a couple of months before you can afford it. Porte4 bills itself as a selective shop with the highest levels of customer service and satisfaction. To be sold here, all merchandise must score highly in four areas: quality of craftsmanship, uniqueness of design, rarity, and value. Porte4 also features unique home and personal accessories from the United States and Europe.

Browne Trading Company

If you've ever ordered caviar from Williams Sonoma or Dean and Deluca, it's likely that your order was packed right here in Portland.

Down on the waterfront, on Merrill's Wharf, you'll find one of the country's top seafood and caviar purveyors. Browne Trading Company counts among its clients some of the nation's best-known chefs, including Daniel Boulud, Jean-Louis Palladin, Charlie Trotter, Eric Ripert, Wolfgang Puck, and Emeril Lagasse.

Rod Mitchell, the founder of the company, has become a legend in the whole-sale seafood business for his dedication to quality and freshness and for his wide selection of seafood carefully harvested from waters all over the world. He is also the country's largest importer of farm-raised caviar.

On any given day, 50 to 75 different kinds of fish and shellfish may pass, briefly, through Browne Trading's 10,000-square-foot warehouse and local retail market. It doesn't stay in Portland long—much of the wholesale seafood is out the door within hours, and no fish stays in the retail market more than a day.

Thanks to the retail market, located in a plain brick building on Commercial Street, Portlanders have access to the same variety and quality of local and inter-

Inside Browne Trading Company. BROWNE TRADING CO.

national seafood as restaurants like New York's Le Bernardin. In addition to plump Maine diver scallops, North Atlantic halibut, and newly harvested Maine peekytoe crab meat, Browne Trading's customers can sample fresh Dover sole, sashimi-grade mahimahi from Hawaii, line-caught tai snapper harvested from the waters between New Zealand and Japan, wild turbot from Portugal, and wild or farm-raised loup de mer from Europe.

Rod Mitchell, who hails from an old New England family (they claim their roots stretch back to the Mayflower), fished the Maine coast with his grandfather and uncle when he was growing up. In the early 1980s he owned and operated a gourmet wine and cheese shop in Camden, and that's where he met Jean-Louis Palladin. It was Palladin who suggested that Mitchell get into caviar, and soon Mitchell was also hunting down hard-to-find seafood for the chef. He found ways to get Palladin glass eel, lamprey, sea urchin, and monkfish livers. He hired divers to hand-harvest scallops. Word began to spread in the culinary world, and the business took off from there. Chefs liked more than just the variety of seafood Mitchell could offer them. They also appreciated the way Mitchell handled the food. He preferred hooks to nets, which he believed were too stressful on the fish thrashing around in them. Whenever possible, he bought dayboat catches to ensure freshness. His delicate approach even extended to storing the fish in shaved ice, which resulted in less bruising.

By 1991 Mitchell and his wife, Cynde, had started Browne Trading Company. They grew the caviar side of the business as well, and today, in addition to offering caviar from American waters, they import caviar from the Caspian Sea and farm-raised caviars from places like Italy and Germany. They are the exclusive distributors of Astara Iranian caviars.

Browne Trading has also developed a line of smoked seafood products that are produced in the company's own smokehouse. Smoke master Ken Meuse creates such delicacies as scotch-cured smoked Scottish salmon, citrus-and-basil-smoked Atlantic salmon (made with citrus oil and vodka), hot-smoked rainbow trout, and Scottish-style finnan haddie made from Gulf of Maine haddock. Locals can tell when there's a batch of maple-syrup-smoked Atlantic salmon in the works because the sweet smell wafts over Commercial Street.

All of this is sold in the retail store, alongside the fresh seafood, a huge selection of cheeses, caviars, imported oils and vinegars, and a wine selection that includes more than 3,000 labels. The market recently started offering seafood-based soups and sandwiches for takeout. Corporate chef Jason Kennedy creates offerings such as smoked trout salad sandwiches, seared tuna sandwiches with blue cheese, smoked pastrami salmon sandwiches, squid scampi, and fish cakes made from opah—also known as moonfish—shipped in from Hawaii.

Visitors come to Portland to sample lobster, clam chowder, and other New England specialties, but with a stop at Browne Trading they'll get all that, plus a taste of the world.

Shipwreck and Cargo
207 Commercial Street
(207) 775–3057
www.shipwreckandcargo.com
Shipwreck and Cargo along the water on Commercial Street features two packed floors of nautical knickknacks, artwork with maritime themes, ship models, antiques and reproductions, and touristy trinkets like stuffed lobsters and moose. Be sure to check out the upstairs, where the nautical clothing and hats are kept—you might find that navy peacoat you've always wanted, with a pair of wool pants to match.

Treehouse Toys
47 Exchange Street
(207) 775–6133
www.treehousetoys.com
Treehouse Toys features toys from around the world, including games, puzzles, collectibles, trains, dolls, and tons of adorable stuffed animals. Treehouse Toys also carries a good selection of books for children at all levels of development. Almost all of the toys have display examples, so you can pick them up and try them out.

Northern Portland

Artist & Craftsman Supply
540 Deering Avenue
(207) 772–7272, (800) 876–8076
www.artistcraftsman.com
A favorite resource for local artists and students attending Portland's Maine College of Art, the Artist & Craftsman Supply store (located on a side street of outer Forest Avenue) is a great place to find all manner of arts supplies, from paintbrushes to handmade paper to frames of all sizes. Check out their selection of unusual or quirky toys—perhaps to get your creative (or silly) spirit going. Members of the staff, many of whom are artists themselves, are knowledgeable, and the store makes a point of stocking the newest paints and crafting tools. Artist & Craftsman is open Monday through Friday from 8:00 A.M. to 7:00 P.M., Saturday from 9:00 A.M. to 7:00 P.M., and Sunday from 10:00 A.M. to 6:00 P.M.

Caravan Beads & Fibers
915 Forest Avenue
(207) 761–2503, (800) 230–8941
www.caravanbeads.com
Caravan Beads started in 1991 on the back porch of co-owner Jean Kahn's house. Over the years Kahn and her friend and business partner Carolyn Mitchell have expanded this bead store from a shoestring operation to a large warehouse store on Forest Street. Caravan is also a bead and yarn supplier on the Internet and helps establish other bead stores around the country. At the Portland location you can choose from thousands of beads and a wide selection of fabrics and yarns to make your craft item. Caravan offers free instruction on knitting and beading techniques. A knitting circle meets here on Tuesday from 6:00 to 8:00 P.M. Caravan is open Monday through Saturday from 11:00 A.M. to 6:00 P.M. and Tuesday to 8:00 P.M.

SPECIALTY FOOD SHOPS
Downtown/Old Port

Beal's Ice Cream
12 Moulton Street
(207) 828–1335
The Portland Beal's, located in the Old Port, is the purveyor of one of the area's most beloved ice-cream brands. Beal's is a small ice-cream manufacturer based in nearby Scarborough. Their ice cream is made in small batches and tastes it. The Moulton Street shop offers plenty of flavors, like butter pecan, grapenut, and blueberry ice cream in the summer. Chocolate-based flavors and the old standbys will also whet your palate. Why is Beal's so popular in these parts? Because the smooth, creamy flavor tastes like Mom made it.

Browne Trading Company
Merrill's Wharf
(800) 944–7848
www.browne-trading.com

Seafood supplier to many of the country's most talented chefs, Browne Trading Company operates its business on Commercial Street on Portland's waterfront. In the small store here, you too have access to the sushi-grade fish Browne is known for, as well as a small, but diverse, selection of specialty foods like foie gras, truffles, and fresh caviar. If you want a taste of Browne's offerings before you buy or ship your choice to anywhere in the country, stop in at midday on a weekday for Browne's fish-based prepared lunch selections.

Fuller's Gourmet Candy and Ice Cream Shoppe
43 Wharf Street
(207) 253–8010

Fuller's is so small that you might miss it, but don't. Located near the block of Fore Street best known for its bars, Fuller's candy and ice-cream shop keeps regular daylight hours during the week, unlike most of its neighbors. Inside this small shop the owner has dipped and churned nearly every kind of sweet she sells. There are truffles and chocolate bark aplenty, as well as traditional candy and about a dozen flavors of homemade ice cream. Be sure to try something with chocolate here, since there's nothing sweeter than homemade chocolate. The ice cream with candy or chocolate, which is made with homemade sweets from the shop, is also outstanding.

Harbor Fish Market
9 Custom House Wharf
(207) 772–6557

A local favorite, Harbor Fish Market supplies frozen and fresh fish caught in the waters of Casco Bay. The store sells all the old standards—crab, lobster, scallops, and all kinds of whitefish—as well as other kinds of seafood. Really, it's best to swing down and check out the place yourself to see what's available, as options change depending on the catch that day. Harbor Fish is located on a narrow side street off Commercial Street, in a fire-engine-red wood-frame building. If you don't like the smell of seafood, stay away from the unloading area for local fishermen—there's seawater and fish juice aplenty.

Northern Portland

Big Sky Bread Co.
536 Deering Avenue
(207) 761–5623
www.mainebread.com

Big Sky Bread Co. has been supplying bread, sandwiches, and other homemade treats to hungry Portlanders since 1994. The flagship store on Deering Avenue is located in an old firehouse. Here, Big Sky employees mill their own wheat and make all of their breads from scratch. On any given day the store usually sells about a dozen varieties of bread—from honey wheat to sourdough to English muffin bread (one of our favorites). Some sweeter breads and monthly specials are always available as well, to mix things up. Besides bread, you can also choose from scones with fresh fruit, muffins in both regular and low-fat varieties, sandwiches during regular lunchtime hours, and homemade granola. There's usually a run on bread in the mornings, especially over the weekend, so if you need a particular kind of bread, it's best to call a day ahead and reserve your loaves. Big Sky's main bakery is open Monday through Friday from 7:00 A.M. to 6:00 P.M., Saturday from 7:00 A.M. to 5:00 P.M., and Sunday from 8:00 A.M. to 2:00 P.M.

Haven's Candies
542 Forest Avenue
(207) 772–0761
www.havenscandies.com

To satisfy a sweet tooth, visit Portland's only organic ice creamery and bakery. Maple's Organics (796 Forest Avenue; www.maplesorganics.com) sells homemade gelato-style ice creams, sorbetti, and baked goods that are all certified organic. The ice creams come in flavors such as Maine maple, vanilla, ginger, banana, chai, peanut butter, dark chocolate, and toasted coconut.

Haven's Candies has been dipping chocolate strawberries, stretching saltwater taffy, and making all other manner of delectable confections in the Greater Portland area since 1915. This locally owned and operated candy manufacturer is best known for its chocolates, and you can get a sample or a year's supply at the retail outlet store in Portland. If you have a special occasion coming up or simply a yearning for a one-of-a-kind chocolate bar, ask about their custom chocolate moldings, an art for which this candy mecca is well known.

The Maine Mall
364 Maine Mall Road, South Portland
(207) 744–0303
www.mainemall.com
The Maine Mall is the largest retail, commercial, and office complex north of Boston. The central building contains 140 stores and restaurants and a Food Court that can seat up to 550 people. Here, you'll find chain department stores like Macy's and Sears, along with chain boutiques like Gap, the Body Shop, Bath and Body Works, Victoria's Secret, and Olympia Sports. Next to the mall is a large cinema at Clark's Pond, where you can take in a new release before or after your shopping trip.

The 137 acres on which the Maine Mall was built was home to Dwyer's pig farm before the city of South Portland purchased it in the late 1960s. In 1971 the Maine Mall opened its doors with 20 stores. Today, thousands of people visit the mall every year, more than 3,000 people work here, and the mall just keeps growing. In recent years several smaller malls adjacent to the central complex have sprouted up, anchored by such retail chain notables as Bed Bath & Beyond, Old Navy, Wal-Mart, and Target. The Maine Mall area is also host to dozens of chain restaurants and eateries, including Chili's, Ruby Tuesday, Dunkin Donuts, Panera Bread, and Starbucks.

The Maine Mall is a little more than 6 miles from downtown Portland. To get there, take Interstate 295 South from Portland to exit 1 (Maine Mall Road/Maine Turnpike North). Bear right off the exit toward Maine Mall Road to the first stop sign. Continue straight to enter the parking lot of the Maine Mall's central complex.

OUTLET SHOPPING BEYOND PORTLAND

If you still have a hankering for more shopping after hitting the stores in and around Portland, don't forget to check out some of the region's most famous shopping less than an hour's drive from the city. Here are some must-see spots for every true-blue shopaholic.

The Kittery Outlets
Route 1, Kittery
(888) 548–8379
www.thekitteryoutlets.com
Roughly one hour's drive south from Portland is the town of Kittery, a small seaside village that has become regionally renowned for its 1-mile stretch of outlet stores along Route 1. Kittery contains hundreds of A-list retail outlet stores, all conveniently clustered in mini-malls side by side along the road. You'll find discount retail outlets for stores such as Jones of New York, J. Crew, Anne Klein, Polo Ralph Lauren, Gap, Tommy Hilfiger, Brooks Brothers, Nautica, and Eddie Bauer. The Kittery Outlets also include dozens of restaurants, specialty shops, sports shops, shoe stores, and home furnishing stores—all from popular designers and brands. And don't forget to check out the area's flagship store, the Kittery Trading Post, which features Maine-inspired activewear for women and men as well as camping and sporting equipment. Call ahead for store hours. To get to the Kittery Outlets, take Interstate 95 South from Portland and get off at exit 4 (York/Berwicks). Turn left at the end of the exit ramp and take a right at the next intersection onto Coastal Route 1 South. Continue straight until you come to the Kittery Outlets.

Perfect Shopping Mecca

Freeport, where the L.L. Bean Flagship Store is located, is also home to dozens of top-quality retail outlets, including Patagonia, J. Crew, and Banana Republic, many of which are located along Main Street off exit 20 on I–295 North. Freeport is designed to be a walkable, outdoor shopping experience, with everything from large flagship outlets to smaller chains and restaurants. It seems as though everything you need to buy is within a 3-block radius. Follow Main Street until you get to the Banana Republic store on your left. This is the center of town, where most of the stores, including L.L. Bean, are located. Follow the signs for parking in the lots nestled behind the stores on Main Street. Parking is free. Also, don't forget to head down the hill below the L.L. Bean Flagship Store to check out L.L. Bean's factory outlet. This is where you can pick up some real bargains.

L.L. Bean Flagship Store
Route 1, Freeport
(877) 552–3268
www.llbean.com
The L.L. Bean Flagship Store in the heart of Freeport's village center is the nexus of the L.L. Bean retail company, which since 1912 has made a name for itself as a reliable purveyor of quality clothing and sporting gear. Today, the company ships its items nationally and internationally and has become famous for its 100 percent guarantee. If you buy something at L.L. Bean and it fails you—even years down the road—you can bring it back for a refund or store credit. According to the store's Web site, founder L.L. Bean placed a plaque on the store's wall in 1916 that states, "I do not consider a sale complete until goods are worn out and the customer is still satisfied."

The L.L. Bean Flagship Store is open 24 hours a day, seven days a week, and is visited by more than 3.5 million people a year. A trip to the store is quite an experience. Both the interior and exterior are outfitted to make the shopper feel one step (and one purchase) away from the wilds of Maine. Outside the entrance is an enormous representation of the store's signature item—the durable, all-weather L.L. Bean boot. Inside, three floors of gear and clothing are featured alongside life-size models of deer and black bears. There's even a small pond with real fish at the base of the main staircase.

L.L. Bean prides itself on its customer service, and employees here are knowledgeable and thorough. If you glance at a tag and half of the high-tech material in the product reads like Greek to you, don't hesitate to ask a staffer to decode it for you in layman's terms. And if you want to know not only which products best suit your needs but also where and how to enjoy yourself in the outdoors, L.L. Bean offers year-round Outdoor Discovery Schools for novices interested in learning more about traditional Maine sports like paddling, cycling, and fly fishing. From Portland, take I–295 North to exit 20 at Freeport and follow Route 1 north to the L.L. Bean store in the center of town.

i L.L. Bean's Outdoor Discovery School offers a range of outdoor sporting workshops on subjects like fly fishing, outdoor leadership, and clay shooting. Call (888) 552–3261 for more information.

Tom's of Maine Outlet Store
52 Main Street, Kennebunk
(207) 985–2944, (800) 367–8667
www.tomsofmaine.com
Tom's of Maine has been making natural

house products since it was founded in 1970. A family-owned company, Tom's is most famous for its toothpaste, although in recent years it has expanded to make everything from body soap to natural cough and cold care. The ingredients in Tom's products are always explained in detail on a user-friendly label on each product. At the factory outlet you can buy Tom's products at a discount at their "factory seconds" store. "Seconds" means the product has some minor defect (like a crooked label) that makes it unsuitable for regular retail sale, so it's sold for less at the outlet. You'll also find plenty of first-quality Tom's products, like Tom's T-shirts, hats, and bags. The outlet is open Monday through Saturday from 9:30 A.M. to 5:00 P.M.

BOOKS AND MUSIC
Downtown/Old Port

Books Etc.
38 Exchange Street
(207) 774–0626
www.mainebooksetc.com
Books Etc. in the Old Port carries a selection of fine literature, books on history and philosophy, travel guides, and children's books. The store specializes in "Maine books"—those either about Maine or written by Mainers. There is also a small used-book section.

Bull Moose Music
151 Middle Street
(207) 780–6424
www.bullmooose.com
Bull Moose Music is easily the hippest place to buy music in the city. Located in the basement of 151 Middle Street, Bull Moose offers new and used CDs of all genres. The staff here is very knowledgeable, if disaffected, and you may end up purchasing an album from a new artist you'll later come to love based on an insightful Bull Moose staff endorsement. Bull Moose is also the place to go to get the latest information on upcoming local concerts and ticket sales. And, if you're

truly at a loss on a weekend night, it's always fun to wander into the store and hear the latest bizarre music the staff is playing on the store speakers.

Casco Bay Books
151 Middle Street
(207) 541–3842
www.cascobaybooks.com
Casco Bay Books features a uniquely diverse selection of small press, independent, and arts books. Here, you might find philosophy and literary classics sharing a display table with an independently produced left-wing poetry chapbook. If you love literary culture, Casco Bay Books is the place to go. And you can even sip a latte from the store cafe while you peruse the newest literature.

Longfellow Books
1 Monument Square
(207) 772–4045
www.longfellowbooks.com
Longfellow Books is stocked with plenty of quality reading, including classics, new nonfiction and fiction, and quirky children's books. This bookstore is crafted for the lifelong reader, and as a nod to this philosophy, Longfellow will send you a store gift certificate every year on your birthday if you register at the counter. Longfellow also hosts regular literary and theatrical readings and acoustic music performances. Call or visit their Web site for upcoming events.

Beyond Portland

Borders Books and Music
430 Gorham Road, South Portland
(207) 775–6110
www.bordersstores.com
This Borders at the Maine Mall is part of the national chain of gigantic book and music stores. Borders carries an impressive selection of specialty books, new releases, literature, and poetry. The store also features a great children's section and a diverse assortment of music for sale.

Select Stores for Used Books

Portland is a bibliophile's city. Along with the assortment of bookstores selling new offerings, the city also has a handful of eclectic used-book purveyors. Here are a few of our favorites.

Carlson & Turner Antiquarian Books & Book Bindery
241 Congress Street
(207) 773–4200, (800) 540–7323
www.carlsonturnerbooks.com

Cunningham Books
188 State Street (at Longfellow Square)
(207) 775–2246

F. M. O'Brien Antiquarian Booksellers
38 High Street
(207) 774–0931

Yes Books
589 Congress Street
(207) 775–3233

CONSIGNMENT STORES
Downtown/Old Port

Encore
521 Congress Street
(207) 775–4275
Encore features designer vintage and contemporary clothing with pizzazz. The store specializes in vintage formal and casual attire from the 1800s to the 1970s and features an impressive selection of old-time accessories, including purses, hats, shoes, and jewelry. The style here is bold—silver lamé and sequins are common—and it's a favorite for local women keen to revisit the rush of raiding their eccentric aunt's closet.

Material Objects
500 Congress Street
(207) 774–1241
Material Objects in Portland's downtown carries a great selection of trendy used and new clothing. The majority of the garments come with a history, and you can find everything you need— including shoes, hats, jackets, and accessories—to pull off your favorite retro look. Material Objects has long been a mainstay of Portland's consignment scene.

Beyond Portland

Tots to Teens
474 Main Street, Gorham
(207) 839–7839
Tots to Teens, located in a town 10 miles west of Portland, carries a wide selection of used furniture, toys, children's equipment, clothing, and accessories.

ANTIQUES SHOPS
Downtown/Old Port

L'Antiquaire
395 Danforth Street
(207) 828–9660
www.antiquaireusa.com
L'Antiquaire, predictably, specializes in French antiques. Their inventory features items from 18th-, 19th-, and early-20th-century France, including furniture, the decorative arts, textiles, pottery, urns, and more. They frequently get cases of new items in from France, so the selection is constantly changing. Many of the items are one-of-a-kind. L'Antiquaire is open by appointment only. Visit their Web site for information on new arrivals.

Portland Antiques & Fine Art
223 Commercial Street
(207) 773–7052, (800) 896–8824
www.portlandantiques.com
Portland Antiques features furniture, fine art, and accessories from 1700 to 1900 in its showroom in the Old Port. The styles range from country to formal, and the store specializes in American antiques. Here, you'll find

i The Maine Antiques Dealers
Association has a list of its Portland
members on its Web site at www.maine
antiques.org.

paintings, folk art, nautical items, and oriental
rugs, among other things. Wednesday is free
appraisal day. The store is open Monday
through Saturday from 10:00 A.M. to 6:00 P.M.
and Sunday from 11:00 A.M. to 5:00 P.M., or by
appointment.

Beyond Portland

F. O. Bailey
35 Depot Road, Falmouth
(207) 781–8001
www.fobailey.com

Formerly located in downtown Portland, F. O.
Bailey moved to the more serene scene in
nearby Falmouth a few years ago. F. O. Bailey
is one of the most well-known antiquarians in
the area. The shop has been open since 1819
and is the state's oldest continuing business.
It is also the second-oldest auction house in
the country. A visit to Bailey's showroom will
present you with some of the finest estate
antiques, collectibles, fine art, jewelry, rugs,
and more. F. O. Bailey has also made a name
for itself as a consultant and appraiser to
estates, collectors, and buyers from around
the country, so you can bring that old ring you
found in your grandmother's jewelry box and
finally learn everything about it. The shop is
open Monday through Friday from 9:00 A.M.
to 5:00 P.M. and Saturday from 10:00 A.M. to
4:00 P.M.

ATTRACTIONS

Here in Portland, you'll find plenty to occupy you and your family for hours. In this chapter are listed some of the best places to visit—from homes rich with local history to crazy amusement parks and cultural museums with local flair. We have noted some of the best-known spots as well as some of the tiny out-of-the-way sites that locals like to keep to themselves.

We have grouped attractions by subject rather than by location. Most of the attractions listed here are located in or around Portland and are easily reachable on foot or by car.

The chapter also gives a rundown of the city's guided tours (which seem to have multiplied exponentially in recent years). These tours are a great way to get your bearings when you first arrive in the city and also a good way for natives to better understand their own backyard.

Whatever attraction you choose, you're bound to have a great time. After all, wherever you go—whether it's to the former home of the nation's premier prohibitionist or to the thundering light show in Saco's Funtown Astrosphere—you won't be able to escape the distinctive mix of quirkiness and courteousness that defines Portland.

AMUSEMENT PARKS AND ZOOS

Funtown/Splashtown
Route 1, Saco
(207) 284–5139
www.funtown.usa
Funtown/Splashtown is the largest amusement park and water park in Maine. It includes rides like Dragon's Descent (a 220-foot drop from a tower), the Excalibur roller coaster (a must for any thrill seeker), and the

Thunder Falls Log Flume. We encourage at least one trip on easily the strangest ride we've ever encountered—the Astrosphere. It involves a scrambler ride, an enclosed dome, and an amped rendition of "Fire on High" by the Electric Light Orchestra. To tell you more would be to ruin the fun. Funtown and Splashtown are both open from June 12 to September 6. Call for hours of operation. An adult ride pass is $23.50; a child ride pass is $16.00. Those who want to wander and not ride must pay $8.00 to enter the park.

Palace Playland
1 Old Orchard Street, Old Orchard Beach
(207) 934–2001
www.palaceplayland.com
Palace Playland is Greater Portland's answer to the boardwalk amusement parks common in southern California and Florida. The Playland offers rides like a 75-foot-high gondola Ferris wheel, a brilliantly decorated carousel, and some robust spinny/flippy contraptions that can promise you'll lose track of the ground faster than you can say "How many tickets?" The Playland is located along the strip of clubs, bars, and video arcades that line the boardwalk at Old Orchard Beach. For this reason, a nighttime trip to the Playland is more for big kids and adults than the little ones, although a daytime trip can be less rowdy.

> **i** For decades, Portland natives have made the drive with friends and family from downtown Portland to Old Orchard Beach for one reason only: Pier Fries. These thick-cut, ridged french fries cost about $5.00 and are a favorite with locals. Snag a box and chow down like a native at any number of fry outlets near Palace Playland. Don't forget the vinegar.

Touring Port City

Perhaps the best way to get a handle on Portland is to take a guided tour around the city. All of the tours are led by experienced guides with information about the culture and history of the area. A few tour options are listed below. For tours of the waters of Casco Bay, see the Beaches and Ocean Activities chapter.

Downeast Duck Adventures
(207) 774–DUCK
www.downeastducktours.com
This land-and-sea tour of Portland and Casco Bay takes place on an "amphibious touring vessel." Tours last from 60 to 90 minutes and cost $22 for adults, $17 for seniors and children ages 6 to 12, and $5.00 for kids age 5 and under. (see the Beaches and Ocean Activities chapter for more details about this tour).

Maine Historical Society Tours
(207) 774–1822
www.mainehistory.org
Volunteers with extensive training in local history host seasonal and special tours, including "The Longfellow Trail," which covers the Portland the famous poet might have known. The cost is $4.00 for adults, $2.00 for children and members.

Mainely Tours
(207) 774–0808
www.mainelytours.com
Trolley tours cover downtown Portland and nearby lighthouses. The cost is $15.00 for adults, $14.00 for seniors, and $8.00 for children. Land and sea sightseeing tours are also offered.

Ocean View Tours
(207) 741–2776, (866) 251–3626
www.mountainviewtours-online.com
Ocean View offers year-round tours of Portland and beyond in luxury vehicles. A three-hour tour costs $55 per adult, with a sliding scale for groups.

Summer Feet/Maine Coast Cycling Adventures
(207) 828–0342, (866) 857–9544
www.summerfeet.net
Half-day bike tours of Portland cost $28 to $40 per person, including bike and helmet rental.

Still, the Playland offers the best in amusement parks if you're also looking to wander around and shop for a lobster T-shirt, shoot a round of skeeball, and snag some crab cakes. To sweeten the deal, the Playland launches fireworks every Thursday night at sunset. The Playland is open seven days a week from June 15 to Labor Day. An unlimited-ride pass costs $22.95 for adults and $15.95 for children. Individual tickets are also available. There is no charge to enter the park.

York's Wild Kingdom
Route 1, York Beach
(207) 363-4911
www.yorkzoo.com
York's Wild Kingdom, located in the scenic oceanside town York Beach, is the local zoo and amusement park. At the Wild Kingdom you will see hundreds of exotic animals from around the globe, including the wallaby, black swan, two-toed sloth, and Maine's only white Bengal tiger. The Wild Kingdom also has an

amusement park and arcade. The park is open every day from late June through August, with limited hours in early June and in September. Admission is $15.25 for adults, $11.75 for children. The zoo is open during peak season from 10:00 A.M. to 6:00 P.M.

CULTURAL MUSEUMS

Center for Maine History Museum
489 Congress Street
(207) 774–1822
www.mainehistory.org
The Maine Historical Society, founded in 1822, runs this museum, which sits beside the Wadsworth-Longfellow House in downtown Portland. The museum houses an eclectic permanent collection of about 10,000 artifacts—including paintings, prints, costumes, political memorabilia, domestic artifacts, and Native American artifacts—and also runs a rotating schedule of special exhibits that in the past have included "Homes Away: Victorian Life at Sea," "Rum, Riot, and Reform: Maine and the History of American Drinking," and "All the Arts That Please: Folk Art of the Maine Historical Society." The museum is open year-round, Monday through Saturday, from 10:00 A.M. to 5:00 P.M. Tickets cost $4.00 for adults, $3.00 for seniors and students, and $2.00 for children. Admission is free for Maine Historical Society members.

The Maine Historical Society also runs a library, tours of the city, and local history seminars and maintains the Wadsworth-Longfellow House. Special research access to the museum is available by appointment. Contact the museum curator at (207) 774–1822, ext. 224, for details.

Maine Narrow Gauge Railroad Co. & Museum
58 Fore Street
(207) 828–0814
www.mngrr.org
Tucked into a clearing near the East End footpath at Commercial Street sits a narrow set of tracks on which you'll find a train that was once part of the Maine Narrow Gauge Railway line used from 1878 to 1945. Back in those days, trains like these snaked all across the state, providing necessary transportation to Maine's rural towns. The railroad's popularity waned, however, during the Great Depression and later when cars became popular. Today, almost the entire track around the state has been pulled up.

But don't despair—a small group of dedicated train enthusiasts at the Maine Narrow Gauge Railroad Co. & Museum have salvaged some of the old-time rail for you to experience. Hop on for a short ride that will take you a few hundred yards and back, or wander into the nearby museum and see the Maine Narrow Gauge Railroad Co.'s collection of locomotives and coaches from the turn-of-the-century Bridgton and Saco River Railroad; the Sandy River and Rangeley Lakes Railroad; the Wiscasset, Waterville and Farmington Railway; and the Monson Railroad. The Maine Narrow Gauge Railroad Co. has everything a train enthusiast could ask for—boxcars, tank cars, flatcars, and cabooses.

And here's an extra flourish the Narrow Gauge guys are particularly excited about: Most of the time, the passenger train is run by a modern diesel engine; however, during holidays and extra-special days in Portland (such as local festivals), the Co. will haul out the steam engine for a run. You can also catch a ride powered by steam during the appropriately titled Steam Days, which always land sometime in September—call ahead for the exact dates.

The museum is open year-round, and the outdoor train runs daily, every hour, from mid-May to mid-October. Fares for the train are $6.00 for adults, $4.00 for children, and

> **i** During the years bracketing the turn of the 20th century, Maine was the only state in the country to rely on an extensive network of 2-foot-wide narrow-gauge railroads for statewide transportation.

$5.00 for seniors. The museum is wheelchair accessible.

Museum of African Culture
122 Spring Street, #1
(207) 871–7188
www.tribalartmuseum.com

The Museum of African Culture (formerly the Museum of African Tribal Art) is the only museum in New England dedicated exclusively to sub-Saharan African art. More than 1,500 pieces make up the museum collection, including large wooden masks, bronze figures, tools, and textiles. The oldest mask in the collection dates from A.D. 1600. The museum director, Oscar Mokeme, has been with the museum since its opening in 1998. He is not only the museum curator and tour guide but also the educational outreach coordinator, often spending half of his week out of the museum at local schools, summer camps, and community centers teaching about African art and culture. Workshops for educators and social workers and a new "Discover Africa" day camp are also offered through the museum. The museum is open Tuesday through Friday from 10:30 A.M. to 4:00 P.M. and Saturday from 12:30 to 4:00 P.M., and by appointment. A $5.00 donation is requested for admission.

Portland Harbor Museum
382 Fort Road
(207) 799–6337
www.portlandharbormuseum.org

Located on the campus of Southern Maine Community College, overlooking Casco Bay, the Portland Harbor Museum is the place to go for local maritime history. The highlight of the museum's collection is the 17-foot reconstructed bow of the Snow Squall, the only surviving American clipper ship. The museum and gift shop are located inside the walls of the former 19th-century Fort Preble and adjacent to the squat Spring Point Ledge Lighthouse (see the "Lighthouses" section for more information). Both the lighthouse, which was built in 1897 and is still used today, and the former fort are available for guided tours

during the summer. Admission is $4.00 for adults, $2.00 for kids ages 6 to 16, and free for kids under 6.

FORTS

Fort Gorges
Casco Bay

OK, it's kind of a tease to list a fort that you can't visit on foot, but Fort Gorges is such a landmark that we would be remiss to leave it out. You can view the fort from a charter boat or with a good pair of binoculars from Willard Beach. Construction on the fort began in 1859; during the Civil War it was used to protect the area around Hog Island in Casco Bay. The squat fort has a mossy green camouflage covering and low windows so that cannonballs fired from it would skim over the water and strike enemy ships. It was a good design, but the war ended before the fort could be completed. During World Wars I and II, Fort Gorges was used to store naval mines. It is now owned by the city.

Fort Preble
Southern Maine Community College, South Portland

Fort Preble abuts the Spring Point Ledge Lighthouse and the Portland Harbor Museum on the campus of Southern Maine Community College in South Portland (see listings under "Lighthouses" and "Cultural Museums" for more on the lighthouse and the museum). The fort is on the shore and faces Fort Gorges in the bay. It was built in 1808 and was added to during the Civil War and at the turn of the 20th century. Today, there is little left to see of the fort, save a couple of exterior walls and lookout points. Still, if you're in the neighborhood, which you may well be since the lighthouse and museum are on the same campus, a walk through the fort is a must.

Fort Williams Park
1000 Shore Road, Cape Elizabeth
(207) 799–2868 (for event registrations)
www.capeelizabeth.com/fort/home.html

Fort Williams Park has it all—breathtaking

views of the ocean, a small beach, the oldest lighthouse in Maine (Portland Head Light, discussed later in the chapter), and, of course, a few very interesting old forts. The 14 acres that would become Fort Williams was purchased in 1872 as a subpost to Fort Preble at Spring Point (see the Fort Preble listing in this section). Fort Williams was active during World War I and World War II and served as the headquarters of the Harbor Defenses of Portland during the latter war. Today, the park is a popular stop for picnickers, joggers, and kite flyers. The park has a great set of swings for kids (and their parents) near the rocky beach and a few hills popular with sledders during the winter. Be sure to check out the remaining military batteries, which are built into the ground as camouflage; and, overlooking the park, the castlelike skeleton of the Goddard Mansion, which housed Colonel John Goddard and his family during the 1800s. Admission to the park is free, and the gates close at sunset. To get here, cross the Casco Bay Bridge and bear left onto Broadway. Follow Broadway to Cottage Road and take a right. At Red's Dairy Freeze (the next light), bear left to remain on Cottage Road. Cottage Road becomes Shore Road once you're in Cape Elizabeth. Follow Shore Road for about a mile until you see the entrance to Fort Williams on your left. Parking is free in lots inside the park.

HISTORIC HOMES

Neal Dow Memorial
714 Congress Street
(207) 773–7773
www.mewctu.org

The Neal Dow Memorial is located in the former home of Neal Dow, a famous prohibitionist and a former mayor of Portland. Dow was a devout Quaker who was raised in early-19th-century Portland when it was the center of the rum trade with the West Indies. According to Dow's papers, drink was everywhere in Portland during his childhood—in the dozens of pubs, in the streets, and even given out as

free samples in some grocery stores. Dow was appalled and deeply concerned about what he viewed as a weakening of the moral fiber of his fellow Mainers. He began a movement to change state law so as to abolish alcohol. The world-famous "Maine Law," which made Maine in 1851 the first state in the nation to ban the manufacture and sale of alcohol, was written in the first-floor study of this small Federal-style home.

The building was built in 1829, and its second floor currently houses the state headquarters of the Maine Women's Christian Temperance Union (MWCTU). Dow's son bequeathed the house to the MWCTU, which now offers tours of the site. Tours are free and run Monday through Friday from 11:00 A.M. to 4:00 P.M. Large groups should call ahead to book a tour. (See the Close-up in the History chapter for more on Neal Dow.)

Tate House Museum
1270 Westbrook Street
(207) 774–6177
www.tatehouse.org

In 1751 Captain George Tate arrived in Portland with his wife and four sons to accept a position as the mast agent for the Royal Navy of King George II. This basically meant that Tate was in charge of finding lumber to build ship's masts for the British navy—simple enough in theory, but a tough haul when the town you live in wants nothing to do with the British and even less to do with their military.

Despite ominous political tides, Tate built his Georgian-style home in the Stroudwater neighborhood of Portland in 1755. Today, the Tate House is the only remaining colonial home in Portland open to the public and stands as a solemn testament to the ill-fated dreams of Captain Tate. After arriving in Portland, Tate's luck took a turn for the worse. His wife died mysteriously, his fortunes deteriorated, and local distaste for the British mast trade was one of the reasons Portland was burned to the ground by the British in 1775.

Still, swing by the Tate House for a glimpse into happier times before all of that mess with the British. Thanks to the preservation efforts of the Maine branch of the Colonial Dames of America, the group that now manages the museum, the home's interior has been carefully re-created in keeping with the way a prominent Portlander like Tate might have lived during the last half of the 18th century. The Tate House Museum is open for tours from June 15 through September 30, Tuesday through Saturday from 10:00 A.M. to 4:00 P.M. and Sunday from 1:00 to 4:00 P.M. Admission is $7.00 for adults, $2.00 for children under 12, and free for kids under 6. A senior discount is available. The Tate House Museum has "Herb Garden Days" every Wednesday during the summer season. Guided tours of the home's herb garden, with plants used by colonists in pre-Revolutionary Maine, provide information about the herbs' medicinal, culinary, and cosmetic uses. Call the Tate House for details.

Victoria Mansion
109 Danforth Street
(207) 772–4841
www.victoriamansion.org

Also known as the Morse-Libby Mansion or "the Vic," the Victoria Mansion (built circa 1860) has been called the finest surviving Italian villa in the country and was recently included in America's Castles, an A&E documentary. The Vic has an impeccably preserved interior, complete with 90 percent of the house's original contents (for more on the mansion's famous architecture, see the Architecture chapter). The Vic's original owner, Ruggles Sylvester Morse, was a Maine native who made his fortune as the proprietor of a number of lavish hotels in New Orleans. The decadent taste he developed in the bayou is evident not only in his mansion's flamboyant exterior but also in its carefully preserved interior, which includes stained-glass windows; oriental carpeting; gas lighting fixtures; porcelain china, silver, and glassware dinner sets; and elaborate murals.

The interior of the mansion was designed by Gustave Herter of the New York City design firm Herter Brothers. It is the earliest known Herter commission and the only one still complete. But Morse didn't stop at just decadent designs; he also insisted on installing the latest technology available in his mansion—then-revolutionary systems like central heating and hot and cold running water. After Morse's death, his widow sold the house and its contents to Joseph Ralph Libby. In the early 20th century, retired educator William Holmes purchased the house and renamed it the Victoria Mansion in honor of Britain's Queen Victoria. Guided tours of the mansion are available from May through October. Tours begin at quarter after and quarter to the hour. Admission is $10.00 for adults and $3.00 for students. Seniors and AAA members receive a discount. During the winter, the Victoria Mansion is lavishly decorated and open to tours to celebrate the winter holiday season. See the Festivals and Annual Events chapter for more information.

Wadsworth-Longfellow House
489 Congress Street
(207) 774–1822
www.mainehistory.org

The Wadsworth-Longfellow House was built in 1776 and became the boyhood home of the great American poet Henry Wadsworth Longfellow. It is now owned and managed by the Maine Historical Society, which operates from the carriage house behind the home on Congress Street. The home has been restored to reflect its appearance during the 1850s and is open for tours from May through October, Monday through Saturday from 10:00 A.M. to 4:00 P.M. and Sunday from noon to 4:00 P.M. Tickets are $7.00 for adults, $6.00 for seniors

i During your tour of the Wadsworth-Longfellow home, be sure to sneak a peek at graffiti attributed to the poet Henry himself. The words "How dear is the home of my childhood," scrawled on a third-floor window frame, are believed to be his.

and students, and $3.00 for children. The Wadsworth-Longfellow House is covered extensively in the Architecture chapter.

LIGHTHOUSES

Breakwater Light
Pickett Street, South Portland
This lighthouse is also known as "Bug Light" because of its relatively small size compared with other lighthouses. The octagonal tower is complemented by six fluted columns. It was first lighted in 1875 and was modeled after the Greek Choragic Monument of Lysicrates, which was built in the fourth century B.C. In 2002 restoration of the Bug was completed, including a fresh coat of paint inside and out and a brand-new light. The Bug Light is not open for tours, but you can park for free in the adjacent Bug Light Park and walk the breakwater wall to examine the exterior up close. To get here, cross the Casco Bay Bridge from Portland to South Portland, take a left onto Broadway, and follow it east to Benjamin W. Pickett Street. Take a left on Pickett, continue through an industrial area, and turn right just before the boat launch booth. Follow the road to Bug Light Park.

Portland Head Light
1000 Shore Road, Cape Elizabeth
(207) 799-2661
www.portlandheadlight.com
Portland Head Light was completed in January 1791 on a spot that had historically been used as a defensive lookout for British attacks during the Revolutionary War. The tower measures 72 feet from base to lantern. The light and fog signals are manned by the U.S. Coast Guard, but the surrounding land is owned by the town of Cape Elizabeth. There is a museum in the former Keeper's Quarters, which is open daily from Memorial Day to the Friday after Columbus Day and on weekends from mid-April to Memorial Day and from Columbus Day to Christmas. Hours are 10:00 A.M. to 4:00 P.M. Admission is $2.00 for adults, $1.00 for children ages 6 to 18, and free for

kids under 6. Museum tours are designed to be self-guided; the tower is not open to the public. To get there, cross the Casco Bay Bridge into South Portland, bear left onto Broadway at the end of the bridge, and then take a right at Cottage Road. At Red's Dairy Freeze a block down, bear left, remaining on Cottage Road. Cottage Road becomes Shore Road once you're in Cape Elizabeth. Continue on Shore Road until you see the gates and sign for Fort Williams on your left, about a mile down. There is ample free parking inside Fort Williams.

On Christmas eve 1886, the *Annie C. Maguire* ran aground on the rocks at the base of the Portland Head Light. The keeper and his family managed to rescue all of the ship's passengers by using a ladder as a makeshift gangplank.

Spring Point Ledge Lighthouse
Fort Road, South Portland
(207) 699-2676 (information hotline)
www.springpointlight.org
The Spring Point Ledge Light was built because of complaints by shipowners who kept losing their cargo to the dangerous underwater ledge here. The lighthouse and its breakwater were completed in 1897. The tower now shines an automated beam of white light visible to ships properly positioned in the channel. The lighthouse, located next to the Portland Harbor Museum (see the "Cultural Museums" section earlier in this chapter), is maintained by the nonprofit Spring Point Ledge Light Trust. Guided tours of the tower are available for a small fee and are sponsored by the museum. Beginning in 2007, the trust will host open houses at the lighthouse every Saturday from 11:00 A.M. to 3:00 P.M. from June 16 through Labor Day weekend. A fee will be charged to support the trust's preservation efforts. Visit the Spring Point Light Web site or call the hotline for information on upcoming tours. Information is also available by contacting the museum at

(207) 799–6337 or visiting www.portland harbormuseum.org. To reach the lighthouse and museum, cross the Casco Bay Bridge to South Portland, bear left on Broadway, follow it 1.3 miles to Benjamin W. Pickett Street, and take a right and then a left onto Fort Road. The lighthouse and museum are at the end of this road. Parking is free.

Two Lights State Park
66 Two Lights Road, Cape Elizabeth
(207) 799–5871
Located off Route 77 in Cape Elizabeth, Two Lights State Park features 40 acres of shore-front land, a rocky shore with views of the bay, the remains of a World War II coastal defense system, picnic table and group sites, and, of course, the famous twin lighthouses. The lighthouses were originally made of stone but in 1874 were replaced with 65-foot towers of cast iron. Today, only the eastern light is active, and it is the brightest lighthouse in Maine. The automated station can be seen 17 miles away at sea. Neither lighthouse is open to the public, but the park is open year-round from 9:00 A.M. to roughly a half hour before sunset. The peak-season entrance fee is $3.00 for adults, $1.00 for children ages 5 to 11, and free for children under 5 and adults over 65.

i Ready for a snack break? Check out the Two Lights Lobster Shack Restaurant, an award-winning seafood joint with spectacular views of the ocean and the lighthouses. It is located in Two Lights State Park.

POINTS OF INTEREST

Children's Museum of Maine
142 Free Street
(207) 828–1234
www.childrensmuseumofme.org
For the young and the young at heart, no trip to Portland is complete without a visit to the Children's Museum of Maine. Located next to the Portland Museum of Art, the Children's

Museum is known for its interesting and fun interactive exhibits. On the first floor, kids can play grown-up in Our Town, an exhibit that includes a fire truck, a farm, and an interactive supermarket. On the second floor, young explorers can check out the natural resources of Maine at the Explore Floor, which includes a climbing wall, a tree house, and a tidal pool tank. The museum also features daily art programs, a dress-up theater, and a packed calendar of special events, programs, and temporary exhibits. If the weather is clear, check out the camera obscura, a giant optic contraption that provides a panoramic view of Portland. It is one of only three of its kind in the country.

Kids who can't get enough of adventure at the museum can join in at one of the museum's summer camps, which explore topics in the museum more in-depth or take kids out in the city to learn about the area's culture and environment. During the summer the museum is open Monday through Saturday from 10:00 A.M. to 5:00 P.M. and Sunday from noon to 5:00 P.M. The museum is closed on Monday from Labor Day to Memorial Day. Admission is $6.00 for children and adults; kids under age one get in for free. If you're only interested in checking out the camera obscura, admission is $3.00. The museum participates in Portland's First Friday Artwalk (see The Arts chapter for more), which means that admission is free on the first Friday of every month between 5:00 and 8:00 P.M.

Desert of Maine
95 Desert Road, Freeport
(207) 865–6962
www.desertofmaine.com
This attraction is about a half-hour drive from Portland and isn't really even in the Greater Portland area, but, hey, it's a desert. In Maine. We think that might be worth stretching the rules a bit. The desert was created by a glacier slipping down from the north 10,000 to 12,000 years ago. The entire expanse covers 500 acres of sand from Oxford to Freeport. The Desert of Maine company owns 44 acres, part of which can be toured.

Fun in the Country

Just outside Portland is a 500-acre working dairy farm that's been in the same family since the 1700s. Smiling Hill Farm in Westbrook packages its milk in old-fashioned glass bottles and also churns out ice cream, fresh butter, and a variety of cheeses (under the Silvery Moon Creamery label), all for sale in its dairy store. There's cross-country skiing in winter. Call (207) 775–4818 for more information.

Each spring, Maine sugarhouses throw open their doors so the public can see how maple syrup is made and can try some on pancakes and ice cream. Maine Maple Sunday, always the fourth Sunday in March, is fun for the kids because there are lots of free tastings, wagon rides, sleigh rides, and live demonstrations. For a list of participating sugarhouses and directions, visit http://getrealgetmaine.com/visit/maine_maple_sunday.html.

If you're visiting Portland in the fall, go apple picking and learn the difference between a McIntosh and a Gravenstein. A half-dozen apple orchards in Cumberland County open to the public in autumn, selling produce and Maine-made apple cider. To find which farms are open, visit http://getrealget maine.com and click on "apple orchards."

But this desert is not like any you may have tromped through in the American Southwest. These desert sand dunes are made of silt pulverized by the glacier thousands of years ago, creating a soft, sandlike powder. The sand covers acres of rolling dunes to the distant tree line. Be sure to check out the abandoned barn—200 years ago, an unlucky family tried unsuccessfully to farm this land. These days, the only evidence of their failed attempt is the old barn perched strangely on the sand, with antique farming equipment still inside. A sand artist and a gemstone hunt for kids 12 and under are also part of the daily Desert of Maine experience. Guided tours cost $7.75 for adults, $5.25 for teens, and $4.25 for kids. You can also wander around the desert on your own for free on designated trails. The desert is open from mid-May to mid-October.

Scarborough Downs
Route 1, Scarborough
(207) 883–4331
www.scarboroughdowns.com

Just a 20-minute drive from Portland, this harness racetrack has been a popular site with locals for more than 50 years. Scarborough Downs touts itself as the largest racetrack in the state and the site of New England's fastest half-mile track. Enjoy a meal in the Downs Club Restaurant while watching a live race or any of the up to 20 simulcast races shown on television screens in the dining room and around the grandstand and clubhouse. The live racing season at the Downs runs from March 20 through December 19. Simulcast TV is open year-round. Post times are Wednesday, Friday, and Saturday at 7:00 P.M. and Tuesday at 2:00 P.M. You must be at least 18 to wager.

Umbrella Cover Museum
62-B Island Avenue, Peaks Island
(207) 766–4496
www.umbrellacovermuseum.tripod.com

The Umbrella Cover Museum (UCM) is by far one of the weirdest collections of off-the-wall art we've come across. Billing itself brazenly (and, most likely, accurately) as the world's only museum dedicated solely to umbrella covers, the UCM is run by curator, director, and founder Nancy 3 Hoffman, a local musician who lives on Peaks Island. Covers at the museum include everything from the traditional print and colored nylon to those made out of bizarre materials like bubblegum wrappers and bulletproof Kevlar. To get to the museum, you'll have to take a 20-minute ferry from the mainland; but if you enjoy extreme, off-the-beaten-path kitsch, the UCM is worth the ride.

The UCM was first conceived of in 1992 when, according to the museum Web site, Hoffman realized how enchanting umbrella covers are when she was compelled to steal one off an umbrella in a dime store. Since the museum's grand opening in Hoffman's kitchen in 1996, the 80-plus cover collection has grown so large that it's been transferred from Hoffman's home to its own building on Island Avenue. The Umbrella Cover Museum is open during the summer, and guided tours are available for a suggested donation of $2.00 per person. As an added bonus, Hoffman treats every tour group to her rendition of the song "Let a Smile Be Your Umbrella," complete with accordion accompaniment. Call ahead for museum hours, as they can change.

ARCHITECTURE

In 1961 one of the city's most beloved buildings was destroyed. Union Station, a sprawling granite train station on St. John Street in Portland, was razed to make way for a mini-mall. The image of the ornate granite clock tower, the building's trademark, as it crashed to the ground amid plumes of dust and debris stuck in the minds and hearts of Portlanders concerned that unchecked development might ruin the character of their city. In the wake of the controversial Union Station demolition, preservation activists converged to form Greater Portland Landmarks (GPL) in 1964. For more than 40 years GPL has worked to preserve hundreds of Portland's architectural treasures, from colonial homes to postmodern museums. Today, Portland has some of the best-preserved historic districts in the country and in 2004 was designated one of the nation's "Dozen Distinguished Destinations" by the National Trust for Historic Preservation. Thanks to a city ordinance passed in 1991, designated landmarks in the city's historic districts are protected by law against destruction or development that might compromise the building's architectural integrity.

In this chapter we have organized significant architectural monuments geographically into three main historical districts on the peninsula: the West End, Congress and State Streets, and the Old Port and Waterfront. For those of you set on a particular century, we have listed the date of each building's construction in its heading.

Thanks to the tireless efforts of Portland's preservationists, this chapter can never encompass *all* of the architectural wonders of the peninsula and beyond. Nearly every street in every neighborhood is gifted with well-preserved, beautiful buildings. Instead, we have highlighted notable structures on the peninsula from the West End to Munjoy Hill, where many of Portland's most famous buildings can be found. While you explore Portland, it is a good idea to remember that preservation efforts in the city have focused largely on neighborhoods rather than on landmarks. If you discover a house or building you particularly enjoy, chances are it will be flanked by other structures with similar detail and designs. For this reason, one way to use this chapter is to zero in on the structures you are most interested in, plant yourself on their sidewalk, and then wander around the neighborhood. For those of you interested in a more organized approach, we've come up with our own Insiders' Walking Tour. This tour will take you through the commercial district in Portland and down streets that have remained virtually unchanged since the 19th century.

If you're thirsty for more details on the city's architectural heritage, we have also listed resources for self-guided and guided tours. The book *Portland,* published by the nonprofit Greater Portland Landmarks, was an indispensable source for much of the architectural information in this chapter.

ARCHITECTURAL PERIODS

Portland is old. If you don't believe us, just take a look around. Buildings on the peninsula date back as far as 1785. The first brick house in Portland was built between 1785 and 1786 by the grandfather of the poet Henry Wadsworth Longfellow. It currently sits in the center of Portland's modern downtown, but when it was built in the late 18th century, its location on the outskirts of the settlement along the waterfront was considered dangerous.

In the early 19th century, Portland became a world-class port. The city's economy flourished, despite a temporary setback caused by the Embargo Act of 1807, and by 1832, when Portland was incorporated as a city, its commercial fleet was the largest on the eastern seaboard. With prosperous business comes prosperous Portlanders, and before long the city's wealthy merchants were rushing to erect grandiose mansions to show off their financial success. Local preservationists call this period of construction between 1800 and 1866 the "revivals period." Greek Revival, Gothic Revival, Federal, and Classical Revival architecture were all popular during this time. The Victoria Mansion, one of the nation's most famous Italian-villa-style homes, was completed in 1860 and stands as an elaborate example of the decadence of the age. It was constructed by Ruggles Sylvester Morse, a Maine native who made his fortune in New Orleans. The design of the mansion incorporates elements of Gothic Revival, Greek Revival, and Egyptian Revival architecture.

In 1866 perhaps the most important event in the city's architectural history took place. The Great Fire destroyed nearly all of Portland from Commercial Street to the foot of the Portland Observatory after Fourth of July celebrations along the waterfront got out of hand. In the wake of this devastation, Portland passed a city ordinance requiring all reconstruction be done with brick or stone. The reconstruction efforts in the years following the fire account for much of the historic commercial architecture in Portland. These brick and stone buildings in the city's downtown and Old Port districts are some of the best-preserved Victorian architecture in the country. Our Insiders' Walking Tour ("The Old Port and the Waterfront" section) highlights many of these famous commercial landmarks, including the wonderfully detailed Centennial Block (93–95 Exchange Street), which was designed by the architect Francis Fassett in 1876.

As Portland developed into the 20th century, the romanticism of the Beaux Arts style

| **i** | The oldest building in Portland is located just off the peninsula in historic Stroudwater. The Tate House, at 1270 Westbrook Street, was built by Captain George Tate in 1755. For more information on tours of the house, see the Attractions chapter or call (207) 774–6177. |

was all the rage. The Fidelity Trust Company Building, the first skyscraper in the state, was constructed in 1910 and displays an elegant stone veneer supported by a revolutionary invention at the time—the interior steel frame. Other Beaux Arts buildings erected during the early 20th century include the Porteous, Mitchell & Braun Block (522–528 Congress Street) and Portland's city hall (389 Congress Street).

Today, Portland remains a city deeply rooted in its past but not limited to it. Examples of modern and postmodern architecture in the city include the new Portland Public Library at 455 Congress Street and the Portland Museum of Art at 7 Congress Square.

TWO GREAT ARCHITECTS

No discussion of Portland architecture is complete without a nod to Portland's most famous architects, John Calvin Stevens and Francis Fassett. Fassett is one of the founding fathers of Portland architecture, and Stevens, his apprentice, went on to national renown for his development of the popular Shingle Style.

Francis Fassett was born in Bath, Maine, in 1823. He studied architecture in Boston and New York before moving to Portland at age 40. John Neal, a 19th-century arts patron, writer, and activist, wrote in his book *Portland Illustrated* that Fassett was one of only a handful of townsmen the city could depend on for its "architectural embellishment." Indeed, Fassett worked tirelessly to build new and engaging structures in Portland as it grew from a town to a city during the second half of the 19th century. Fassett is responsible for countless residential and commercial structures in

The Marker Program

As you wander around Portland, you're sure to notice small plaques with a blue design of a lighthouse on the sides of some of our historic buildings. These markers decorate the facades of the city's National Historic Landmarks—buildings that have received a special distinction in the National Register of Historic Places from the secretary of the U.S. Department of the Interior for their architectural and historic merit. Unfortunately, the federal government doesn't always provide an official plaque announcing this distinction. Portlanders intent on showing up their neighbors must instead apply with Greater Portland Landmarks for these historic markers. To be approved, the building must meet strict local and federal standards pertaining to the integrity of its preservation. While no federal laws protect buildings on the National Register of Historic Places, all home owners of a designated historic site in Portland must clear major structural renovations with the city's Historic Preservation Committee.

Howard produced more than 500 works in an array of styles, including the style for which Stevens is best known—the Shingle Style. Stevens was influenced by Boston architects when he developed his Shingle Style cottages, which are distinguished by rounded roofs and wide exterior walls covered with wooden shingles. One of the first houses designed in this manner was Stevens's own residence at 52 Bowdoin Street. Shingle Style cottages were popular at the dawn of the Industrial Age in part because they recalled old-fashioned simplicity. Today, Stevens's influence on Portland continues to recall earlier, simpler times.

ARCHITECTURAL PRESERVATION AND GUIDED TOURS

Greater Portland Landmarks
165 State Street
(207) 774–5561
www.portlandlandmarks.org
Greater Portland Landmarks (GPL) was formed in 1964 to preserve and protect Portland's architectural heritage. Today, GPL not only advocates to protect Portland's great buildings but also offers educational programs in area schools, hands-on workshops in preservation and home renovation, a first-class research library, and consultations for owners of historic homes. If you have any questions on local architecture, GPL is the place to go. After all, who can argue with a group that calls itself "the architectural conscience" of Greater Portland?

In 1983 GPL opened the Francis W. Peabody Research Library at 165 State Street. The research library, named after a former volunteer, contains more than 1,000 books, periodicals, slides, and photographs on subjects like historic preservation, interior design, architecture, and landscaping. It is the most extensive preservation collection north of Boston. The library is open most weekdays from 9:00 A.M. to 5:00 P.M., but it is also used for meetings, so GPL suggests you call ahead before visiting.

Portland, and his work was instrumental in the western development of the business district lining Congress Street. Some of his most important commercial work includes the former Portland Public Library at 619 Congress Street, the original wing of Maine Medical Center, and the Williston West Church at 32 Thomas Street.

In 1873 young Portland-born architect John Calvin Stevens joined the office of Francis Fassett. Eighteen years later Stevens opened his own office in Portland. Over the next 40 years, Stevens and his son John

Greater Portland Landmarks offers numerous tours of the peninsula focusing on the city's history and architecture. Tour guides, or docents, are volunteers from the community who have been trained through one of GPL's docent workshops. Some docents specialize in history, some in architecture. Tours run from June 15 through Columbus Day and cost between $5.00 and $8.00 per person. Visit the GPL Web site for information on special tours such as "Portland's Historic Fire Houses" and October's "Evening Tour of the Western Cemetery."

In keeping with its mission statement to "promote the appreciation, preservation and appropriate use of historic structures and landscapes," GPL also offers an Advisory Service for home owners. For a fee ($25 for members, $60 for nonmembers), two or more GPL volunteers will visit your historic home and advise you on appropriate preservation and restoration, including detail restoration and historically accurate paint colors.

And how do you get access to all of this at a discount? By becoming a GPL member, of course. Individual membership to GPL costs $35 and includes perks like the quarterly newsletter, advanced notice on special events and tours, and a special member price for GPL events.

i   If you'd like to take matters into your own hands, try one of Greater Portland Landmark's self-guided walking tours. Tour brochures, including an easy-to-follow map and landmark descriptions, can be purchased for $2.00 at the GPL office at 165 State Street.

INSIDERS' WALKING TOUR
Downtown Portland

The city of Portland has spent nearly four decades seeing to the preservation of many of its richest architectural wonders. For this reason, any walk around Portland is sure to offer up dozens of architectural treasures. Our own Insiders' Walking Tour will show you some of the best the city has to offer. As one local history docent said, "Portland is an 'in-the-palm-of-your-hand' city," meaning that most of the metropolitan landmarks are clustered together on the peninsula, which can be walked lengthwise from the Western to the Eastern Promenade in about an hour. Our walking tour highlights the downtown area and its fine examples of Gothic, colonial, Federal, Italianate, and modern architectural styles. We've even included a cannonball or two along the way.

The tour takes you from Monument Square, through the Old Port, and finally to Commercial Street. We think it's perfect for the intrepid architecture buff who also wouldn't mind stopping along the way for some homemade ice cream or a local trinket or two. You could race through this tour in about 25 minutes, but we're estimating it should take about two hours if you take a few minutes to stop and admire each site.

Our tour begins at Monument Square, the center of downtown Portland. Parking is notoriously tough in the downtown area, but the square has a parking garage on the south side. You also might be able to find off-street parking on the side streets along Congress Street or in the lot on Free Street, which runs parallel to Congress behind Monument Square. Free Street is often your best bet for parking, lot or otherwise, but just to make things tricky, city planners have designated it a one-way street. Turn off Congress at Brown Street to pick up Free Street in the middle, or drive up Congress to High Street and take a left onto the beginning of Free at the Portland Museum of Art. Whew. We promise, this is the toughest part of the tour.

Once you've disposed of your pesky vehicle, strap on your walking shoes, tuck this book under your arm, and head to our first stop—the regal statue at the center of Monument Square.

Our Lady of Victories Monument, 1891
Monument Square
This bronze sculpture was modeled after Minerva, the Roman goddess of wisdom and war, and was commissioned by the now

defunct Portland Soldiers and Sailors Monument Association in honor of Portland's men and boys who died in the Civil War. The pedestal was designed by prominent New York architect Richard Morris Hunt, and the statue was designed by Portland's own Franklin Simmons. In 1889 the old Kimball-Clapp city hall that once stood here was demolished, and the square was widened and made more accessible to walking traffic. When the statue was erected, the square's name was changed from Market Square to, you guessed it, Monument Square. The statue watches over the downtown as the patron goddess of Portland.

Go ahead and mimic the Lady and stand facing up Congress Street. Step across Center Street and then to the other side of Congress and head toward a small, redbrick house that looks completely out of place on the city's bustling main street. You are now standing in front of the oldest and most famous home on the peninsula, formerly owned by a nice family by the name of Longfellow.

Wadsworth-Longfellow House, 1786
487 Congress Street
National Historic Landmark
(207) 774–1822
www.mainehistory.org
Built in 1785–1786, this three-story brick house was the first wholly brick dwelling in Portland. General Peleg Wadsworth built the home on land that was then on the outskirts of Portland's residential center near the waterfront. Wadsworth was the grandfather of Henry Wadsworth Longfellow (1807–1882), one of America's greatest 19th-century poets (see the Attractions chapter for information on tours of the house). Henry grew up at 487 Congress Street, and in 1901 his younger sister Anne Longfellow Pierce bequeathed the building to the Maine Historical Society as a memorial to her brother. In 2002 the house was reopened for tours after a two-and-a-half-year, $700,000 renovation. Exterior restoration included mortar repair, window sash repair,

and the re-creation of the original 19th-century louvered shutters on the front doors and windows. Today, the Wadsworth-Longfellow House is open for tours every day from May through October and is maintained by the Maine Historical Society, which has its offices beside the building at 489 Congress.

The Wadsworth-Longfellow House is one of the best-preserved architectural gems on the peninsula. In its original incarnation in 1786, the house was a two-and-a-half-story home with a pitched roof. Architectural influences for this part of the construction were late Georgian in nature, such as the projecting stringcourse separating the first and second stories and the softly arched window and door openings. A fire in 1814 destroyed the original gable roof. The third story, a Federal-style hip roof, and the front portico were all added the following year. If you have a sharp eye, you may be able to distinguish the new floor from the original building by the changes in the brick pattern.

Facing the Wadsworth-Longfellow House, turn to your right and head back down Congress Street. Stay on the side of the street opposite Monument Square. Cross Preble Street and look up. You are standing in front of the oldest skyscraper in Maine, the Fidelity Trust Company Building.

Fidelity Trust Company Building, 1910
467 Congress Street
The state's first skyscraper, the Fidelity Trust Company Building, was built in 1910. The building was designed by Boston architect G. Henri Desmond and is a towering example of the romantic extravagance of the Beaux Arts period, otherwise known as the Classical Revival. The stone veneer draping the building is capped by a sculptured roofline of Gothic peaks. This veneer hides the secret structural ingredient that distinguishes the Fidelity Building—its interior steel frame. The steel skeleton revolutionized commercial architecture at the turn of the 20th century. The frame supports much of the building's weight and allowed

architects like Desmond to design lean, decorative exteriors. The Fidelity Trust Company Building stands 10 stories tall and is currently the home of Maine Bank and Trust and other companies. If you are touring during normal business hours, stop and take a peek inside the impressive bank lobby, with its 30-foot-high ceilings, Italian marble floors, and walls covered with violet brachia and Caen stone from France.

Back outside on Congress Street, continue walking to your left past the new **Portland Public Library,** at 455 Congress Street. The library is a great example of modern cubist architecture in the downtown area. Erected in 1979, it was designed by James R. Clapp Jr., David Schurman, and Shepley, Bulfinch, Richardson and Abbott Inc.

Continue down Congress Street, crossing Elm Street. Just beyond Elm, the trees along the sidewalk clear, and a wide set of granite stairs leads up from the brick sidewalk to the narrow red doors of the oldest church in Portland.

First Parish Church, 1826
425 Congress Street
National Historic Landmark
(207) 773–5747
www.firstparishportland.org
This granite church was built in 1825–1826 with stone shipped from Freeport, Maine. John Mussey, a parishioner, is credited with designing the First Parish. The design is a replica of the original wooden meetinghouse erected by Portland's first colonists on this site in 1740. Mussey's granite version represents a stylistic transition from early-18th-century churches with a fully projecting central tower to later Federal and Greek Revival styles, which were distinguished by a full portico and a tower rising from the roof. The tower of the church is divided by a balustrade, which marks the beginning of an octagonal, domed belfry. Above the belfry a lantern and spire reach toward the heavens. The clock on the tower was repaired in the

mid-1990s and, last time we checked, runs about 10 minutes fast. Otherwise, the structure has undergone few changes since its completion in 1826. As proof of this church's colonial heritage, the golden banner atop the spire is the same weathervane that spun atop the original wooden meetinghouse, which was known as "Old Jerusalem."

Cannonball One: The first of two cannonballs on our walking tour can be found inside the First Parish Church. In 1775 British naval captain Henry Mowatt bombarded the revolution-minded Portland with cannonballs and destroyed the town. First Parish Church officials claim to have "three or four cannonballs rolling around" that were plucked from the walls by their colonial predecessors after the Mowatt raid. At least one of the cannonballs can easily be accounted for—it is woven into the chain of the crystal chandelier hanging just above the church's center aisle.

> **i** If you're interested in getting married in the First Parish, pick up a brochure in the church office.

You are now at the head of Temple Street. Look to your right along Temple and make a note of it—you will return to Monument Square at the end of the tour via this main road. But now is not the time to linger on thoughts of home. Press on, brave explorers, and continue down Congress Street to the largest granite structure in the city. This is city hall, home of the recently renovated Merrill Auditorium.

Portland City Hall, 1912
389 Congress Street
(207) 874–8300
www.ci.portland.me.us
Now, you've heard about Portland's problem with fire (see this chapter's introduction if you're still in the dark). Well, no building in town has been more terrorized by conflagration than our dear old city hall. The building standing before you is the third city hall this

site has known. The first city hall, a three-story sprawling granite structure, burned in the fire of 1866. Portlanders rebuilt their central government building immediately, only to lose it in another fire in 1908. Both previous incarnations of city hall were classical in detail, with three-part entrances and octagonal domes on top. Not to be kept down, in the early 20th century, Portland hired renowned New York City architects John Carrere and Thomas Hastings (designers of the New York Public Library in Manhattan) to re-reconstruct city hall for the third and, knock on wood everyone, final time. The city hall you see before you was built between 1909 and 1912 and mirrors many of the design elements of the first two buildings. The three-part entrance of the first two buildings is mimicked in the three archways at the building's main entrance. The bell tower at the top of the building recalls the octagonal domes that capped the lost city halls. Carrere and Hastings loosely based the design of the building on the French Renaissance Hôtel de Ville and added classical linear flourishes to suggest academia. The central portion is set back from the sidewalk, and the wings stretching forward create an entrance court. The detailing of the iron grillwork at the top of the arches reflects the slenderness of the building's bell tower, reaching 200 feet above the street. Break out the binoculars and check out the weathervane on top of the building. The sailing ship motif was designed by John Carrere.

Inside city hall is the gold-gilded Merrill Auditorium, an architectural landmark in its own right. The original 1912 auditorium was

> **i** Take a look at the top of the older buildings in town. Many of the brick structures display two dates: the date of the first building's construction before it was burned in the Great Fire and the date of its rebirth afterward. The dates are often carved into the building's facade near the roof.

renovated in 1996 by Winton Scott Architects and was reopened the following year with improved acoustics and sightlines. Merrill has hosted many famous performers over the years, including George Gershwin, John Philip Sousa, and Sergei Rachmaninoff. Tours of the theater can be arranged by calling the city at the number listed above. Be sure to check out the famous Kotzschmar Organ, which is embedded in the interior of the auditorium.

The Old Port and the Waterfront

Cross Congress Street and walk to your left to turn down Exchange Street. You are now heading into the most visited area of the city—the Old Port. English settlers first established themselves on this part of the peninsula in 1632. Since then, the Old Port has remained the commercial center of Portland, despite being almost thoroughly razed during the Great Fire. On this part of the tour, wander along some of the oldest streets in the country and check out building after building of impeccably preserved Victorian architecture. One local historian says that she likes to wander around the narrow streets of the Old Port and imagine away the modern cars. If you can manage this, she says, you can see the Old Port almost exactly the way a 19th-century resident would have.

In this part of the tour, keep an eye out for major commercial designs from several of Portland's most famous architects, including Francis Fassett, John Calvin Stevens, and Charles Quincy Clapp.

Continue 1 block down Exchange Street, which has remained the main street in the Old Port in one incarnation or another since 1724. When you arrive at Federal Street, look diagonally across the intersection to the brick office building twisting around the corner at Federal and Exchange. This is the Printers' Exchange, which was designed by Portland's most famous self-taught architect, the ubiquitous Charles Quincy Clapp.

Printers' Exchange, 1866
103–107 Exchange Street

Charles Quincy Clapp (1799–1868) was a tireless land speculator and self-taught architect who was responsible for more than 600 real estate transactions in Portland during the 19th century. The Printers' Exchange is an example of one of Clapp's commercial designs. The building, which was erected in 1866 just after the Great Fire, utilizes Italianate architectural detail, including a deep hip roof and arched windows. Originally, a twin building sat opposite the block where the Salt Gallery now stands.

Continue walking down Exchange Street until you are standing in front of 90 Exchange Street. Across the street is the **Centennial Block** (93–95 Exchange Street). This block was built in 1876 by the city's premier architect of the time, the hometown boy Francis Fassett (you might remember him from this chapter's introduction). Note the building's exquisite patchwork granite and sandstone facade. Fassett reportedly sketched a plan for the Centennial Block that included the shape and color of each stone. He was so obsessed with the pattern of the facade that he allegedly rented an office across the street to monitor its construction.

Cannonball Two: Look up. You are standing under the second cannonball on our tour, this one wedged into the side of 90 Exchange Street, the **Cotesworthy Building.** The original building was burned during the 1866 fire. During reconstruction the building's owners discovered a grapefruit-sized cannonball in the basement that dated back to, you guessed it, Captain Mowatt's attack on Portland in 1775 (it appears that Mowatt was nothing if not thorough). Hardly ones to let an opportunity like this pass them by, the owners incorporated the cannonball into the new building's facade. Is it a thumb to the nose of any malicious force, human or otherwise, that might try to destroy the new Cotesworthy Building, or just a little creative design? It's your call. The cannonball is readily visible

peeking out of the brick just under the Cotesworthy banner facing Exchange Street.

Continue on Exchange until you reach two small parks on opposite sides of the street. Standing with your back to city hall, **Tommy's Park** is to your right, and **Post Office Park** is to your left. Take a moment to look at the mural painted on the side of the Natasha's restaurant building facing Tommy's Park. This is one of two *trompe l'oeil* ("fool the eye") murals in Portland's downtown (the other is on Free Street). It was painted in 1985 and designed by local artists Michael Lewis and Chris Denison. The mural incorporates architectural elements from the 1867 post office building that once occupied the Tommy's Park lot. Eight shades of paint were used to simulate the granite facade of the old post office. Denison and his assistants completed the mural in 10 weeks.

Tommy's Park and Post Office Park are local gathering places for everyone from lawyers and artists to teenagers with body piercings and bongo drums. The parks are popular rendezvous spots and great for snagging a quick bite on lunch break. If you're feeling weary, now would be a good time to grab a snack from one of the sandwich shops surrounding the parks and take a break on a granite bench. If you're taking our walking tour during the summer, there's a good chance you'll happen upon a musical performance or two in the parks, sponsored by Portland's Downtown District. But don't rest too long because the heart of the Old Port is just a few steps away.

Continue down the street to what's known as the **Widgery Block,** at 36–40 Exchange Street. It was built by William Widgery Thomas in 1871, when this block on Exchange Street was the heart of the commercial district. Today, not much has changed—this block plays host to some of the trendiest coffee shops and boutiques in the Old Port. The storefronts of the Widgery Block are all original. Take a look up at the top of the building, where a semicircular pediment distinguishes this building from the flat rooflines of its neighbors. All of the buildings on this block are worth a closer look. Many have intricate original carved details and brickwork. After taking your time on this block of Exchange Street, take a left at Fore Street. Three storefronts down you will find our next stop, the Seaman's Club Building.

Seaman's Club Building, 1866
373–375 Fore Street
The Seaman's Club Building (so named for a restaurant that formerly occupied the location) was constructed just after the 1866 fire and currently houses one of the most popular Irish pubs in town, Bull Feeney's (see the Nightlife chapter for more information). Its designer was Charles Quincy Clapp, and it is notable for its two enormous Gothic windows. Four intertwining pointed arches divide the windows and balance three carved wooden medallions on their peaks. This window-dominated facade includes design elements that would later influence Victorian commercial facades. You may want to step across the street for a better view. Once you've finished admiring these windows, do an about-face. Say hello to the second-oldest church in the city.

Mariner's Church, 1829
366–376 Fore Street
National Historic Landmark
(207) 774–7016
www.oldporttavern.com
In the decades immediately following the War of 1812, Portland was the fifth-largest commercial port in the world. Dozens of ships came in and out of port every day, along with hundreds of hardworking and often rowdy seamen. Portlanders quickly grew tired of the party habits of some of these offshore visitors, and so, in 1829, they built a church a stone's throw from the docks. The Mariner's Church was constructed to introduce Portland's sailors to the Christian faith. The architectural plan of the building was designed by Asa Clapp (Charles Quincy's father) and mimicks Faneuil Hall in Boston. It is an eclectic combination of Federal and Greek Revival styles. The shape of the building and its windows reflect the Greek Revival school, but the dainty cornice outlining the pediment and the fan window are Federal-style flourishes. Despite altruistic intentions, Mariner's Church was built with a shrewd sense of practicality. The bottom floors were designed to house apartments and stores, with the chapel relegated to the top floor. Apparently, the building's designers had a good dose of foresight. The congregation has long since departed Mariner's Church, and the building now houses a banquet hall, a pub, and several popular shops.

Cross Market Street and continue on past Silver Street to a small baby-blue house beside Rosie's Pub.

Samuel Butts House and Store, 1792
332–334 Fore Street
This unassuming little building was constructed in 1792 and is the second-oldest surviving structure on the peninsula (after the Wadsworth-Longfellow House). The roof just above the third-story windows, the small windows themselves, and the large central chimney are all classic elements of colonial architecture. Note the change in the brickwork between the second and third stories, betraying the addition of the top floor at a later date.

After you are finished admiring this building, continue to walk down Fore Street to the corner. Across the street is the city's stately Customs House.

United States Customs House, 1871
312 Fore Street/468 Commercial Street
National Historic Landmark
The Customs House was designed by the supervising architect for the U.S. Treasury Department, Alfred B. Mullet. At the time of it construction between 1868 and 1871, it was standard for all major federal buildings around the country to be designed by this

central office. The U.S. Customs House was built during the rush of building activity after the Civil War. It is set on a slope from Fore Street to Commercial Street, which allows a two-story facade facing Fore, with an additional story on Commercial. The division in the building's facade created by the rounded columns, projected pilasters, and double arches and doors suggests its width and robustness and is characteristic of the Baroque Revival style popular at the time. Light-colored granite from New Hampshire was used to suggest more expensive marble. Both the interior and exterior of this building have been preserved to maintain much of their original appearance. Take a right off Fore and walk down to Commercial Street along the building's side so you can admire the waterfront facade.

Take a right along Commercial Street, walk 1 block, and look across the street. This is the last building on our tour, the Elias Thomas Block.

Elias Thomas Block, 1860
102–103 Commercial Street
William Widgery Thomas was a local banker and businessman in Portland in the early 19th century. He had this block erected in 1860, and a strong sea breeze saved it from a scorching in 1866. It is the largest mid-19th-century commercial building on the street. The building is divided into eight sections, each with three windows looking out over Casco Bay. The Thomas Block is notable because it conforms to the S-shape of Commercial Street. The concave building's curve is mirrored in the curved pediment crowning the central axis of the building. To see the curve, cross the street and look down the length of the building.

The Thomas Block exploits the width that Commercial Street allowed—the granite storefronts on the ground floor alternate between narrow and wider openings complemented by wide Doric pilasters. Each windowsill and lintel rests on two small, square

blocks, providing nice visual relief. The projecting cornice is supported by brackets separated by inset panels in the brickwork. The roundel originally contained a clock that was donated by the building's namesake, Elias Thomas, who was William Widgery's father.

Now you are in the center of the Old Port, the nexus of shopping, food, fishing, and all-around fun in Portland. When you're ready to return to your car, head back to Monument Square by walking up Commercial Street past DiMillo's Restaurant. Take a right at Union Street and follow it until it turns into Temple Street a couple of blocks up. Just beyond the Nickelodeon Cinema, you should see the tower of the First Parish Church. Head toward the church and take a left onto Congress Street. One block up, you'll find Monument Square and our old friend Minerva.

OTHER ARCHITECTURE IN DETAIL
West End

John J. Brown House/Gothic House, 1845
387 Spring Street
National Historic Landmark
This little house, which looks as though it's made out of gingerbread, retains the square central plan scheme of many of its classical predecessors, but architect Henry Rowe dressed up the exterior with plenty of elaborate Gothic details. Note the pier buttresses bracketing the building at its corners, the projected pavilion at the entrance topped by a sharply pointed gable and a small enclosed porch. The house was modeled after a Gothic church and was originally located closer to the downtown amid other Federal, Greek, and Gothic Revival buildings that have since been lost.

Charles Clapp House, 1832
97 Spring Street
Charles Quincy Clapp came from one of early Portland's most enterprising families. For his family home on Spring Street, Clapp designed

a uniquely bold Greek Revival mansion. Instead of a traditional peripteral temple facade, Clapp used an Ionic colonnade and colonettes to frame his building's facade, with a wide, overhanging pediment connecting the fluted columns. The effect is a lean building that emphasizes a vertical reach to the roofline, punctuated by large urns crowning each of the three pedestals. This building is now owned by the Maine College of Art.

Thomas Delano House, 1800
127 Pleasant Street
Thomas Delano was famous for his superhuman strength (he is reputed to have once lifted a ship's anchor). In 1800 he built this Federal-style home for his family. Little about the original architecture has been altered since then. Although the design is simpler than other examples of Federal architecture in Portland, it does display a few typical Georgian flourishes, such as the symmetrical arrangement of windows around the doorway and chimneys close to the interior. The sidelights and door panels are transitional Federal details.

Francis H. Fassett Houses, 1876
117–119 Pine Street
In 1876 Francis Fassett built this eclectic duplex home for himself and his son Edward. Fassett was known for designing buildings in the mansard and Queen Anne styles and, later, in the Romanesque and Classical Revival traditions popular during the end of the 19th century. With this pair of residences, however, Fassett displayed a flair for High Victorian Gothic details. Fassett utilized a rich variety of building materials—including brick, granite, sandstone, red marble, slate, and iron—in a facade whose many projections and recessions add a deep linear texture to the building. The vertical framework of the building is accentuated by its bold chimney stacks, slim portico colonettes, and squat side porches.

McLellan Mansion, 1800
107 Spring Street
National Historic Landmark
www.portlandmuseum.org
In 1908 one of the largest mansions on the West End, the Hugh McLellan Mansion, was bequeathed to the Portland Museum of Art. After years of renovation on both the interior and exterior, the mansion was finally reopened as an extension of the museum in 2002. In 1800 McLellan commissioned local master builder John Kimball Sr. to design the house. The resulting mansion displays typical Federal-style details, including a central arched light surrounded by two pilastered sections and a projecting entrance portico. A graceful balustrade is accented by slender Doric columns supporting the portico and hand-carved urns dotting the original fence. The windows of the ground floor were lengthened by Charles Quincy Clapp during the 1820s, and the brick was painted a delicate cream to appear as though it was cut from a single piece of marble.

Samuel and Andrew Spring Mansions, 1854–1855
300 and 306 Danforth Street
Samuel and Andrew Spring were uncle and nephew, business partners, and neighbors who lived side by side in these two mansions on Danforth Street. The mansions were originally part of a small cluster of stately homes that included the now-demolished Storer and Hershey mansions across the street. Designed by Charles Alexander, the twin residences rely on the cubist hard angles that John Calvin Stevens's Shingle Style homes sought to erase. These Italianate mansions were built to rival the Victoria Mansion (see below for more on the Vic).

i Nearly every home on the block of Bowdoin Street between the Western Promenade and Vaughn Street is the work of John Calvin Stevens. These Shingle Style homes were Stevens's trademark.

John Calvin Stevens Home, 1884
52 Bowdoin Street
National Historic Landmark
Just after founding his own architectural firm in Portland in 1884, John Calvin Stevens built a residence for himself and his family half a block from the Western Promenade. The informal style of the home, with a low, broad profile and projecting second floor, broke the earlier traditions of cube-shaped buildings and introduced Portland to a new style that would influence building aesthetics into the 20th century. The Shingle Style, for which Calvin Stevens became famous, is characterized by reduced gables, recessed porches, and exterior walls covered with shingles.

Victoria Mansion, 1859–1860
109 Danforth Street
National Historic Landmark
(207) 772–4841
www.victoriamansion.org
The Victoria Mansion (also known as the Morse-Libby Mansion or "the Vic") is widely regarded as the greatest and most outrageously decadent Italian-villa home in the country. The residence was built by Ruggles Sylvester Morse, a Maine native with a checkered past (for more on the mansion and Morse, see the Attractions chapter). The building was designed by Henry Austin of New Haven. Austin, a risk taker when it came to architectural styles, was influenced by everything from Gothic Revival to Greek Revival and even Egyptian Revival architecture. Although the Victoria Mansion is often categorized as an Italianate structure, it is actually a dense mixture of various architectural styles. Perhaps the most unique element of the building's exterior is its glaring asymmetry. Instead of a simple central-hall scheme common to mansions at the time, the Vic appears to be a hodgepodge of unequal, interpenetrating blocks. For example, the mansion's square tower rises a story above and a bay out from the flat-roofed rectangular block to the west. Austin's textured structure is further enhanced by rich, rust-colored brownstone

that was shipped from Connecticut and finished on the Portland pier. The porous stone allowed the architect to manipulate light and shadow on the porches, windows, and arches of the tower, creating that haunting air of mystery that makes the Vic so enchanting. To learn more about tours of this national treasure, turn to the Attractions chapter.

George C. West House, 1911
181 Western Promenade
The enormous West House sits like a beacon to traffic entering Portland on the Veterans' Memorial Bridge. On a clear day, the yellow brick mansion, with its enormous white colonnade and ruby-red roof, sits like a sentinel watching over the Fore River. The mansion was designed by Frederick A. Thompson and is one of the most grandiose examples of residential architecture in Portland. It has a gambrel rook and colossal Ionic portico.

Congress and State Streets
John B. Brown Memorial Building
523–543 Congress Street
National Historic Landmark
The Brown Memorial Building is one of several Portland commercial buildings designed by the architect Francis Fassett. The Lancaster Building at Monument Square, the Eastland Hotel on Congress Street, and Maine Medical Center's original wing all bear Fassett's stamp. The Brown building incorporates basic elements of the Queen Anne vocabulary, which characterize all of Fassett's commercial work in the city, including narrow chimney stacks and window bays topped with pointed gables. Stand across the street and look for John Brown's signature inscribed above the entrance to 537 Congress Street.

Hunnewell House/Portland Club, 1805
156 State Street
The Hunnewell House—now the home of the Portland Club, a private organization—was built for Richard Hunnewell in 1805. Famed local architect Alexander Parris was the building's designer. The home was remodeled in

the 1920s in the Colonial Revival theme, which was actually based on Federal-style architecture, then seen as a romanticized version of the past. Remodelers JCS & Son added a Palladian window above the entrance and a balustrade to the original portico.

John Neal House, 1836
173–175 State Street

In 1836 John Neal built this duplex-style home and hoped it would be the first in a series of row houses on State Street. The idea didn't catch on as Neal had hoped, and today this granite structure remains a silent tribute to the ill-fated plans of one of Portland's early developers. The duplex displays simplified Greek Revival details, including a segmented arched dormer in the attic roofs, a cast-iron fence along the sidewalk, and second-story iron balconies.

The Portland Observatory, 1807
138 Congress Street
National Historic Landmark
(207) 774–5561
www.portlandlandmarks.org

In 1807 retired naval captain Lemuel Moody organized the construction of Portland's most recognizable landmark, the Portland Observatory maritime signal tower on Munjoy Hill. The wooden structure stands 221 feet above sea level and was used during the 19th century to alert shipowners and dockhands that their ship was sighted heading into Portland. The structure was designed by Moody, who modeled the building after similar observatories he had seen in Nantucket and Boston while in the navy. The octagonal base of the tower is held in place by 122 tons of granite rocks placed on a crisscross of wooden beams. A cupola with a small lantern deck tops the structure. For more on tours of the observatory, see the Close-up in this chapter.

Porteous, Mitchell & Braun Block, 1904
522–528 Congress Street
National Historic Landmark
www.meca.edu

In 1950 the Porteous, Mitchell & Braun Block was the shopping mecca of Portland. These days, it is owned by a different MECA (the Maine College of Art). Architect George Burnham designed the 1904 building in the Beaux Arts classical style. Cherub heads dot the tops of the building's Ionic pilasters. Other details have been carved into the limestone, including the crested rondels and the garlands on the top story, the rondels and plaques at the building's middle, and the leafy brackets of the cornice.

Portland Museum of Art
Charles Shipman Payson Wing, 1983
7 Congress Square
(207) 775–6148
www.portlandmuseum.org

This postmodern brick building was opened in 1983 to honor a gift of 17 Winslow Homer paintings from Charles Shipman Payson. The Payson Wing was designed by Henry N. Cobb of Pei, Cobb, Freed & Partners of New York City. The firm is responsible for some of the best designs of the 20th century, including the John Hancock Tower and the John F. Kennedy Library, both located in Boston. Coincidentally, Cobb is a direct descendant of Matthew Cobb, the former owner of the mansion that originally occupied the site. The modern-day Cobb modeled the museum's Great Hall on a domed clerestory, the glassed portion of a church that rises above neighboring rooftops to allow sunlight into the interior. The front of the building recalls the Doges Palace in Venice, with its sheer front mounted on a ground-level loggia.

Portland Public Library, 1888
619 Congress Street
(207) 871–1700

Local architect Francis Fassett was influenced by the ornate facades of Romanesque churches when he designed the original Portland Public Library (now a Maine College of Art building) in 1888. The wide facade reaching toward the sky suggests a church's central nave and side aisles. Eight large arched win-

 Close-up

Old Faithful

No visit to Portland is complete without a trip to the Portland Observatory Maritime Signal Tower. Located at the top of Munjoy Hill, this red wooden tower has stood as a beacon of Portland's ingenuity and connection to her maritime trade for more than 200 years. Since its construction in the early 19th century, the observatory has survived everything from blizzards, hurricanes, and the Great Fire to a nasty case of termite infestation. Although it was never home to anyone, the observatory remains one of the city's most visited monuments.

Captain Lemuel Moody built the observatory in 1807 after a career spent in the navy. In those days, before telephones, electricity, or telegraphs, Portland merchants would send their ships out to sea and never know when they had returned until word traveled through the grapevine that the ship was back in port. Moody knew that a watchtower such as those he had seen in Boston and Nantucket would be useful in Portland. Moody, a relentless entrepreneur, already owned a dance hall, a banquet hall, a bowling alley, and a riding stable, all of which he rented out for a fee. But in the observatory, Moody saw a unique opportunity. He could build a watchtower and charge area merchants for his lookout services.

Today, you can climb the very same stairs Captain Moody climbed (103 to be exact, from the first step on Congress Street) to the cupola in which he once stood as he looked down the main ship course from Casco Bay. The golden telescope that Moody gazed through is now lost, but a re-creation of the compass rose painted on the cupola's ceiling recalls the observatory's long history. Two or three times a day, Moody would walk from his house near the base of the tower, through the cow pastures, to the top of the observatory. If he saw a ship, and the ship's merchant was on his registry of paying clients, Moody would fly the corresponding flag from the tower to alert the ship's owner that his ship had arrived. Moody, ever the businessman, also charged for tours of the tower.

The Great Fire of 1866 (see the History chapter for details) devastated much of downtown Portland and nearly leveled the observatory. Local lore holds that the

dows face the street, with a recessed main entrance. The eye is directed upward to a large roundel above the main entrance.

Old Port/Downtown

Board of Trade Building, 1867
34 Exchange Street
Built in 1867, this is the only stone building in a brick neighborhood. It housed the Board of Trade, which advocated for healthy trade in Portland, and the Merchants National Bank, the Bank of Portland, and the National Traders Bank. The formal design of this banking block, which includes arched windows and doors and rusticated pilasters, was intended to contrast with the business block. Matthew Stead, the building's designer, wanted to reflect the conservatism of banks and boards of trade in his more traditional facade.

only reason that the wooden tower didn't burn was because men were stationed at each of its windows with buckets of water to douse any sparks that fell on the building's shingles.

These days, all tours of the tower are guided, although 19th-century graffiti on the interior walls recall the days before tour guides. When you make it to the top, don't be afraid to take a step out onto the lantern deck to check out the view of the White Mountains just across the border in New Hampshire. You might even try to imagine how it looked to Captain Moody, early on a Saturday morning, while all of the city's cows grazed below him on Munjoy Hill.

The tower is located at 138 Congress Street. Call (207) 774–5561, ext. 104, or visit www.portlandlandmarks.org for information.

The Portland Observatory. COURTESY OF GREATER PORTLAND LANDMARKS; PHOTO BY BILL HALL

Cumberland County Courthouse, 1911
142 Federal Street

Like the Custom House and city hall, the Cumberland County Courthouse was built during a time when many American architects were trained at L'École des Beaux Arts in Paris. In fact, the neoclassical tradition taught at this school had become so influential and widespread that it had become somewhat passé.

The courthouse was completed in 1911 and designed by a Beaux Arts–trained architect, George Burnham. Despite the overuse of the Beaux Arts form, Burnham managed to craft a courthouse that is both handsome and functional. The tall basement story of large granite blocks contrasts with the slender lines created by the series of Doric colonnades on the building's facade. The colonnade effect is carried to the side of the building, giving the court-house a unique texture.

The State of Maine Armory, 1895
20 Milk Street
The armory was built by the state in 1895 and was designed in the Romanesque Revival style by Frederick A. Thompson. The building once housed several National Guard units and now contains one of the nicest hotels in the city, the Regency. The design of the armory was meant to recall a fortress, with corner turrets and brick dentils in the corners, suggesting military defenses.

HOUSES OF WORSHIP
West End

Park Street Church/Holy Trinity Greek Orthodox Church, 1828
133 Pleasant Street
(207) 774-0281
The Park Street Church, now known as the Holy Trinity Greek Orthodox Church, was constructed three years after the First Parish and reflects much of the First Parish's architectural vocabulary, although with a sleeker, simpler overall design. Like the First Parish, the Park Street Church, with its full portico and slightly setback tower, exemplifies the transitional style from early-18th-century designs to the later Federal and Greek Revival styles. The church has a similar side door and main tower construction as the First Parish, but its shorter tower rises in one continuous line to a square wooden belfry topped with a large lantern and spire. An arched window set high above the entrance mirrors the lunette of the First Parish, while the sleek, clean brick facade creates an overall sense of modernity that distinguishes it from its stylistic brother.

St. Dominic's Church, 1888
34 Gray Street
(207) 780-0118
www.maineirish.com
St. Dominic's congregation was founded in

i Greater Portland Landmarks has published several books on Portland's architectural heritage. *Portland,* which details the city's architectural history from 1628 to the present, includes plenty of black-and-white photographs and illustrations of the city's landmarks, including those lost to development. The book is available at the GPL office or online at www.portlandlandmark.org.

1822, and growing attendance led to the construction of the church in 1888. The building is characterized by its colorful, Gothic stained-glass windows. It is a strongly vertical structure with narrow windows and buttresses, graceful moldings, and clean brick. In 1998 the run-down building was closed to parishioners. Today, St. Dominic's houses the Irish Heritage Center.

State and Congress Streets
Cathedral Church of St. Luke, 1869
133 State Street
(207) 772–5434
www.cathedralofstluke.org
St. Luke's is the city's second-oldest cathedral in Portland, after the Cathedral of the Immaculate Conception at 307 Congress Street. It was built in the English Gothic form, with light-blue limestone from Cape Elizabeth. Apostles are depicted in animal form in the church's stained glass. The bell tower was added in 1958 to harmonize with bells at nearby St. Dominic's and State Street Church. Take a peek inside; the church is best known for the painting *American Madonna,* by John LaFarge, which hangs over the altar in St. Luke's Emmanuel Chapel.

Cathedral of the Immaculate Conception, 1869
307 Congress Street
(207) 772–6597
www.portlandcathedral.org
The seat of the archbishop of the Catholic

i The Woodman Block at 133–141 Middle Street is one of the few structures in the city boasting a plaque with the architect's name. The plaque is located at the foot of the building, on the corner of Middle and Pearl Streets.

Diocese of Maine, the cathedral—with the high ceilings of its main hall and an interior embellished with Brescia and Numidian red marble—displays modified French Gothic vocabulary.

First Parish Church, 1826
425 Congress Street
National Historic Landmark
(207) 773–5747
www.firstparishportland.org
The First Parish Church is the oldest house of worship in the city. It is covered extensively in the Insiders' Walking Tour earlier in the chapter.

St. Lawrence Church, 1897
76 Congress Street
(207) 775–5568
www.stlawrencearts.org
Sitting atop Munjoy Hill, St. Lawrence Church is easily the most eclectic former house of worship in Portland. Its chunky, Richardsonian Romanesque facade was designed by Arthur Bates Jennings, complete with Gothic turrets, finials, and a central bell tower. Inside the building, the floor slopes to the pulpit, with pews arranged in a semicircle around it.

Today, part of the church is used as an arts and community center. In 2006, the St. Lawrence board announced plans to destroy the badly decayed sanctuary.

State Street Church, 1851
159 State Street
(207) 774–6396
www.statestreetchurch.org
State Street Church was built in 1851 and designed by William Washburn of Boston. The church today has changed dramatically from its original design, which featured a central wooden spire atop a tower with a nasty habit of being struck by lightning. The spire was removed in 1871, and in 1892 John Calvin Stevens covered the building with the present red freestone facade. The addition of the heavy stone facade stripped State Street Church of much of its original elegance and speaks to the aesthetic sensibilities of the late 19th century.

Old Port/Downtown

Mariner's Church, 1829
366–376 Fore Street
National Historic Landmark
(207) 774–7016
www.oldporttavern.com
The Mariner's Church was constructed in 1829 as a commercial space and a chapel. See the Insiders' Walking Tour for more details.

THE ARTS

Portland is widely regarded as one of the most dynamic arts communities in northern New England. Nationally, the city has been called one of the best small arts towns in the country (if you don't believe us, check out the 1998 book *The 100 Best Small Arts Towns in America,* by John Villani, which ranked Portland fourth). And lately, it seems as though the arts scene in this city just keeps growing. In recent years Portland officials have begun banking on the arts community to add texture to the city's overall image as a working port town.

To highlight the progressive, hip arts culture here, officials created the "Arts District," which stretches somewhat arbitrarily from Longfellow Square along Congress Street to the Old Port. The Arts District marketing ploy did indeed help highlight the local arts scene, although a lot of Portlanders think the notion of an "arts district" is somewhat of a joke simply because the city's arts are hardly limited to the district corridor. In fact, the arts culture here has grown so diverse and has become so widespread—thanks in part to the Maine College of Art, the Portland Museum of Art, and the efforts of local arts activists—that the arts scene has overflowed beyond Portland to the suburban and rural towns nearby.

These days, you'll find not only traditional galleries but also experimental performance spaces (like the appropriately named "Space" gallery on Congress Street) as well as "guerrilla art" graffiti walls around town. But balancing the needs of artists and the demands of a hot real estate market has proven to be challenging—many Portland artists can no longer find an affordable place to live and work on the peninsula. The real estate market has changed significantly since the 1970s and 1980s, when studio space in the Old Port was priced within artists' budgets. Today, real estate on the peninsula is at a premium, and many buildings that had long housed artists are being renovated and sold as condominiums (see the Neighborhoods and Real Estate chapter for more on the market). But everyone in Portland seems to agree that the progressive and quirky character of this city comes in large part from the local arts community. To this end, the Portland city council and arts activist groups like Portland Artist Dwellings and Studios (PADS) are working to secure living/working spaces for artists on the peninsula, with limited success so far. As Portland continues to grow and develop, this struggle to foster resident artists will no doubt continue. It will be up to the city, private developers, and local arts activists to make sure creative types continue to call Portland home.

This chapter lists a number of events, venues, galleries, and resources for the artist and the art lover in all of us. Listings are grouped according to type (galleries and museums, literary arts, film, etc.), and those few that are not in the downtown area are noted clearly in the description. Here, you'll find information on both traditional and experimental arts venues and performers, including theater, music, literary, and mixed-media offerings. You'll no doubt note that the section on galleries is by far the largest. Portland has plenty of galleries for all tastes; in fact, there is such an interest in showing art that establishments which are not traditional galleries (like restaurants and coffee shops) have recently begun showcasing local artwork on their walls.

The museums listed in this chapter are art museums—for cultural museums or historic homes, see the Attractions chapter. We have not included community theaters in this chap-

Summertime Arts

Portland's Parks and Recreation Department sponsors the annual "Summer in the Parks" concert series in July and August. All performances are free and open to the public. For details, call Parks and Recreation at (207) 756–8275.

The Bates Dance Festival at Bates College in Lewiston presents internationally renowned dancers as part of its summer schedule. Contact Bates College at (207) 786–6381 for more information.

ter. To find out about performances from any of the wonderful community theaters in Portland and beyond, including the Lyric Theatre and the Portland Players (both in South Portland), check out the *Portland Press Herald* and its Thursday "Go" entertainment section. If you are interested in music, visit www .mainemusic.org for information on Maine musicians, composers, festivals, upcoming performances, and music education. The University of Southern Maine's School of Music regularly produces theatrical and musical performances. Call the School of Music box office at (207) 780–5555 for details

If you're an artist who wants to connect to the statewide community and explore grant options, contact the Maine Arts Commission (MAC) in Augusta. The commission is funded by the state and the National Endowment for the Arts and is a wonderful resource for Maine's visual and performance artists. MAC awards a number of grants every year for emerging and established artists and works to enhance the public image of the arts in the state. For more information, call (207) 287–2724 or visit the Web site at www.maine arts.com.

For a small city of just more than 60,000 people, Portland's arts scene certainly packs a punch. This chapter will familiarize you with

many of the key players. Nonetheless, as is typical of any arts scene, offerings and venues are in a constant state of flux. Be sure to call ahead or check out local papers like the *Portland Phoenix* (the free arts-and-entertainment weekly) to find out about the latest hot new thing. Our advice is to be bold—arts finds are waiting around every corner in this city, as long as you take the time to look.

MAJOR VENUES

The Cumberland County Civic Center
1 Civic Center Square
(207) 775–3481
(207) 775–3458 (tickets)
www.theciviccenter.com
The Cumberland County Civic Center is hard to miss. This hulking gray-and-brown ice arena and performance space dates back to 1977 and has the boxy design and sharp angles to prove it. The Civic Center is currently the largest concert venue in town (it can hold up to 7,000 screaming fans), although there has been talk lately at the city level to build a larger venue. For the time being, though, this is the favorite indoor venue for big-name rock 'n' roll bands, Disney on Ice, and pretty much any other loud, funky performance that rolls through town. The Civic Center is relatively cozy when compared with arenas in Boston or New York City that can hold three to four times as many people—which means that those $100 tickets to Cher might be worth it since here you can actually make out the famous face without the aid of binoculars. The Civic Center is also the home turf of Portland's minor league hockey team—the Portland Pirates (see the Parks and Recreation chapter for more on these guys).

Merrill Auditorium
20 Myrtle Street
(207) 874–8200
(207) 842–0800 (tickets)
www.portlandevents.com
The Merrill Auditorium at city hall has been a

staple of the Portland arts scene for nearly a century. In 1997 the city completed a multi-million-dollar renovation of this 1,900-seat auditorium, which improved the acoustics and the view of the stage. Merrill Auditorium, or "the Merrill" as it is known to locals, dates back to 1912. It is the home theater for the Portland Symphony Orchestra and also regularly hosts first-rate touring shows, including Broadway productions, opera, and performances from legends like the late Ray Charles and Bruce Hornsby. The Merrill is also the permanent home of the Kotzschmar Memorial Organ, a 5,000-pipe instrument that was donated by publishing tycoon Cyrus Curtis in 1912. The Merrill hosts frequent organ recitals to spotlight the instrument. Tours of the Merrill are available on request.

Friends of the Kotzschmar Organ, Inc., a nonprofit group, is the self-described "caretaker" of the famous instrument located in Merrill Auditorium. The group hosts concerts and tours of the organ. For more information, visit their Web site at www.foko.org.

Portland Performing Arts Center

25A Forest Avenue
(207) 774–1043
(207) 774–0465 (tickets)
www.portlandstage.com

The Portland Performing Arts Center is located in a brick building on a busy downtown throughway lined with restaurants and shops. The main theater here is the home of Portland Stage, the professional theater troupe that owns and operates the arts center. Portland Stage often hosts guest performers from New York City and beyond. The main theater is small (it seats only 290 people), so performances have an acutely intimate atmosphere. The center also contains a studio theater, which is available for short-run performances, one-act plays, or guest artists, as well as troupes unaffiliated with Portland Stage.

Out on the Town

Every insider needs to know where to go to get the skinny on the weekend's best performances. Locals turn to the *Portland Phoenix* and the *Portland Press Herald's* "Go" section. The *Phoenix* tends to be geared more for the funky set, while "Go" has the latest on orchestral and operatic performances as well as touring Broadway shows. Portland is a small city, though, and there is a lot of crossover. The *Phoenix* is free and published every Wednesday. You can pick it up nearly anywhere, but if you're at a loss, try one of the red distribution boxes along Congress Street downtown. The "Go" section comes out on Thursday in the daily *Portland Press Herald*, which is sold in white distribution boxes downtown.

St. Lawrence Arts and Community Center

76 Congress Street
(207) 775–5568
www.stlawrencearts.org

The St. Lawrence Arts and Community Center is located in half of the former St. Lawrence Street Chapel (which dates back to 1854), on the top of Munjoy Hill. The other half of the building is still mired in renovations and fundraising for said renovations. In the meantime, the 110-seat Parish Hall is up and running, and the nonprofit group that owns the space attracts an eclectic lineup of musicians, performance artists, and theater and dance troupes. The St. Lawrence is friend to all things original and funky. In 2004 the *Portland Phoenix* recognized the originality of the performances here and called the "rebirth" of the St. Lawrence Arts and Community Center one of the five most significant state arts events in the last five years.

DANCE

Maine Ballroom Dance
614 Congress Street
(207) 773–0002
www.maineballroomdancing.com
Maine Ballroom Dance focuses on teaching various forms of ballroom dance but does occasionally perform for festivals and small functions. For more on Maine Ballroom and lessons, see the sidebar below. Visit their Web site for information on upcoming performances, classes, and open dances.

Maine State Ballet
348 Route 1, Falmouth
(207) 781–7672
www.mainestateballet.org
The Maine State Ballet (MSB) was incorporated in 1982 by artistic director Linda MacArthur Miele, a former member of George Balanchine's famous New York City Ballet. The company includes 36 professional dancers who are often joined in performances by students from the Maine State School for the Performing Arts—the ballet school affiliated with MSB. Past MSB performances have included *Cinderella, Don Quixote,* and, of course, *The Nutcracker.*

New Dance Studio
61 Pleasant Street
(207) 780–0554
www.newdancestudio.com
The New Dance Studio features dance performances year-round by local and professional choreographers. The troupe often performs at the Portland Performing Arts Center in downtown Portland. New Dance also runs the Center for Dance Development, which offers a two-week residency to emerging choreographers from Maine and beyond. New Dance is a relatively new troupe, but the group is quickly making a name for itself for producing quality, contemporary dance performances. It's worth keeping your eyes peeled for New Dance performance announcements in the local papers.

Ballroom Dancing

Dancing in all its forms is popular in this city, whether it be impromptu bouncing to the beat of a street musician in Tommy's Park or swirling around in a series of planned moves with an experienced partner. For those of you interested in the latter, Portland has three respected ballroom dance schools—Maine Ballroom Dance, the Maplewood Dance Center, and the American Ballroom Dance Academy. Maine Ballroom Dance, located near the art museum downtown at 614 Congress Street, is an area favorite in part because of its enormous picture windows, which give even the most disinterested passerby a great view of the tango, salsa, or swing. Maine Ballroom Dance teaches both American and international styles in group or private classes and sponsors dance events for both the clumsy and the smooth. Call (207) 773–0002 or visit www.maineballroomdancing.com for information.

If you're looking for love, the Maplewood Dance Center at 383 Warren Avenue hosts regular dances for singles. Call (207) 878–0584 or visit www.maplewood
dancecenter.com for more information.

The American Ballroom Dance Academy at 62 Forest Avenue offers private and group lessons in Latin, swing, and ballroom, and holds weekly dance parties. Call (207) 879–5761 for information.

i Movies on Exchange is the city's only cinema devoted exclusively to independent and foreign films. It's located at 10 Exchange Street. For more information about this tiny theater, visit www.moviesonexchange.com or call the box office at (207) 772–8041. A recorded movie schedule can be heard at (207) 772–9600.

Portland Ballet Company
517 Forest Avenue, Suite 2
(207) 772–9671
www.portlandballet.org

The Portland Ballet Company was founded in 1985. This small, classically oriented company is directed by Eugenia L. O'Brien and has performed full-length classic ballet pieces as well as modern works. It was the first ballet company to premiere in Portland and the first to work with internationally acclaimed dancers. The annual *Victorian Nutcracker,* which sets the famous ballet on a stage modeled after Portland's Victoria Mansion (see the Attractions chapter), is the performance for which the company is perhaps best known. Portland Ballet also hosts a dance school for children and adults.

FILM

Human Rights Watch International Film Festival
Space Alternative Arts Venue
538 Congress Street
(207) 828–5600
www.space538.org

The Human Rights Watch International Film Festival is a traveling event sponsored by the nonprofit organization Human Rights Watch. The festival touches down in Maine at the Space Gallery in downtown Portland thanks to sponsorship from local businesses. The festival takes place each fall and includes several short and feature-length documentaries related to human rights issues worldwide. In 2004 the film that would go on to win the Academy Award for Best Documentary that year, *Born into Brothels,* premiered in Maine at the Human Rights Watch International Film Festival. Tickets are $5.00 per screening for adults and $4.00 for students and seniors.

Maine International Film Festival
177 Main Street, Waterville
(207) 861–8138
www.miff.org

Although Waterville is a solid two-hour drive north, plenty of Portland's filmmakers and film lovers make the trek every year to enjoy one of the state's finest film festivals. The Maine International Film Festival (MIFF) was founded in 1998 by the nonprofit group Friends of Art and Film in Central Maine. Every July the festival screens more than 80 domestic and international films in 10 days at two locations in Waterville, and many of the screenings are accompanied by discussions with directors, actors, writers, musicians, and producers. MIFF also bestows its Mid-Life Achievement Award (past winners have included Peter Fonda and Sissy Spacek) and honors Maine student filmmakers with the Maine Student Film and Video Festival, a one-day event during the MIFF festivities. A full-festival pass costs $150, a partial-festival pass costs $75, and individual admission to most screenings costs $8.00.

Maine Jewish Film Festival
10 Exchange Street (Movies on Exchange)
(207) 831–7495
www.mjff.org

The Maine Jewish Film Festival runs in the spring and features some two dozen short and feature-length films by Jewish filmmakers and/or about Jewish culture. The films are screened at venues in downtown Portland (historically, the Portland Museum of Art, the Movies on Exchange, and Nickelodeon Cinemas), and tickets are available by the show or for the entire festival. Opening and closing galas mark the weeklong event. Tickets for individual screenings cost $7.00 for adults, $5.00 for students under 18 and seniors over 65.

GALLERIES AND MUSEUMS

Abacus Fine American Crafts
44 Exchange Street
(207) 772–4880
www.abacusgallery.com
Abacus's colorful Portland gallery has caught the eye of shoppers on Exchange Street for almost 30 years. This gallery and retail store features eclectic artwork, jewelry, furniture, and crafts from American artists. Much of the artwork is whimsical and colorful—past pieces have included children's furniture hand-carved with inspirational quotes—and a visit to Abacus can bring out the kid in everyone. Abacus is open Monday through Saturday from 10:00 A.M. to 9:00 P.M. from mid-June through the end of August. During the winter the gallery is open Monday through Thursday from 10:00 A.M. to 6:00 P.M. and Friday and Saturday from 10:00 A.M. to 9:00 P.M.

The Clown
123 Middle Street
(207) 756–7399
www.the-clown.com
The Clown is an eclectic retail store and gallery with a world-class wine cellar, an antiques shop, and a selection of contemporary art. The gallery features a new artist every month; visit the Web site for details. The Clown is open Monday through Wednesday from 10:00 A.M. to 6:00 P.M. and Thursday through Saturday from 10:00 A.M. to 7:00 P.M. For more information see the Shopping chapter.

Due Gallery
81 Market Street
(207) 879–1869, (207) 773–7730
www.duegallery.com
Due Gallery is named after the Italian word *due* (meaning "two") for the pair of painters who own and operate the business. The gallery always includes work by these artists, Stephen Lanzalotta and Ian Factor, and also showcases other painters. Many of the paintings here are bold and bright, ranging from the abstract to the realistic. Due also hosts artist talks, spoken-word events, and other happenings. Due shares space with Sophia's Bakery, a popular Italian lunch and Sunday brunch spot that is run by Lanzalotta. The gallery is open Tuesday through Friday from 9:00 A.M. to 4:00 P.M. and Saturday and Sunday from noon to 5:00 P.M.

Earth and Soul Gallery
34 Washington Avenue
(207) 775–1089
www.earthandsoulpottery.com
Earth and Soul Gallery features pottery from owner Sarah Sorenson-Coppi and indigenous artwork from local and international artists, with special emphasis on artists from Africa and Colombia. All objects from indigenous artists are fairly traded. The gallery is open Tuesday through Saturday from 10:00 A.M. to 1:00 P.M. and from 3:00 to 7:00 P.M. and Sunday from noon to 5:00 P.M.

Fore Street Gallery
372 Fore Street
(207) 874–8084, (877) 874–8084
www.forestreetgallery.com
The Fore Street Gallery opened in 1998 and features framed artwork by 20 artists as well as matted originals, prints, and photographs. Artwork here depicts Maine's landscape, coast, and surf and ranges from lighthouse scenes to depictions of ocean kayaking. The gallery is open Monday through Saturday from 10:00 A.M. to 6:00 P.M. and Sunday from noon to 6:00 P.M.

Greenhut Galleries
146 Middle Street
(207) 772–2693, (888) 772–2693
www.greenhutgalleries.com
Native New Yorker Peggy Greenhut Golden opened Greenhut Galleries in 1977, years before the Old Port enjoyed the arts renaissance that it is now known for. Golden continues to spearhead this local gallery giant, which is the oldest year-round gallery in the city. Greenhut represents more than 20 artists and artists' estates, and the gallery hosts

monthly exhibits and receptions for featured artists. The paintings and sculpture featured here range from the realistic to the abstract. The gallery is open Monday through Friday from 10:00 A.M. to 5:30 P.M. and Saturday from 10:00 A.M. to 5:00 P.M.

Institute for Contemporary Art at the Maine College of Art
522 Congress Street
(207) 879–5742 (recorded information; press 3 for the ICA)
www.meca.edu

The Institute for Contemporary Art is a gallery and educational resource for contemporary art. The ICA, as it is known here, is run by the Maine College of Art, a private art school situated in the heart of Portland's Arts District. The ICA galleries are located in the former Porteous retail building on Congress Street; exhibitions showcase emerging contemporary artists and new trends in the contemporary art domain. The ICA also hosts educational programs that are open to the public, including artists' talks, forums on current topics in the art world, and arts workshops for youth. Admission to the ICA is free. The ICA is open Wednesday, Friday, Saturday, and Sunday from 11:00 A.M. to 5:00 P.M. and Thursday from 11:00 A.M. to 7:00 P.M. On the first Friday of every month, the closing time is pushed forward to 8:00 P.M. to allow for the First Friday Artwalk.

Jameson Gallery
305 Commercial Street
(207) 772–5522
www.jamesongallery.com

Realism is the focus at Jameson Gallery, and many of the artists represented here are from Maine. Established in 1992, the gallery also includes a frame shop and the adjacent Jameson Estate Collection, LLC, which features artwork from American artists of the 19th and 20th centuries. The gallery is open Monday through Saturday from 10:00 A.M. to 6:00 P.M. and by appointment.

June Fitzpatrick Gallery
112 High Street
(207) 772–1961

522 Congress Street
(207) 879–5742, ext. 283
www.junefitzpatrickgallery.com

Since opening in 1992, the June Fitzpatrick Gallery has developed a reputation as one of the finest galleries for contemporary art north of Boston. The gallery features both established artists and select newcomers. In 2001 the Congress Street location at the Maine College of Art (MECA) opened to supplement the original spot on High Street. The High Street location now features only framed and unframed works on paper, while the MECA location features works in other media. Exhibits change monthly. The galleries are open Tuesday through Saturday from noon to 5:00 P.M. and by appointment.

Art Party

If you love visiting galleries, don't miss the First Friday Artwalk on the first Friday of every month from 5:00 to 8:00 P.M. Dozens of Portland Galleries from the very smallest to the very biggest stay open late on this night so that art lovers can wander around, meet the artists showing, and snack on wine and cheese. The Portland Museum of Art, in the spirit of the night, offers free admission and a small band of young artists showcase themed one-night-only art shows in a rented truck that migrates around the downtown. You can pick up a listing of the week's participating galleries in stores up and down Congress Street or visit www.firstfridayart walk.com for details.

ℹ️ The Maine College of Art in Portland offers an assortment of short-term art workshops through their Continuing Studies Department. Visit www.meca.edu or call (800) 639–4808 for more information.

Museum of African Culture
122 Spring Street, #1
(207) 871–7188
www.tribalartmuseum.com

The Museum of African Culture (MAC), formerly the Museum of African Tribal Art, is a nonprofit organization founded in 1998. The museum features a collection of more than 1,500 pieces of sub-Saharan African tribal art, including masks, bronze figurines, and tools. The museum also sponsors educational outreach programs. MAC is open Tuesday through Friday from 10:30 A.M. to 4:00 P.M., Saturday from 12:30 to 4:00 P.M., and by appointment. A donation of $5.00 for admission is encouraged. For more information, see the Attractions chapter.

Portland Fiber Gallery and Weaving Studio
229 Congress Street
(207) 780–1345
www.portlandfibergallery.com

The Portland Fiber Gallery and Weaving Studio is a member of the Maine Crafts Association and the Maine Fiber Arts Organization and represents 25 local and regional weavers. The gallery showcases fine fiber arts, including clothing and accessories, and also offers a handful of fiber-related arts classes. Portland Fiber is open Tuesday through Saturday from noon to 5:00 P.M.

Portland Museum of Art
7 Congress Square
(207) 775–6148
www.portlandmuseum.org

The Portland Museum of Art is the city's principal art museum and features a large collection of fine and decorative arts from the 18th century to the present. Works by Maine greats like Winslow Homer and Andrew Wyeth are permanent parts of the museum's collection. The museum also features a rotating collection of American and European modern and classical artwork, which in the past has included everything from experimental lithographs to Rodin sculptures. A cafe and a gift shop round out the offerings. Admission is $8.00 for adults, $6.00 for seniors and students, and $2.00 for youth ages 6 to 17. Hours are Tuesday, Wednesday, Thursday, Saturday, and Sunday from 10:00 A.M. to 5:00 P.M. and Friday from 10:00 A.M. to 9:00 P.M. There is free admission from 5:00 to 9:00 P.M. on Friday. From Memorial Day to Columbus Day, the museum is also open on Monday from 10:00 A.M. to 5:00 P.M. The museum is closed on Thanksgiving, Christmas, and New Year's Day.

Radiant Light Gallery
615 Congress Street, Suite 409
(207) 252–7258
www.radiantlightgallery.com

Radiant Light focuses on contemporary and vintage photography, including the male and female nude, portraiture, and documentary imagery. The gallery represents world-class photographers; past shows have included work from industry luminaries such as Annie Liebowitz, Thom Adams, and Jock Sturges. The gallery is open on Saturday from noon to 6:30 P.M., during the First Friday Artwalk from 6:00 to 8:30 P.M., and by appointment. The gallery hours change during July and August; during these months, Radiant Light is open Thursday through Saturday from noon to 7:00 P.M. and for First Friday Artwalks until 8:00 P.M.

Running with Scissors
34 Portland Street
(207) 780–6252
www.runningwithscissorsartists.com

This working artists' collaborative and gallery was the brainchild of three Maine College of Art graduates who wanted to maintain the artistic exchange they enjoyed at MECA after graduation. Running with Scissors opened in 2002 and features a dozen or so artists who rent studio space and exhibit here. Because of the gallery's collaborative nature, artwork runs the gamut from painting to sculpture to welding. Some of the artists have no formal training. Gallery hours vary depending on the artist showing, so call or visit the Web site before you drop by.

Spindleworks
7–9 Lincoln Street, Brunswick
(207) 725–8820
www.spindleworks.org
Spindleworks is a nonprofit collaborative serving adult artists with physical and mental disabilities. More than 35 artists work at the studios in Brunswick (about a half-hour drive north of Portland) in a variety of media, including painting, sculpture, poetry, performing arts, and, of course, weaving. The artists receive 75 percent of the selling price of their work; the remainder goes to Spindleworks to help purchase supplies. The gallery is open Monday through Friday from 8:00 A.M. to 4:30 P.M.

Whitney Art Works
45 York Street
(207) 780-0700, (207) 615–ARTS
www.whitneyartworks.com
Whitney Art Works, which was originally located on Long Island, New York, moved to Portland in 2003. The Art Works can be found in the Old Port, on a street lined with former warehouses that have been transformed into office buildings. Whitney showcases contemporary artists in a variety of media, including photography, printmaking, and sculpture. The space is home to a gallery with a rotating series of featured artists and hosts the occasional event or performance. Whitney Art Works also provides a range of arts services, like packaging and shipping, and acts as a liaison with major American customs brokers for international shipments. Whitney Art Works is the official shipper and installer of the annual "Arts in the Capitol" show in Augusta, which is sponsored by the Maine Arts Commission. For rates or to make an appointment for services, call the Art Works at the number above.

The gallery is open Wednesday through Saturday from noon to 5:00 P.M.

Zero Station
222 Anderson Street
(207) 347–7000
www.zerostation.com
Zero Station owner Keith Fitzgerald opened this contemporary art gallery in 2003 to showcase what he calls "thin art"—work like drawing, photography, printmaking, and digital media. The front gallery features changing exhibitions, while the back gallery is home to a file portfolio featuring works of Zero's stable of innovative artists. In keeping with the progressive theme, Zero's snazzy Web site features digital renditions of works in the gallery's portfolio. Zero Station is open Tuesday through Saturday from 10:00 A.M. to 6:00 P.M.

LITERARY ARTS
The Brown Bag Lecture Series
Portland Public Library
5 Monument Square
(207) 871–1700
www.portlandlibrary.com
The Brown Bag Lecture Series features bestselling authors from Maine and beyond in an intimate setting during lunch hour. Programs run from noon to 1:00 P.M. in the Rines Auditorium at the bottom floor of the library and include free coffee and snacks, a reading from the author, and, usually, a question-and-answer period. Past readers have included Tobias Wolfe and Stephen King. All readings are free.

Maine Writers and Publishers Alliance
318 Glickman Family Library at University of Southern Maine
(207) 228–8263
www.mainewriters.org

i The Maine Arts Commission awards several Good Idea Grants (GIGs) every year to artists working in a variety of media. For more information, call the MAC at (207) 287–2724.

The Maine Writers and Publishers Alliance (MWPA) counts both beginning and established writers among its almost 1,000 members. The group was founded in 1975 to connect the state's writers, poets, and small-press publishers. After some internal friction in 2004, in which the former executive director resigned and the group considered disbanding, MWPA is now back on track with new programs and a renewed sense of purpose. MWPA sponsors regular readings, workshops, and competitions and recently launched a mentoring program in which writers can pay a base fee to have a manuscript critiqued by one of the alliance's established writers. In December 2005 MWPA moved from its Bath offices to room 318 at the Glickman Library in Portland (Glickman is the University of Southern Maine's library on Forest Avenue). Visit the new offices and sign up to be a part of MWPA. Membership costs $35 per year and includes a subscription to the alliance's newsletter and discounts on workshops and books.

MUSIC

Portland Conservatory of Music
116 Free Street
(207) 775–3356
www.portlandconservatory.net
The Portland Conservatory of Music was founded in 1995 to provide music instruction to people of all ages and at all levels of ability. The conservatory currently works with more than 400 students in the state and employs more than 40 musicians to teach. Along with its continuing schedule of individual and ensemble teaching, the conservatory regularly sponsors events and concerts, including its annual International Piano and Chamber Music Festival each summer.

Portland Opera Repertory Theatre
P.O. Box 7733
Portland, ME 04112
(207) 879–7678
www.portopera.org
The Portland Repertory Theatre (PORT) was

i Like a little music with your lunch? Check out the Portland Conservatory of Music's "Noonday Concerts," held from October to April at the First Parish Church on Congress Street. All performances begin at 12:15 P.M. and are free. Call the conservatory for a schedule.

founded in 1994 and is a small, part-time company with only one show a year in the summer. Organizers hope to expand PORT as it moves forward, eventually offering two or three shows a year at Merrill Auditorium. Despite its small size, PORT has made a name for itself both locally and nationally as a great place for young, talented singers to get their start. The company's Emerging Artists program fosters homegrown talent by casting a full-length opera with Maine singers and taking the show on the road throughout the state.

Portland Symphony Orchestra
477 Congress Street
(207) 773–6128
www.portlandsymphony.com
The Portland Symphony Orchestra (PSO) was established in 1923 and is the premier orchestra of the city of Portland. Many of the PSO musicians are solo performers and music teachers. The 85 musicians perform a series of classical and pop programs from September through June, a special Independence Pops picnic concert to celebrate July 4, and a Magic of Christmas performance in December. The symphony also runs two ongoing series—Classical Tuesdays and Classical Sundays—in which the PSO performs pieces by great composers like Bach, Beethoven, and Tchaikovsky. Sunday is family day at the symphony and features the PSO Music Camp—activities to help children nine and older understand the performance—prior to each show. The PSO performs in Merrill Auditorium. In spring 2006 longtime PSO music director and conductor Toshiyuki Shimada retired; whoever replaces him will have big shoes to fill indeed.

THEATER

Acorn Productions
P.O. Box 44
Portland, ME 04112
(207) 766–3386
www.acorn-productions.org

Acorn Productions is a nonprofit, professional theater troupe featuring local talent. Acorn was founded in 1995 and has a reputation for not shying away from heady plays and works by established playwrights—during its 10-year history, the troupe has performed works by Sam Shepard, David Mamet, and Anton Chekhov, to name just a few. Acorn also sponsors the annual Phyzgig Festival of physical comedy in December, works with local playwrights and performers on the Maine Short Play Festival in March and April, and organizes the Cassandra Project festival of female performers in June. As if this weren't enough, Acorn actors offer acting lessons as well. Acorn's home theater is the Parish Hall in the St. Lawrence Arts Center on Munjoy Hill.

A Company of Girls
East End Children's Workshop
215 Congress Street
(207) 874–2107

A Company of Girls has encouraged girls to explore their theatrical flair for the past decade. Founded in 1996, this nonprofit after-school program presents traditional and original plays with a cast made up completely of girls ages 8 to 18. Plays that are traditionally staged with male actors are tweaked to allow the girls to take over (take, for example, the company's recent performance of *Lord of the Flies*, in which the traditionally all-male cast was played entirely by girls). In the audience, of course, both genders are welcome. Tickets are usually $5.00 for children and $10.00 for adults, although prices vary by performance.

The Good Theater Company
P.O. Box 347
Portland, ME 04112
(207) 885–5883
www.goodtheater.com

The Good Theater Company was founded in 2001 by actor Stephen Underwood and director Brian Allen. This professional, nonprofit theater troupe performs, well, "good" plays and musicals, many of which have won Tony Awards or have become hits on Broadway. Recent plays staged by Good Theater include *Master Class,* by Terrance McNally; *Barrymore,* by William Luce; and *California Suite,* by Neil Simon. Tickets range in price from $10 for seniors and students to $18 full price. Good Theater performs at the St. Lawrence Center for the Arts on Munjoy Hill.

Lucid Stage Productions
Bakery Studios, 61 Pleasant Street
(207) 773–4601

Lucid Stage Productions, one of the city's newest theater troupes, has already made a name for itself by staging traditional works like Shakespeare's Macbeth with a funky twist (like casting a woman to play Macbeth). Founder Adam Gutgsell was formerly an actor with the Children's Theatre of Maine before launching the troupe. Lucid might be a bit hard to track down between performances (the address above is not their permanent home but rather one of their performance spaces), so your best bet is to check out listings in the local newspapers for upcoming shows.

Mad Horse Theatre Company
Portland Performing Arts Center
25A Forest Avenue
(207) 730–2389
www.madhorse.com

Mad Horse is a professional theater ensemble that has made a local name for itself for producing hard-hitting, often gritty depictions of the struggles of the human spirit. According to the group's Web site, Mad Horse performances focus on "areas of social concern, personal transformation, and the building of lasting community relationships." To put it simply, drama Mad Horse–style packs a punch. Mad Horse usually performs at the Portland Performing Arts Center.

Maine State Music Theatre

22 Elm Street, Brunswick
(207) 725–8760
(207) 725–8769 (tickets)
www.msmt.org

The Maine State Music Theatre (MSMT) is a nonprofit, professional theater troupe that presents classic American musicals for all ages. MSMT was founded in 1959 and is the only resident, professional music theater in the country. It is based in Brunswick, north of Portland. Many of the actors, directors, and designers are professional artists who work year-round in theater. MSMT puts on several musicals a year at their theater in Brunswick and also teaches young theater students how to stage professional plays.

Portland Stage Company

25A Forest Avenue
(207) 774–1043
(207) 774–0465 (tickets)
www.portlandstage.com

The nonprofit Portland Stage Company (PSC) was founded in 1974 and is northern New England's largest professional member of the League of Resident Theaters, a national trade organization. Portland Stage presents a wide range of plays year-round, many featuring talent from New York City, Boston, and other large cities. PSC's home stage at the Portland Center for the Performing Arts on Forest Avenue has hosted both world-premiere works and theater classics, including works by Tennessee Williams, William Shakespeare, and Molière. PSC also produces two festivals: the Little Festival of the Unexpected, which showcases new plays and young writers; and From Away, in which international writers come to Portland to present their work and share ideas. PSC's annual performance of Charles Dickens's *A Christmas Carol* has become a favorite holiday event in Portland. Every year PSC recruits the best local and from-away talent to give new life to this timeless story. PSC also frequently presents lectures and discussions with actors, directors, and writers before or after the performance about the methods behind theatrical production.

The Stage

P.O. Box 5183
Portland, ME 04101
(207) 828–0128
www.thestagemaine.org

The Stage is a nonprofit theater troupe that performs free outdoor theater in the summer at Spring Point Park in South Portland. It is sponsored in part by Southern Maine Community College (which owns the campus at Spring Point) and the city of South Portland. The Stage presents classic drama, including works by Shakespeare. The Stage also sponsors the Young Actors Institute, a three-week intensive program that trains 10 selected students in the methods of theater and the real-world challenges of a career as an artist.

The Theater Project

14 School Street, Brunswick
(207) 729–8584
www.theaterproject.com

The Theater Project was founded in 1971 in Brunswick, a town about a half-hour drive north of Portland. Over the past 30 years, the nonprofit Theater Project has grown to include a professional ensemble company, a children's theater troupe, and touring productions. Along with the year-round series of stage plays (many of which are family-oriented), the Theater Project also sponsors acting classes for all ages and community festivals. In keeping with the Theater Project's nonprofit roots, all shows are pay-what-you-can, with suggested ticket prices ranging from $6.00 to $15.00.

ARTISTIC AND LITERARY SUPPORT GROUPS

Bluegrass Music Association of Maine

P.O. Box 154
Troy, ME 04987
(207) 948–5819
www.bmam.org

The Bluegrass Music Association of Maine provides information about festivals, local bands and bluegrass enthusiasts, and "pickin' parties," where you can jam with other bluegrass musicians. Membership in the group is

Statues

Portland has a variety of public artworks on display, but three statues in particular have interesting stories behind them.

John Ford
Gorham's Corner, junction of Center, Danforth, and Pleasant Streets

John Ford won six Academy Awards, was the recipient of the first American Film Institute Lifetime Achievement Award, and is considered by many film critics to be America's greatest director. But few people know he was born and raised right here in Portland. Born John Martin Feeney in Cape Elizabeth in 1895, Ford grew up in a third-floor apartment on Sheridan Street in Portland's Munjoy Hill neighborhood. His father ran a pub called Feeney's at Gorham's Corner, which at the time was a neighborhood of Irish immigrants. In 1913 Ford played fullback on Portland High School's state champion football team and became known by the moniker "Bull Feeney." Bull Feeney's, a pub in the Old Port, is named in his honor. When Ford turned 14, he followed his brother Francis out to Hollywood. His brother, an actor, was calling himself Ford, and so John decided to take on that name as well. He appeared as an extra in D. W. Griffith's Birth of a Nation but by 1917 was working solely as a director. The rest is film history. John Ford went on to direct such classic films as *The Quiet Man, The Grapes of Wrath, How Green Was My Valley, Stagecoach,* and *The Man Who Shot Liberty Valance.*

The 10-foot-tall statue of Ford at Gorham's Corner was created by New York sculptor George Kelly for Linda Noe Laine, a philanthropist and old friend of Ford's who made a gift of the statue to Portland. This bronze depiction of the director shows him seated in his director's chair. Six granite tablets describing each of his Oscar-winning movies are spread in a semicircle at his feet. The unveiling in July 1998 was accompanied by the first-ever weeklong celebration of Ford's life, career, and connection to the city. There was a John Ford Film Festival and a Saturday-evening gala attended by actors who had appeared in his films. Speakers included Harry Carey Jr., who was the star of many of Ford's westerns; Claude Jarman Jr., star of *Rio Grande;* and Patrick Wayne, the son of the late John Wayne. Billy Yellow, a stunt rider in many Ford westerns, chanted a prayer in Navajo, and a local choir sang songs from Ford's films.

Ford died in 1973 at age 79. Throughout his long career he never forgot his roots. In the 1945 film *They Were Expendable,* he named a ship after Lucien Libby, his former English teacher at Portland High School. The director surely would be pleased that his hometown has not forgotten him, either.

Henry Wadsworth Longfellow
Longfellow Square, junction of Congress, State, and Pine Streets

This stately representation of Portland's most famous son was designed by Franklin Simmons, a neoclassical sculptor who is also responsible for the Soldiers and Sailors Monument (1891) in Portland's Monument Square. Simmons was born poor, outside of Lewiston, but lived much of his life in Italy. He became famous for his portraits of Civil War–era generals before creating this seated likeness of Longfellow looking contemplative. The bronzed poet has a scroll under his left arm, and three books are stacked underneath his chair. The statue was erected in 1888, and ever since it has held a soft spot in Portlanders' hearts. At the end of World War II in 1945, impromptu celebrations in Portland's streets included residents hopping into Longfellow's lap. In the early 1990s local schoolchildren collected $300 in pennies to help clean and restore the statue. And just as another poet, Edgar Allan Poe, is celebrated every year on his birthday with cognac and roses, so too is Longfellow honored each year, at Christmastime. The statue is decked out with a bright-red winter scarf wound around his neck and shoulders, and brightly wrapped gifts mysteriously appear at his feet.

The Maine Lobsterman
Canal Plaza, corner of Temple and Middle Streets

The Maine Lobsterman is a kind of cultural touchstone for this state, a representation of the quintessential Mainer who makes his living from the sea. The statue depicts a Maine lobsterman kneeling in his boots, pegging a lobster's claw. "Pegging" means jamming a small wooden plug into the joint of the lobster's claw so it can't harm other lobsters—or you! (Today, rubber bands around the claws serve the same purpose.) The model for the statue was H. Elroy Johnson, a Bailey Island lobsterman who was born in 1894 and began fishing when he was 10. At age 71 he was still making his own old-fashioned wooden lobster traps and still going out to sea, hauling 400 traps himself. The lobster in the statue was modeled after a real lobster.

The statue was originally sculpted in plaster for the 1939 World's Fair in New York. The artist, Victor Kahill, was a native of Beirut and followed his brother Joseph, a portrait artist, to Maine when he was just 14

The Maine Lobsterman. MEREDITH GOAD

(continued)

years old. He soon decided to follow in his brother's footsteps. Just four years after Victor Kahill arrived here, he was getting major commissions in the United States. He studied and taught at the Fine Arts Academy in Philadelphia and at the Boston Museum of Fine Art. When World War I broke out, Kahill enlisted and then stayed to study in Europe after the war was over. Ultimately, he returned to Maine, and when the 1939 World's Fair rolled around and people were clamoring for something special to be sent to the Maine Pavilion, a Portland attorney commissioned Kahill to make the lobsterman statue.

There was never enough money to have the statue cast in bronze, so Kahill painted it a bronze color and sent it to the World's Fair as hard plaster. After the fair it was stored in the Columbia Hotel, then in Portland's city hall. Vandals continually picked the statue apart, breaking off hands and feet and making away with parts of the lobster. By this time, World War II had broken out, and Kahill had left Portland for North Africa, where he rubbed elbows with Winston Churchill in Casablanca. Kahill's brother Joseph tried several times to fix the statue, but it always ended up damaged again. Finally, he gave up and said he wouldn't touch it again unless it were moved to a safer place. Eventually, it ended up in a warehouse in Boothbay, where it was almost forgotten. Interest in the statue bubbled up again in September 1973, after the death of Elroy Johnson. The legislature finally approved a bronze casting, and it was unveiled at the Maine State Museum in Augusta in 1975.

Ultimately, three castings were made. In 1983 a group of Campfire Girls raised enough money to have the Augusta statue placed on Maine Avenue in Washington, D.C. Another casting went to Portland's Canal Plaza in 1977. And residents of Bailey Island, Elroy Johnson's home, raised money for a third casting, which now serves as a fisherman's memorial at Land's End.

And what became of Victor Kahill? After serving in the army and running a nightclub in France, he and his wife returned to Casablanca in 1947. There he opened a well-known nightclub called the Red Fez. Kahill returned to the United States in 1965 and died in San Francisco that year at the age of 70.

The Maine Lobsterman statue is 8.5 feet tall and weighs more than 800 pounds. Today, it's clear that he was meant to be outside, interacting with people, not locked up in a warehouse somewhere. If you walk by on any given day, you're likely to find flowers and other little offerings laid at his feet. Once, on a rainy day, someone gave him an umbrella. He's also been seen with a wool fisherman's cap on his head. And, of course, people love to have their photo taken with him. Somewhere, Victor Kahill must be smiling.

$10 for individuals, $15 for a couple. Down-home fun is included free of charge.

Maine Crafts Association
P.O. Box 8817
Portland, ME 04104
(207) 780–1807
www.mainecrafts.org
The Maine Crafts Association (MCA) has promoted the art of crafting since 1983 with contemporary craft exhibitions, educational programs, artistic and business mentoring, and a bimonthly newsletter. MCA also publishes a listing of all registered Maine crafters in its annual *Maine Guide to Craft Artists and Culture*. Annual membership costs $50, $40 for students and seniors.

Maine Film and Video Association
P.O. Box 2225
South Portland 04116-2225.]
www.mainefilm.com
The Maine Film and Video Association has more than 100 members who are involved in the state's film industry on either a full- or part-time basis. The association serves as a networking hub for film professionals; it sponsors workshops, holds regular meetings, and informs members of industry events. The association's Web site lists the names of members and information about each member's specialty. Membership is $45 per year, $25 for students.

Maine Writers and Publishers Alliance
318 Glickman Family Library at University of Southern Maine
(207) 228–8263
www.mainewriters.org
The Maine Writers and Publishers Alliance is an association connecting writers, readers, and publishers in the state. See the "Literary Arts" section of this chapter for more extensive information.

Portland Media Artists
(no address)
www.portlandmediaartists.com
Organized by local photographer Franklin McMahon, this is an informal group comprised of area artists, including writers, filmmakers, photographers, and actors. The purpose of the group is to promote collaboration among members. The group meets twice a month at JavaNet Café at 37 Exchange Street in downtown Portland. For more information, visit their Web site.

FESTIVALS AND ANNUAL EVENTS

There are few things Portland residents like better than a good festival, and who can blame us? Festivals and annual events are an opportunity to meet new people, check out new things, and catch up with old friends in a city small enough to offer up familiar faces at practically every gathering. Year-round, you'll find events to pique your interest, whether your tastes lean toward home renovation, sports, traditional national holidays, or just a good old-fashioned block party. This chapter focuses on some of the best and biggest festivals in Greater Portland, including June's Old Port Festival, July's Yarmouth Clam Festival, and January's Winterfest, as well as popular events within an hour's drive of the city.

As any local will tell you, Portland's social scene really picks up in the summer. You'll notice in this chapter that many of the area's largest festivals fall in the months of June, July, and August. This list is by no means exhaustive. If you sniff around, you can find some kind of event to attend nearly every week here. The local newspapers are a good resource—you'll find information on some of the area's smaller happenings, including dozens of church fairs and activities sponsored by the city and area merchants and organizations.

Unless noted, events are free of charge. Where entry fees are charged, we have noted the current price. Still, ticket prices are subject to change, so it's best to double-check before you go. And make sure to bring enough money for snacks at the event. Since this is Portland, most events offer great seafood, homemade sweets, and ethnic cuisine that you won't want to pass up.

Also, the dates and times of events listed may change from year to year. For events that run longer than one month, we have listed the event in the month in which it traditionally begins. Some annual fund-raisers and arts festivals occur in different venues from one year to the next. For these events, we have listed the address of the sponsor. Be sure to call ahead or check local listings to confirm that your intended event has not migrated to other pastures.

And finally, in this chapter we have replaced geographic organization with month-by-month chronology. This way you can mark your calendar and make sure to hit the events that most excite you. Have fun!

FEBRUARY

The Maine Home, Remodeling, and Garden Show
Cumberland County Civic Center
(866) 295–6438
www.dicksonandmcgonigle.com/maine show.cfm
The Maine Home, Remodeling, and Garden Show celebrated its 15th anniversary in 2005. The sprawling show occupies the Cumberland County Civic Center in downtown Portland for two days around February 11. Here, you'll find examples of the latest in home remodeling techniques and appliances, how-to segments from experts, a new cooking series with regional chefs, and booths from more than 150 exhibitors. Admission is $6.00 for adults, $5.00 for seniors. Children under 10 years of age get in free.

Homelessness Marathon
Monument Square
www.homelessnessmarathon.org
Each year, several nonprofit groups in Portland participate in the national 24-hour Homelessness Marathon, a radio and community event that originated in New York state in

Since 1976 mysterious red hearts printed on simple white pieces of paper have appeared on storefronts throughout the city on Valentine's Day. The culprit is the famed (and anonymous) "Valentine's Phantom," whose largest heart is usually draped over the front of the Portland Museum of Art.

1998. Here in Portland, local community radio WMPG 90.9/104.1 FM (see the Media chapter for more information) joins with prominent nonprofits like the Preble Street Resource Center, area shelters, and concerned citizens and activists to broadcast a local marathon on homelessness from a "homeless awareness village" in Monument Square, where dozens of Portlanders spend the night in tents to call attention to the problem of homelessness. WMPG broadcasts local and national marathon reports all day. Tune in to WMPG or swing by the square to join or chat with activists. Usually held in mid-February, exact dates of the marathon change yearly, so visit the Web site for information.

Maine Winterfest
Falmouth and Freeport
(207) 772–2811
www.mainewinterfest.com
The Maine Winterfest, held the last week in February, has celebrated the state's infamous chilly season since 2000. In honor of what many locals consider the most formidable of seasons, the Falmouth/Cumberland Community Chamber of Commerce, the Freeport Merchants Marketing Association, and the Portland Regional Chamber sponsor events at the Winterfest, including a luge run, family entertainment, and dozens of intricate snow and ice carvings by amateur and professional artists from around the world. The events take place in the Portland suburbs of Freeport and Falmouth. Some events are free. Admission to either the snow park or the ice park is $2.00 per person ($3.00 for admission to both parks). Times vary. Most events are outside, so remember to bundle up.

MARCH
Maine Boatbuilders Show
58 Fore Street (The Portland Complex)
(207) 775–4403
www.portlandcompany.com/bshow.html
The weekendlong Maine Boatbuilders Show in mid-March gathers some of the best examples of fiberglass and wooden custom-built boats on the East Coast. Here, you'll find canoes, kayaks, sailboats, powerboats, and rowboats, along with the builders themselves. Several boating equipment manufacturers also exhibit at the show. Seminars on boatbuilding and boating culture run throughout the weekend. Admission is $15 per person for one day, $25 per person for two days, and $35 per person for three days.

Maine Jewish Film Festival
10 Exchange Street (Movies on Exchange)
(207) 831–7495
www.mjff.org
The Maine Jewish Film Festival in mid-March presents films related to Jewish culture. For details, see the Arts chapter.

St. Patrick's Day at the Maine
Irish Heritage Center
34 Gray Street
(207) 780–0118
www.maineirish.com
St. Patrick's Day (March 17) is a popular holiday throughout Portland, although festivities tend to be limited to the evening hours at local pubs and bars. The Maine Irish Heritage Center, however, hosts a handful of family-oriented events for the true-blue Irishman, or those who just wish they were. The day always starts with an early-morning parade from the center, followed by a flag-raising ceremony at Harbor View Park at dawn and a breakfast. Other events in the past have included an Irish dance and a play later in the day. Most events cost between $10 and $15. For more information, visit the Web site or call the center.

The Chocolate Lovers' Fling and Auction
Sexual Assault Response Services of
Southern Maine
(207) 828–1035
www.sarsonline.org

This fund-raiser and sugar-fest held the last week in March supports Sexual Assault Response Services of Southern Maine, a nonprofit that helps victims of sexual assault. The Chocolate Lovers' Fling has been an area favorite for nearly 20 years, and it's no wonder—here, you can sample some of the best chocolate desserts from dozens of the area's bakeries and restaurants while also supporting a very worthwhile cause. A ticket to the event gets you unlimited access to the dessert samples and the auction, which includes artwork, chocolate sculptures, weekend getaway packages, and more. Don't forget to vote for your favorite dessert—area chocolatiers proudly display their winning plaques from this event even years later. Advance tickets are $23 ($25 at the door). VIP tickets (including silver-platter wait service) are $50.

Maine Maple Sunday
Various farms throughout Maine
www.getrealmaine.com

Every spring, Maine's maple producers invite guests to their farms to get a closer look at how sap becomes syrup. Hundreds of farms throughout the state participate in the event, which is always held on the fourth Sunday in March. Cumberland County is home to a good number of participating producers, all within an easy drive of Portland. Each sugarhouse offers different events to entice visitors—from free syrup-friendly food (like pancakes and homemade ice cream) to sleigh and wagon rides. All of the participating sugarhouses (visit the Web site for a complete listing) sell homemade maple syrup.

APRIL

Spring Thing
Ingraham
(207) 874–1055
www.ingraham.org

The Spring Thing has raised money for Ingraham, a nonprofit social service agency, since 1994. The Spring Thing is held in April and attracts many area notables who join together to bid on a variety of fine merchandise and services, sample food from the city's best restaurants, and enjoy quality wine from local vendors. Tickets are $55 in advance, $60 at the door.

JUNE

The Old Port Festival
Portland's Downtown District
(207) 772–6828
www.portlandmaine.com

The Old Port Festival, held the first weekend in June, is the state's largest one-day festival and consistently attracts tens of thousands of people. The annual event is over 30 years old and includes street performances, food from around the world, and sidewalk sales from area retailers. The festival, which is regarded as a kickoff to summer, is nearly all outside, sprawling over blocks in the downtown Portland neighborhood known as the Old Port. This is a family event, and admission is free. Be sure to snag a map of the event in the *Portland Press Herald* before attending, as there's a lot to see. The festival is held rain or shine.

International Piano and
Chamber Music Festival
Portland Conservatory of Music
116 Free Street
(207) 775–3356
www.portlandconservatory.net/piano
festival.htm

This recently inaugurated festival promises to enhance the arts culture of an already culturally rich city. The International Piano and Chamber Music Festival marked its third year

During the summer, many of Portland's neighborhoods hold block parties that often include games and food. Visit the city's Web site for registered neighborhood associations, www.living inportland.org, for upcoming events.

in 2006. Usually held in the second week of June, the festival features a weeklong series of performances from some of the world's best pianists and chamber musicians. The festival also allows conservatory students to take master classes with the visiting artists. Single recital tickets cost $15 for adults, $12 for seniors and students. A series ticket to all five recitals costs $75.

La Kermesse Franco-American Festival
Biddeford
www.biddefordmaine.org
La Kermesse is a celebration of all things French, French-Canadian, and Franco-American in a state that has strong French-Canadian influences. La Kermesse is an outdoor festival featuring music, entertainment, food, and "La Kermesse Idol"—a singing contest a la *American Idol*. Fireworks kick off the weekendlong event held the third week in June. La Kermesse is a family event, but you do need an official La Kermesse button to attend. Daily admission is $10 for Friday and Sunday, $12 for Saturday. Weekend passes are $12 in advance, $15 at the gate. Biddeford is about a half-hour drive south from Portland.

Bowdoin International Music Festival
6300 College Station, Brunswick
(207) 373–1400
www.summermusic.org
The Bowdoin International Music Festival attracts internationally known musicians each year to the Bowdoin campus in Brunswick to participate in a six-week music school and chamber music festival. The festival starts in late June and continues through July and the first week of August. Students ranging in age from 12 to 42 attend this competitive pro-

gram, and a range of concerts featuring guest artists, students, and faculty are presented weekly. Tickets for professional concerts range in price from $10 to $25, and season passes are available. Admission to student concerts is free, with a suggested donation of $5.00.

JULY
Fourth of July Fireworks
Eastern Promenade
www.ci.portland.me.us
Every year on July 4, thousands gather on the Eastern Promenade in Portland at dusk to watch the city-sponsored fireworks display. That evening, automobile access to the hill is limited to local traffic, so most residents walk to the event by way of Commercial Street or Congress Street. The throngs of people walking transforms this residential neighborhood into one giant street party. Food and games are part of the party on the hill, and some enterprising residents have even been known to sell snacks from their doorstep. Don't forget to bring a blanket to sit on. Also, keep a close eye on friends; the crowd on the hill on July 4 is as dense as Bourbon Street in New Orleans. The event is free.

Independence Pops Fourth of July Concert
Fort Williams Park, Cape Elizabeth
(207) 773–6128
(207) 842–0800 (tickets)
www.portlandsymphony.com
The Portland Symphony presents its annual Independence Pops Concert on an outdoor stage along the water at Fort Williams Park. The orchestra plays a rousing series of patriotic tunes, finishing with a grand finale march

Although fireworks are illegal in Maine, plenty of Portlanders head to New Hampshire to buy them and set them off during the Fourth of July Munjoy Hill festivities, with some partygoers even launching them on crowded streets! Keep a sharp eye out to avoid any mishap.

that ends with fireworks. This is a picnic concert, so bring a blanket and some munchies. Advance tickets cost $18 for adults ($22 at the gate), $14 for children and students ($18 at the gate), $16 for seniors ($20 at the gate). Group discounts are also available. Organizers say ticket prices vary by the year, so be sure to call ahead before arriving without a ticket.

Beachfest
Ocean Park, First Street, Old Orchard Beach
(207) 934–2500
The city of Old Orchard (about a 15-minute drive south of Portland) ushers in the July 4 weekend every year with an action-packed roster of beach activities befitting this coastal town. Beachfest features a parade, concerts throughout the weekend, and a giant sandcastle-building contest. Admission is free.

Bates Dance Festival
Bates College, Lewiston
(207) 786–6381
www.bates.edu
This festival of dance, with workshops and performances for children and adults, runs throughout July and August. Nationally known dancers flock to the Bates College campus (about an hour's drive north of Portland) to train professionals and children in everything from ballet to hip-hop dance. Needless to say, the performance series that accompanies this artists' camp is incredible. Performance dates, times, and ticket prices vary each season. Contact the festival for more information.

Moxie Festival
Main Street, Lisbon Falls
(207) 353–5354
www.moxiefestival.com
The Moxie Festival is one of the most eclectic and distinctly Maine events of the summer season. Located in the small town of Lisbon Falls (about a 40-minute drive north of Portland), the Moxie Fest celebrates that most bitter of New England sodas—Moxie. Moxie is purely Maine. It's only sold in these parts, and, like Australians and their Vegemite, it's really enjoyed only by Mainers. When Mainers think someone is brave, they sometimes say, "He's full of Moxie."

This three-day event to celebrate the Maine soda regularly attracts some 30,000 visitors, who enjoy events like the Chowder Dinner, the 5K Moxie Fun Race, a parade, a car show, and a Moxie raffle. You can also, of course, buy vintage-style Moxie T-shirts to make all your friends jealous. Admission to this event held the second weekend in July is free, although food and awesome T-shirts will cost you. To get to Lisbon Falls, take Interstate 295 North about 25 miles to exit 31/Route 196 toward Lisbon/Topsham. Turn left onto New Lisbon Road (Route 196) and continue 5.3 miles onto Route 196 North. Turn right onto Main Street after half a mile and continue to the Moxie Store at 2 Main Street.

YMCA Peaks to Portland Swim
www.cumberlandcountyymca.org
The Cumberland County YMCA in Portland has sponsored the Peaks to Portland Swim race since 1981. Swimmers start on Peaks Island in Casco Bay, the island closest to the mainland city, and swim 2.4 miles through the brisk waters to the East End Beach in Portland. In 2005, 148 swimmers participated in the event, which is also a fund-raiser for the YMCA's membership scholarships. The race is usually held the third week in July.

Maine International Film Festival
Friends of Art and Film in Central Maine,
Waterville
(207) 861–8138
www.miff.org
This 10-day festival in central Maine features nearly 100 films from American and international independent filmmakers. Screenings often include lectures from directors, actors, and others affiliated with the films. A full-festival pass is $150.00; a partial-festival pass costs $75.00; and tickets for individual screenings are $8.00. This festival, which is usually held the third week in July, is covered more extensively in the Arts chapter.

ℹ️ Throughout the summer, MENSK, Portland's nonprofit events organization, sponsors free movie screenings on the rooftop of a city building. For more information, visit www.mensk.cc.

Yarmouth Clam Festival
Yarmouth Chamber of Commerce, Yarmouth
(207) 846–3984
www.clamfestival.com

The Yarmouth Clam Festival is one of southern Maine's most anticipated summer events. The Clam Fest has been shucking and serving shellfish for more than 40 years. Even if you're not a fan of the aforementioned delicacy, you can still find plenty of things to do here. The festival runs for three days the third weekend in July and features rides, games, a parade, fireworks, free contests and performances, and tons of food, including clams, lobsters, shrimp, and corn on the cob. Admission is free, and the music and entertainment are gratis, but you'll shell out dough for food, crafts, and rides. Yarmouth is a 15-minute drive (about 11 miles) from Portland. Take I–295 North from Portland toward Falmouth, continuing on when the road turns to Interstate 95. Take exit 15 toward Yarmouth/Cumberland and bear right at the end of the ramp. Merge onto Route 1. Paid parking lots line Route 1 close to the fairground (expect to shell out about $5.00), and free parking with shuttle service is available at DeLorme Map Company just off the exit or on North Road off East Main Street.

AUGUST

Beach to Beacon 10K Roadrace
Cape Elizabeth
www.beach2beacon.org

The Beach to Beacon annual roadrace was founded by Joan Benoit Samuelson, a native of Cape Elizabeth, in 1997. Benoit won the first-ever women's marathon at the 1984 Olympics in Los Angeles and is one of Greater Portland's most beloved local heroes. The 6.2-mile run starts at Crescent Beach and ends at Portland Head Light at Fort Williams Park in Cape Elizabeth. It is held the first weekend in August. Some 5,000 professional and amateur runners, young and old, take to the streets every year to participate, and the race attracts some of the best marathoners in the world. The local weekly newspapers list the finishing times. If you want to watch the race and cheer the runners on, you can line up anywhere along the route, but most people go to the finish line at Fort Williams.

Great Falls Balloon Festival
Lewiston and Auburn
(800) 639–6331
www.greatfallsballoonfestival.com

The Great Falls Balloon Festival is New England's largest hot-air balloon festival. Located in the twin cities of Lewiston and Auburn, which are about an hour's drive north of Portland on Route 495, the Balloon Festival usually occurs over the third weekend in August. The festival includes entertainment, food, carnival rides, paragliders and parachutists, and, of course, plenty of rides on hot-air balloons. A striking array of colorful hot-air balloons hover in the skies over Lewiston/Auburn all weekend. Admission to the event is free, but vendors charge for rides on the balloons, and tickets are required for the carnival rides. Activities are scattered throughout both Lewiston and Auburn. Be sure to visit the Web site, which has a chart of activities and their locations, to figure out when and where to go before hitting the road.

Portland Chamber Music Festival
Westbrook College
(800) 320–0257
www.pcmf.org

This festival features nationally acclaimed performers from around the world and has been going strong since 1994. Concerts are held in the Ludcke Auditorium of the Westbrook College campus on Stevens Avenue in Portland. There are two weekends of concerts at the end of August; each weekend features two concerts. Past concerts have included works by Beethoven, Tchaikovsky, and David Horne.

Tickets cost $20 for adults 21 and over. Concertgoers younger than 21 are admitted for free. Festival tickets for all shows cost $70 for adults, $60 for seniors 65 and over.

MS Regatta Harborfest
Maine State Pier
(800) FIGHT–MS
www.msmaine.org

The state's largest sailing race takes place in Portland in late August. The event is a fundraiser for the local chapter of the Multiple Sclerosis Society. Besides the regatta, there are parades for sailboats, tugboats, and powerboats; a charity auction and a party to kick off the weekend; and plenty of activities at the accompanying festival at the Maine State Pier on Commercial Street.

SEPTEMBER

Cumberland County Fair
Cumberland Fairgrounds, Cumberland
(207) 829–5531
www.cumberlandfair.com

Maine is certainly not short on old-fashioned farm and livestock fairs—you can find them throughout the state during the warm months of the year. Sponsored by the Maine Department of Agriculture, the Cumberland Fair is the go-to event for Portlanders who love country fairs, since it's only a 20-minute drive away. The fair traditionally runs during the last week of September. Here, you can purchase livestock, eat cotton candy, play games, shop for crafts, enjoy local music, and watch harness racing and tractor-pull contests. There's also a contest for the most unusually gigantic pumpkin or squash, which should be intriguing to one and all. Tickets are $6.00 a day for adults during the workweek and $8.00 on the weekend. Children age 10 and under are free. Tickets for kids ages 11 and 12 are $2.00.

OCTOBER

The Fryeburg Fair
Fryeburg Fairgrounds, Fryeburg
(207) 935–3268
www.fryeburgfair.com

OK, the Fryeburg Fair is about a 50-mile drive northwest from Portland (heck, it's right near the New Hampshire border), so it doesn't qualify as a Portland-area event. However, this is the largest and most eclectic fair in Maine, and it is one we never miss. Every year, in early October, the tiny town of Fryeburg (population just over 3,000) is taken over for a week by fairgoers. The fair, which dates back to the mid-19th century, has it all—carnival rides, a racetrack, agricultural displays, and tons of shows, including the annual woodsmen's contest (including a riveting hatchet throw) and the largest steer and oxen show in the world.

If you're looking to buy or look at livestock, this is also the place to be since it's the biggest agriculture fair in the state. An eight-day pass to the show costs $38; bracelets for the rides cost an extra $15 per person and are available only on Tuesday, Thursday, and Sunday. All other days, expect to pay per ride. One-day admission costs $6.00 ($8.00 on Saturday); children under 12 get in for free. Also, expect to shell out $5.00 to $10.00 to park near the fair (the prices range according to the whim of the enterprising townie whose front yard you're parking in). Limited camping is available near the fairground, and organizers encourage advance registration. Camping fees vary, so call ahead or register on the Web site.

Annual Christmas Craft Show
772 Stevens Avenue
www.newenglandcraftfairs.com

One of several Maine craft shows scheduled throughout the state during the months before the winter holidays, this craft show features hundreds of local artists and craftspeople selling wares especially designed to be gift-worthy. This weekendlong show runs at the end of October.

FESTIVALS AND ANNUAL EVENTS

NOVEMBER

Maine Brewer's Festival
Portland Expo
www.mainebrew.com
November is "Drink Maine Beer" month and this beer fest in early November has everything the brew fanatic could ask for. Admission to the one-day extravaganza includes 12 tastings (at 4 ounces apiece) and an 8-ounce tasting mug. The Brewer's Fest, organized by local event planners East Coast Events, books several regional bands to provide live music during the two tasting times (happy hour starts at 2:30 P.M., with taps running at 3:00 P.M.; the evening session starts at 8:00 P.M., with taps running at 8:30 P.M.). The Maine Brewers' Guild, a featured participant in the festival, has over a dozen local members, including the Allagash Brewing Company and Gritty McDuff's, all of which are represented here. Only adults 21 and older are admitted. Tickets are $22 in advance, $25 at the door.

Lighting of the Nubble Lighthouse
York Parks and Recreation, York
(207) 363–1040
www.parksandrec.yorkmaine.org
Held the first Sunday after Thanksgiving, the Lighting of the Nubble is one of the most beautiful and folksy events of the holiday season, attracting tourists and locals alike. The seaside town of York, where the Nubble Lighthouse (otherwise known as the Cape Neddick Lighthouse) is located, is approximately 45 miles south of Portland on I–95, but, as long as you bundle up, the trek south is worth it. The Nubble Lighthouse and keeper's quarters sit on a small rocky island just offshore. Completed in 1879, the Nubble Light was manned by a keeper until 1987. Every November, the town strings thousands of white lights around the lighthouse and keeper's quarters. The lighting festival begins at 5:00 P.M. and includes Santa Claus, hot chocolate, cookies, and live music. Then, after a countdown, the lights are turned on around 6:00 P.M. Parking for this event can be tough, so call York Parks and Recreation for advice. In the past, the

i On the last Friday in November, join Portlanders in Monument Square for the annual tree-lighting ceremony.

town has provided a shuttle service from Ellis Park at Short Sands Beach.

Christmas at the Victoria Mansion
109 Danforth Street
(207) 772–4841
www.victoriamansion.org
From November 25 to December 31, the famous Victoria Mansion is decorated for the winter holidays the way it might have been in the mid-19th century, when its original owner, Ruggles Sylvester Morse, lived there with his wife, Olive. Professional interior designers, decorators, and florists outfit the mansion with lavish decorations. During this off-season, tours are self-guided, although history docents are on hand to answer questions. No reservation is necessary for groups of fewer than 10. Call ahead to schedule a group of 10 or more. Tickets cost $12.00 for adults, $5.00 for students ages 6 to 17; children under 6 get in free. Prices are subject to change, so call ahead to confirm. During these months the mansion is open for tours Tuesday through Sunday from 11:00 A.M. to 5:00 P.M.

DECEMBER

The Magic of Christmas
Portland Symphony Orchestra
Merrill Auditorium
(207) 842–0800
www.portlandsymphony.com
If the Maine State Ballet and Portland Ballet's rival productions of *The Nutcracker* and the Portland Stage Company's annual production of *A Christmas Carol* (see the Arts chapter for information on the Portland Stage Company) aren't quite enough for you, then check out *The Magic of Christmas*, a perennial holiday favorite featuring a roster of holiday-themed songs performed elegantly and enthusiastically by the Portland Symphony

i For information on the city of Portland's New Year's Eve celebration plans, visit www.ci.portland.me.us.

Orchestra. Performances, given every weekend in December, include both classical and popular music. There's also a sing-along. Tickets range in price from $15 to $50 for adults, depending on the seat. Discounts are available for students, children, seniors, and groups of 10 or more. Call for more information.

United Maine Craftsmen's Annual Holiday Craft Show
University of Southern Maine Gym
Falmouth Street
(207) 621–2818
www.unitedmainecraftsmen.com
One of the largest and most popular craft fairs during the holiday season, the United Maine Craftsmen's Annual Holiday Craft Show, held the first week in December, features nearly 100 local crafters selling their handmade products. Admission to the show is $2.00 at the door. If you really love crafts, be sure to visit the Craftsmen's Web site for information on other shows throughout the fall season.

Sparkle Weekend
Freeport Merchants Association, Freeport
(207) 865–1212
www.freeportusa.com
The Sparkle Weekend in Freeport, which is home to the famed L.L. Bean store, is held annually during the first week in December to kick off the holiday shopping season in

A Tale of Three Nutcrackers

There are several versions of *The Nutcracker* to choose from in Portland. For more than two decades, the city's two ballet companies—the Portland Ballet Company and the Maine State Ballet Company—have produced rival Nutcracker performances during the winter holiday season. Both traditional Nutcracker ballets are staged at Merrill Auditorium, although the dates for the two shows are staggered. Visit merrill auditorium.com or call (207) 842–0800 for ticket information. Or for something completley different, every December since 2003, local dance troupe Vivid Motion, Inc. has put on *Nutcracker Burlesque*, a sexy, adult version of the classic ballet. Needless to say, tickets sell out quickly. Call the St. Lawrence Arts and Community Center at (207) 775–5568 for more information.

this retail outlet mecca. It's organized by the Freeport Merchants Association, a nonprofit town trade group. Sparkle Weekend includes the Maine Street Magic Parade of Lights (an electric light parade) as well as wandering carolers, a talking Christmas tree, horse-drawn carriage rides, and, of course, appearances by St. Nick himself. Admission is free. Shopping, of course, is not.

BEACHES AND OCEAN ACTIVITIES

If you have come to Portland, chances are that you're a fan of the ocean. How could you not be? The city boasts not only a working waterfront but also countless beaches and activities related to the salty water. This chapter gives you a heaping helping of some of the best coastal activities in the area. Whether you like to get your feet wet in the sea or lounge on a sandy shore, you'll find everything you need to enjoy Portland's rocky coastline just like a local. You could come to Portland and never have anything to do with the ocean, but you'd be missing a good part of the city's soul. As the poet e.e. cummings wrote, "For whatever we lose (like a you or a me) / it's always ourselves we find in the sea."

This chapter lists beaches, whale watches, ocean sports, and more than a dozen tours of the bay and beyond. For those of you who'd like to learn how to tie a hitch or let out a jib, we have also listed a few sailing schools.

The "Beaches" section provides rough directions from downtown Portland to the selected shores, as well as entrance fees and whether a lifeguard is on duty. Most people hit the beach here between Memorial Day and Labor Day, the traditional summer season in Maine. The information provided in this chapter, including entrance fees, is for this warm, sunny stretch. These summer months offer the most activity shoreside and also are the warmest time to take a dip in the notoriously chilly Atlantic Ocean. From June through August, the water normally warms from its winter low of around 33 degrees Fahrenheit to 70 degrees Fahrenheit (which is not as warm as it sounds).

Another element of nature that is constantly changing around here is the ocean tides. Knowledge of the tides is crucial for swimmers, boaters, and seaside strollers alike—an ill-timed picnic at high tide can really swamp your spirits, and strong currents make for potentially dangerous conditions. The local Portland harbormaster (the city official in charge of Casco Bay) runs an updated Web site on the tides, ocean weather, and sunrise and sunset times at www.portland harbor.org. The weather section of the *Portland Press Herald* also has the same information.

When you're ready to hit the beach, remember that entrance fees can change seasonally just like the natural elements, so bring a couple of extra bucks just in case. As for lifeguards, it's always best to take caution when swimming in new waters, even if someone is looking out for you. Dogs, even when leashed, are barred on most beaches. If you must bring man's best friend along, call the area town office ahead of time to make sure the local ordinance allows pets on the sand. Some areas allow pets during off-hours or during the cooler months; be sure to notice any such restrictions posted on signs. Any dog off its leash must be under voice control—a rowdy pet could land you a fine. Owners must pick up after dogs and dispose of droppings.

You'll notice that the "Ocean Tours" section is especially long. Lately, a number of tour companies have launched their own tours around Casco Bay and its islands. Portland has jurisdiction over five islands in the bay—Peaks, Great Diamond, Little Diamond, Long, and Cliff Islands. All are inhabited year-round (Peaks has the largest population), although summer vacationers are becoming more and more prevalent. Besides these five inhabited islands, Casco Bay also contains Chebeague Island to the north (which in April 2006 won its independence from the mainland town of Cumberland) and over 365

Comfort at Sea

If you're going to lie around on the sand all summer, be sure to use strong sunscreen and reapply, reapply, reapply, especially after swimming. Also, if you're spending time on the ocean, you must—repeat MUST—wear a hat and good sunglasses (preferably polarized), because the sun's reflection on the water doubles its brightness and can induce headaches and strained eyes if you're not properly protected. If you plan to head out on an ocean tour, you should bring an extra layer of clothing (sea breezes can get chilly) and some bottled water. Those of you with particularly weak stomachs should bring an anti-seasickness medication like Dramamine.

Calendar Islands, so named because there are as many (or more) islands as there are days in the year. Some of these islands are private and developed, but most are wild. Portland's five inhabited islands, besides being gorgeous and easy to reach by the Casco Bay Lines ferry, also have a notorious independent streak. In 2006 Peaks Island joined Chebeague Island in its quest to secede from the mainland and become an independent town, mostly to avoid what some residents believe are unfairly high tax burdens. Chebeague won its historic battle, but, as of press time, the fate of Peaks Island's secessionist movement remains up in the air.

Politics aside, Casco Bay—its islands, beaches, and ocean—offers enough beauty and character to justify a book limited strictly to its waters. This chapter lists some of the local favorites, each of which offers something a bit different. If you find yourself absolutely overwhelmed by the selection, just wing it and walk down Commercial Street, where most of the ocean tour offices are located. No doubt you'll find a vessel that fits your needs.

BEACHES

Crescent Beach State Park
Route 77, Cape Elizabeth
(207) 799-5871
www.state.me.us/doc/parks

Crescent Beach, a state park run by the Maine Bureau of Parks and Recreation, is one of the most popular beaches in the area and is always packed on sunny summer days with families and beachgoers of all ages. The beach here is expansive, the surf is mild, and the area boasts a rocky coast to the south and Kettle Cove, with fun trails to explore, to the north. There are bathhouses with showers, flush toilets, a large snack bar, and plenty of parking. Lifeguards are on duty from 9:00 A.M. to sunset. The beach is open from Memorial Day through Columbus Day. The entrance fee is $3.50 for people age 12 and older, $1.00 for children ages 5 to 11, and free for seniors over 65 and children 4 and younger. Summer season passes are available for $60. Pets are not allowed on the beach.

To reach Crescent Beach, cross the Casco Bay Bridge into South Portland, bearing left at the end of the bridge to get onto Broadway and to remain on Route 77. Take a right at the Pizza Joint to continue on Route 77. Follow Route 77 (otherwise known as Ocean House Road) for just under 5 miles until you see the sign on your left for Crescent Beach State Park.

East End Beach
Eastern Promenade
East End Beach is a small, rocky beach on the Portland peninsula with fantastic views of Casco Bay. Parking for up to 70 cars, picnic tables, changing rooms, and toilets are available here, but there isn't a lifeguard, so swim at your own risk. To get here from downtown Portland, follow Congress Street east to the

top of Munjoy Hill, overlooking the Eastern Promenade. Parking is located at the base of the Prom, and there is access to the beach from the lot.

Ferry Beach State Park
Black Point Road, Scarborough

Ferry Beach is a small, sandy beach in a sheltered cove, which makes the ocean water here shallower (and often warmer) than at many other local beaches. The beach has an adjacent parking lot (which can accommodate up to 100 vehicles), outhouses, a boat launch, moorings, boat storage, and views of Pine Point, Prouts Neck, and Old Orchard. There aren't any lifeguards. To reach Ferry Beach, take Interstate 295 South from Portland to exit 2 and follow Route 1 South to Oak Hill Plaza. Take a left onto Route 207/Blackpoint Road and follow the road for just over 4 miles to Ferry Road, on the right just past Scarborough Beach (keep an eye out—the street sign is hard to spot!). The beach is located at the end of Ferry Road. Admission is $10 per car.

Higgins Beach
Spurwink Road, Scarborough

The shore at Higgins Beach is rocky and narrow, but the surf here is great. It's no surprise, then, that the beach is popular with surfers and teenagers. No lifeguards are on duty here, so brave the waves at your own risk. You also won't find a changing room or a bathroom on the beach, but, hey, who says surfing is easy? To get to the beach from Portland, cross the Casco Bay Bridge to South Portland and bear left at the end of the bridge onto Broadway. At the Pizza Joint restaurant, turn right onto Route 77/Ocean Street. Follow Route 77 through Cape Elizabeth, past Crescent Beach, and take a left onto Higgins Road (look for the

i The surf during the colder fall and winter months tends to feature large waves and rough conditions, making these months ideal for surfers. Be sure to wear a wetsuit for protection from the frigid Maine waters.

little red farm stand across the street). The beach is located at the end of this road. Parking is available in private lots along Higgins Road. Fees range according to the mood of the local in charge of the lot, so it's best to budget between $5.00 and $10.00 per car.

Kettle Cove
Kettle Cove Road, Cape Elizabeth

Kettle Cove has a small, sandy beach and a network of easily accessible trails through the connecting woods. This beach is perfect for families since there's a lot to do along the shoreline, including walking along the trails and exploring the many large rocks and tidal pools. Kettle Cove has parking (no fee) and outhouses but doesn't have a lifeguard. To reach this beach, cross Casco Bay Bridge to South Portland, bear left on Broadway, and take a right onto Route 77/Ocean Street at the Pizza Joint restaurant. Follow Route 77/Ocean Street to Cape Elizabeth. Ocean Street changes to Ocean House Road once you cross into Cape Elizabeth. Look for the white Kettle Cove Take Out and Dairy Bar after about 5 miles. Take a left onto Kettle Cove Road and follow it to the end.

Old Orchard Beach
Route 5, Saco

Known not only for its enormous shoreline but also the adjacent boardwalk, arcades, and amusement park, the Old Orchard Beach experience is full of stimulation. Besides the renowned stretch of quiet shoreline here, OOB (as it's known to some locals) is also packed with hotels, motels, shops, and restaurants that always attract thousands of visitors during the summer. This is also the site of one of the area's most popular amusement parks, Palace Playland (for more information on the Playland, one of the oldest amusement parks in southern Maine, see the Attractions chapter). To reach Old Orchard Beach, take I–295 South to exit 36 to Saco. Follow Route 5 to the beach. Plenty of parking is available in either metered spots or in private lots (expect to pay $5.00 to $10.00 for a spot, depending on the lot), and admission to the beach is free. Lifeguards are on duty from 9:00 A.M. to sunset.

Pine Point Beach
Pine Point Road, Scarborough

Located at the northern end of Old Orchard Beach, Pine Point includes a rock breakwater and a sandy shore. A popular spot for picnicking, kiting, and dune buggy riders during the off-season, Pine Point is open year-round during daylight hours. The beach has a changing room as well as a popular hot dog stand (both of which are open only in-season) as well as snack bars and toilets. No lifeguards are on duty. To get to Pine Point Beach, take I–295 South to exit 42 (Scarborough). Turn right onto Route 1 and follow it for 4 miles over the marsh. At the Dunstan School intersection, take a left onto Pine Point Road. Follow it to the beach, bearing left at the "T." Parking is available.

Scarborough Beach State Park
Black Point Road, Scarborough

Scarborough Beach State Park is a long, sandy beach that attracts plenty of locals and young people. The surf here is good, and the beach has outhouses and a view of the upscale coastal neighborhood of Prouts Neck. Parking is available, and lifeguards are on duty in-season. To reach the beach from Portland, take I–295 South to exit 2 (Scarborough/Route 1). Bear right on Route 1 to Oak Hill. Take a left at Route 207/Black Point Road (at Amato's sandwich shop). Follow Route 207 until you see a sign for the entrance to the beach on your left.

Willard Beach
Willow Road, South Portland

This small, sheltered beach features a playground, a snack bar, and an outcropping of rocks with tidal pools. Parking and entry to Willard are free, and lifeguards are on duty during daylight hours, so this a popular spot for families with young children. The beach borders one of the most rapidly transforming

i Maine is known for its rocky coast, and many of the beaches listed here have rock clusters that kids love to explore for tidal pools. Be sure they are accompanied by an adult with a sharp eye, as the rocks can be slippery and dangerous to navigate.

neighborhoods in Greater Portland. Once inhabited entirely by working-class South Portlanders and local fishermen, the blocks around Willard Beach have in recent years become hot property. Modest houses within view of the water are now priced in the millions of dollars, and aging family homes have been torn down and replaced with luxury modern residences. Before heading to the beach, take a walk up and down the streets and check out the changing mosaic of properties.

Willard Beach is bracketed by Southern Maine Community College on one end and a small outcropping of rocks with a nice grassy top and benches on the other end. To reach the beach from downtown Portland, cross Casco Bay Bridge to South Portland, bear left on Broadway, and take a right on Cottage Road. Bear left at Red's Dairy Freeze and continue straight on Cottage Road. At DiPietro's Sandwich shop and the blinking yellow light, take a left onto Pillsbury Street. Follow the road to the end (a three-way intersection) and take a left, then an immediate right onto Willow Street. The beach and the adjacent parking lot are located at the end of this road.

OCEAN SPORTS

Maine Island Kayak Company
Peaks Island
(800) 796–2373
www.maineislandkayak.com

Maine Island Kayak Company (MIKCo) leads half-day and full-day kayak tours of Casco Bay starting from its boathouse on Peaks Island, just a short ferry ride from downtown Portland. Guides lead small groups around the islands in the bay, exploring secluded beaches, ocean forts, and majestic lighthouses. MIKCo says all "athletic beginners" are welcome, which means be prepared to paddle. Half-day trips cost $60 per person, full-day trips cost $95 per person, and both include kayaking and safety gear. Lunch (homemade) is included only on the full-day trips. The cost of the ferry ride to and from Peaks Island is not included, so during the summer (peak season) expect to spend $12.50 round-trip for an adult, $6.10 round-trip for a child.

MIKCo's half-day trip runs from 10:00 A.M. to 1:30 P.M., and the full-day trip runs from 10:00 A.M. to 4:30 P.M. Both trips require paddlers to meet at the island boathouse by 9:45 A.M., so you'll have to take an early-morning ferry on Casco Bay Lines (the 9:15 A.M. boat should get you there on time). Trips launch regardless of weather, unless the instructors deem the conditions dangerous, so bring appropriate weather gear as well as a water bottle, sunscreen, sunglasses, and a hat. MIKCo also sells water, cameras, T-shirts, and croakies for your sunglasses. Fees are non-refundable unless MIKCo cancels the trip, in which case you'll receive a full refund. If you're looking for more paddling, check out MIKCo's family trips or multiday trips up the coast.

Rollins Scuba Associates
68 Washington Avenue, South Portland
(207) 799–7990
www.rollinsscuba.com
Rollins Scuba is a small scuba-diving company owned by instructor Paul Rollins and operated out of his home. He has owned the business since 1988 and is certified in YMCA, NAUI, PADI, and CMAS diving. He leads individual and group dives year-round to explore the murky, chilly waters around Portland. Since Rollins is a tiny operation, the business accepts only check or cash payment. Rollins books dives for up to four people at a time as far in advance as possible, and most trips are booked a week or two in advance.

A typical summer dive would start at Kettle Cove in Cape Elizabeth with a beach entry

to an eventual dive depth of 30 feet below the surface. Dives include one hour in the water plus around an hour and a half for prebriefing and a safety check. Rollins leads dives for beginners as well as more experienced divers with proof of open-water certification. The Discover Scuba program, for first-time divers, costs $150 per student. An open-water dive as described above costs $150 per diver. Equipment rental is also available at around $100 per person, though this price varies depending on what is needed.

Scarborough Marsh Audubon Center
Route 9/Pine Point Road, Scarborough
(207) 883–5100 (May through September)
(207) 781–2330 (October through May)
www.maineaudubon.org
The Scarborough Marsh office of the Maine Audubon Society leads a variety of canoe and kayaking tours of Scarborough Marsh during the warmer months of the year. Scarborough Marsh is about a 15-minute drive from downtown Portland. The 3,100-acre estuary is the largest salt marsh in Maine, and it's a magnet for wildlife looking to rest, feed, and breed. You can take a self-guided tour of the marsh in a canoe or kayak (at least one person in the group must be 18 or over). The center also provides guided daytime and nighttime tours.

Kayak and canoe rentals are available daily from 9:30 A.M. to 4:00 P.M. and cost $13 per hour for members, $15 per hour for non-members. You can also rent for a half day for $45 per person. Rentals include a map and a nature guide. A guided canoe tour costs $10 for adults ($11 for nonmembers), $8.00 for children age 12 and younger ($9.00 for nonmembers). Daytime tours last an hour and a half, and guides take care to point out the

i The Maine Island Trail Association maintains 150 miles of ocean trails on Maine islands, from Cape Porpoise Harbor in Kennebunkport to the Canadian Maritimes at the northernmost Maine coastline. For more information, visit www.mita.org.

area's unique flora and fauna. The trips are designed for all levels of paddlers. Also available are the special Full Moon Canoe Tour at night, the Sunset Canoe Tour in the evening, and the Early Morning Canoe Tour just after dawn. These tours run intermittently throughout the summer and cost just $1.00 more per person than the daytime tours.

OCEAN TOURS, FISHING GUIDES, WHALE WATCHING, AND SAILING SCHOOLS

Lately, it seems as though there are as many ocean tours in Casco Bay as there are fish in its waters. Portland has a tour for everyone, whether you want to get your hands dirty hauling traps with a real lobsterman or prefer to just kick back with a glass of bubbly while someone sails you off into the sunset. Most of the tours listed here run only during the summer (usually late May through Labor Day). Be sure to call ahead to confirm ticket prices, as they tend to fluctuate each year.

Bayview Cruises
184 Commercial Street (Fisherman's Wharf)
(207) 761–0496
www.bayviewcruisesme.com
Enjoy Casco Bay aboard the *Bayview Lady,* a yacht available both for scheduled tours and charter trips. During the summer Bayview Cruises offers daily tours, lasting from 40 minutes to two hours. If you want a quick ride around Casco Bay, try the Harbor Lunchtime Cruise (12:10 to 12:50 P.M.) or the Attitude Adjustment (5:15 to 6:15 P.M.). Or, if you're looking for a longer excursion, a seal-watching cruise is available. And you can add a lobster bake meal on most cruises with only 15 minutes' notice. Adult tickets cost $12 for the basic tours; prices for specialty tours change with the season.

Downeast Duck Adventures
177 Commercial Street
(207) 774–DUCK
www.downeastducktours.com

The only "amphibious" tour in Portland, the Downeast Duck Adventures tour bus is a hulking 39-foot boat on wheels that travels around Portland's downtown and Old Port, past must-see landlubber spots like the Victoria Mansion and the Portland Observatory, and then splashes headlong into Casco Bay for a thorough tour of the area's sea sites, such as the half-submerged Fort Gorges and local lighthouses. Tours last from 60 to 90 minutes, with equal time on land and sea. Along the way, you'll hear an informational narrative of area history and legend from a wacky guide, or "Duckaneer." The season runs from late May to mid-October. Tickets are $22 for adults, $17 for seniors and children ages 6 to 12, and $5.00 for kids age 5 and under. Tickets can be purchased at Harbor View Gifts at 177 Commercial Street.

Eagle Island Tours
170 Commercial Street (Long Wharf)
(207) 774–6498
www.eagleislandtours.com
Tour Casco Bay up close in one of Eagle Island Tours' classic motorized excursion boats. These tours are designed to take the stress away from seafaring by offering a smooth, comfortable ride. You can choose from several routes, including the Lighthouse Lovers' Tour and the Eagle Island Cruise, which includes a picnic on the island. Eagle Island Tours also runs charter expeditions for your special event. Prices for the 90-minute cruises vary from $10 to $24; call or visit their Web site for more information. If you like the idea of a sunset cruise, the price is well below the competition's, at just $10 per person.

Go Fish Charters
Spring Point Marina, South Portland
(207) 799–1339, (207) 232–1678
www.gofishmaine.com
Captain Ben Garfield leads offshore and coastal fishing trips on his 22-foot Edgewater boat, docked at the Spring Point Marina. Captain Ben provides all the equipment needed for both amateur and seasoned fishermen,

i Every summer, about 150 swimmers participate in the Greater Portland YMCA's annual Peaks to Portland
Swim, a 2.4-mile race between Peaks
Island and the East End Beach. For
details, contact the Y at (207) 874–1111.

including an array of high-quality reels by
Penn, Shimano, Newell, and Sci Angler and
custom-made rods by Saco Bay Tackle. A four-
hour inshore fishing trip is priced at $275 for a
group of up to six people; an eight-hour
inshore trip costs $475 for the same size
group. Inshore trips focus on light-tackle fishing around the islands in Casco Bay for
species like stripers and bluefish. For the
more adventurous fisher, Go Fish also leads
eight-hour offshore shark-fishing tours, which
cost $550 for up to three people.

Lucky Catch Cruises
170 Commercial Street
(207) 233–2026, (888) 624–6321 (tickets)
www.luckycatch.com
At Lucky Catch you can join a working Maine
lobsterman aboard his 37-foot Maine-crafted
lobster boat as he tours the waters of Casco
Bay hauling traps. Most cruises consist of
pulling 10 lobster traps in five traditional
styles. The boat has extra gloves, pants, and
boots if you're interested in joining in. Popular
local sites are also included on the tour, like
area lighthouses and forts, and the tour
guide/lobsterman talks about lobster habits
and conservation efforts. Anything hauled in
during the tour is available for sale afterward.
Cruises last 80 to 90 minutes and cost $22 for
adults, $18 for juniors and seniors, and $12
for children.

Maine Fishing and Diving Charters
177 Harriet Street, South Portland
(207) 799–9826, (866) 799–9826
www.fishinganddiving.com
Maine Fishing and Diving Charters specializes
in half-day and full-day deep-sea fishing and
diving tours. Captain Rob Odlin has led these

trips since 1997, and if the photos on his Web
site are any testament, he and his guest crew
frequently catch some real-life whoppers.
Inshore fishing charters cost $475 for a half
day or $675 for a full day. Offshore fishing for
cod, tuna, or shark costs $770 per day. All
trips are priced for parties of up to six people
and include bait, tackle, filleting, and freezer
bags. These trips around the outskirts of
Casco Bay are for beginners and experienced
anglers alike. Diving tours require some experience and open-water certification.

Maine Saltwater Fishing
(207) 471–5858
www.mainesaltwaterfishing.com
Join Captain John Ford on his 22-foot fishing
boat to explore some of the shallow, serene
coves of Casco Bay. Ford specializes in
striped-bass fishing in shallow water, also
known as "flats style" fishing. He is a registered Maine guide and a licensed U.S. Coast
Guard captain. Adding to the local summer
fishing trips, Ford also runs a few destination
trips during the colder months to locations
such as the Bahamas and Costa Rica. Local
half-day charters cost $275; full-day charters
are $350. Rates are for two anglers; tackle is
included.

New England Sailing and Cruising School
P.O. Box 1316
Wells, ME 04090
(386) 956–7666
www.newenglandsailing.com
The school offers a variety of basic and inter-
mediate sailing courses, many of which run
for only a few days. The school is based in
Wells but docks its 37-foot Kalliste yacht in
Portland, so be sure to specify that you're
looking for Portland courses when you call.
New England Sailing also occasionally runs
"Gourmet Charters" of Casco Bay, which
include a gourmet meal complete with hors
d'oeuvres, salad, and dessert. Classes and
charter rates vary, so call or visit their Web
site for more details.

North Atlantic Maritime Services
Scarborough
(207) 730–1514
www.namaritimeservices.com

The owners of North Atlantic Maritime Services, Jim Maxner and Keith Fosler, have eight years' combined experience in the U.S. Coast Guard and more than 30 years' combined experience on the ocean. Jim and Keith provide boat management lessons for beginners and experienced boaters, fresh- or saltwater charter cruises, and yacht management services to help you maintain your boat. North Atlantic Maritime charges a flat fee of $50 per hour for any level of maritime instruction.

Old Port Mariner Fleet
170 Commercial Street (Long Wharf)
(207) 774–2022, (800) 437–3270
www.marinerfleet.com

The Old Port Mariner Fleet offers an extensive roster of ocean excursions to suit every taste, with five fishing trips from June through August and weekend trips in September and October. If you can't decide whether you prefer whale watching, deep-sea fishing, or a lighthouse cruise, Mariner Fleet's friendly sales associates will help you decide which tour is right for you. Besides these offerings, they also book sunset cruises, dinner cruises, carriage rides, railroad rides, walking tours, and more. Deep-sea fishing trips, one of the Fleet's staples, cost $63 for adults, $58 for juniors ages 13 to 17 and seniors age 60 and over. A handful of "marathon trips" are offered throughout the summer and into the fall. These trips last from 5:00 A.M. to 5:00 P.M. (rather than the standard 8:00 A.M. to 5:00 P.M.) and cost $125 per angler.

> **i** Check out the Whaling Wall by Michigan artist Wyland at the Marine State Pier next to the Casco Bay Lines terminal on Commercial Street. Wyland, a devout environmentalist, has painted some 60 similar murals on outdoor sites around the country.

Ophelia's Odyssey
Sunset Marina, South Portland
(207) 590–3145
http://captainsearles.tripod.com

Tour Casco Bay on this 40-foot Friendship Sloop, captained by friendly, experienced Tom Searles. You can lie back and enjoy the ride or help Tom skipper the boat, steer a course, or hoist a sail. The number of passengers on board is limited to allow enough space to spread out and relax. Day cruises (which last approximately three hours) cost $35 per person. Two-hour sunset cruises, including complimentary hors d'oeuvres and champagne, cost $50 per person.

Palawan Sailing
170 Commercial Street
(207) 773–2163, (888) 284–PAL1
www.sailpalawan.us

Sail around Casco Bay in style on this 50-foot yacht, which was the first ship of its kind to use a fin keel. The *Palawan* seats up to 24 passengers and runs relaxing trips around the bay during the morning, afternoon, and evening. All-day trips or lobster-bake trips are also available. Prices range from $20 to $95 per person, depending on the type of cruise. The lobster-bake picnic on the beach costs $120 per person.

Portland Schooner Company
Commercial Street
(207) 766–2500, 87–SCHOONER
www.portlandschooner.com

The Portland Schooner Company runs public and private charter trips on its 72-foot wooden schooner, the *Bagheera*. The ship features an interior that has been meticulously maintained since the ship was launched in 1924. These tours of Casco Bay are perfect for passengers of all ages. Most tours last two hours; the crew encourage you to bring a bagged lunch. Wine and beer are also allowed on the ship. The cost is $28 for adults, $12 for children. Be sure to ask about the *Bagheera*'s daily sunset cruise.

Close-up

Portland Fish Exchange

Maine's coastal communities are constantly struggling to maintain a balance between development and retaining the character of their working waterfronts. That task has grown more difficult in recent years as groundfish stocks (such as cod and haddock) have declined and stricter fishing regulations have taken their toll on local fishing communities. A 2002 study found that only 25 miles of working waterfront remain in the 7,000 miles of tidal coastline between Kittery in southern Maine and Eastport, a Downeast fishing town.

Portland has worked hard to maintain a working waterfront in the face of development pressure. One way it does that is through a unique non-profit organization known as the Portland Fish Exchange. When it opened in 1987, the fish exchange was the first display seafood auction in the country. Trawlers, up to four vessels at a time, motor up to the docks to offload their catch. The staff sorts, weighs, and labels the fish, and then it is put on ice for display. The 22,000-square-foot facility can hold up to a half-million pounds of fish. A daily auction held midday Sunday through Thursday brings together fishermen and 25 registered buyers representing restaurants, markets, and other retailers. An independent auctioneer runs the show, assisted by a computerized auction tracking system that follows sales in real time. Sellers have the option of declining any bid price.

More than 90 percent of Maine's groundfish catch, and 20 percent of New England's catch, is sold here. About 150 fishing vessels supply 15 to 20 million pounds of seafood to the fish exchange each year.

School of Ocean Sailing
TLC #1, 5600 Royal Dane Mall, Suite 12
St. Thomas, VI 00802
(340) 998–2042
E-mail: svsamana@sailingschool.com
www.sailingschool.com
This school teaches offshore ocean sailing and navigation through a series of live-aboard trips from Portland up the coast to Canada during the summer and off the coast of St. Thomas in the Virgin Islands during the winter. Classes are conducted on the *Samana*, a 52-foot steel sailing ketch. Several courses are offered for both the beginner and advanced-level sailor. Courses cost between $1,600 and $2,200 per student and run for roughly a week. The instructors are often on the water and away from the phone, so e-mail is the preferred method of inquiry.

PARKS AND RECREATION

Portland offers plenty of things to do during the daytime and at night. If you like to be active, this is the chapter for you. Listed here are some of the best choices for all kinds of recreational sports and activities, as well as information on some of the best urban and area parks in and around Portland. Many of these activities are seasonal, but most parks in the state are open year-round, for hiking during the warmer months and snowshoeing and cross-country skiing when things turn white and icy. If you're looking for information on seaside parks off the peninsula, turn to the Beaches and Ocean Activities chapter. In this chapter, we have limited the park listings to either areas on the peninsula or landlocked parks beyond the peninsula. For your safety, all parks listed here are open only during daylight hours.

Portland is known as Forest City because of its abundance of trees, even in urban areas like the Old Port and the downtown. Here, you'll find a park that was designed by the man who created Central Park in New York City, as well as beautiful lookout points and plenty of places for the perfect picnic. The Portland area also offers a wide variety of recreational sports and activities—everything from birding to ice hockey.

Portland's location in the Pine Tree State means that outdoor activities are a big draw for visitors and natives alike. For those of us who like to meet new people while exploring the great outdoors, there's the Maine Outdoor Adventure Club (MOAC), an all-purpose, nature-lovers organization with more than 100 members in the Portland area. MOAC is listed in the "Hiking" section, but the group participates in a range of activities year-round, from kayaking to snowshoeing. Portland also runs a number of organized activities and intramural

sports on a rotating basis each year. If you'd like more information, contact the city's Parks and Recreation Department at (207) 874–8793. All of the parks listed here, except Bradbury Mountain State Park, are maintained by Portland Parks and Recreation, so, if you have more questions, visit their Web site (www.ci.portland.me.us/rec.htm) or call them at the above number.

In this chapter, you'll find a network of enthusiasts and opportunities for you and your family, whatever your interest. So get excited—there's a lot to do!

PARKS
Portland Parks

Back Bay Cove/Baxter Boulevard
Baxter Boulevard at Franklin Street
The Back Bay and Baxter Boulevard are essentially one and the same to Portlanders, although Back Bay technically refers to the area of seawater just off Washington Avenue around which Baxter Boulevard is wrapped. The Back Bay is known best for its jogging path, an almost 4-mile-long, flat dirt trail that can be jogged, walked, or biked. There's also a field that is used for intramural and school soccer, lacrosse, rugby, and whatever else is on the roster. On the northern end of the bay, be sure to check out Payson Park, which is chock-full of places to run around and have fun. Payson Park has a baseball diamond, an open field, and basketball and tennis courts.

i The "Summer in the Parks" concert series is sponsored by the city's Parks and Recreation Department and runs throughout July and August. For more on these free events, call Parks and Recreation at (207) 756–8275.

Use of all of these parks is gratis. To make things even better, there's a medium-size parking lot off Franklin Street across from the Hannaford Supermarket. During the summer the Back Bay serves as an outdoor gym for many a Portlander.

Baxter Woods Park
Outer Forest Avenue and Stevens Avenue

Given to the city by former governor Percival Baxter and maintained by the Portland Parks and Recreation Department, Baxter Woods is a nature reserve and bird sanctuary that sprawls over 30 acres of forest. Percival Baxter decreed that the land would forever remain a public park. Here, you can meander amid towering oak and pine trees that, sadly, are rarely seen these days elsewhere on the peninsula. You'll find wide hiking trails as well as an off-leash area for dogs and a pond with beautiful lily pads blooming in the warmer months. Most people park on the street on Stevens Avenue or Forest Avenue, but there is also a small parking lot at the end of Percival Road right off Stevens Avenue.

Deering Oaks
Park Avenue between High Street and Deering Avenue

Deering Oaks is Portland's largest and most visited park. Sprawling over roughly 55 acres, this park was designed more than a century ago by the same man who created New York City's famous Central Park, Frederick Law Olmsted. Deering Oaks is home to tennis and basketball courts, a sand volleyball court, a baseball diamond, a duck pond for paddle boating during the summer and ice skating during the winter, and a playground. There's also a new manmade spring for wading during the hotter months. Deering Oaks is the perfect spot for a romantic stroll, a picnic, or a

> **i** Portland has two designated dog parks, one on Valley Street and the other at Presumpscott Street and Ocean Avenue. Call Portland Parks and Recreation at (207) 874–8793 for details.

game of Frisbee with the family. Parking is available in a small lot off Deering Avenue as well as on-street.

Eastern Promenade
Eastern Promenade between Washington Avenue and Fore Street

The Eastern Promenade was created in 1836 when the downtown and the seaports were bustling with activity. The Eastern Prom boasts one of the nicest walkways in the city, a 1.5-mile paved trail starting at the intersection of India Street and Commercial Street along the water and wrapping around the eastern end of the peninsula to Washington Avenue. The promenade itself begins at the crest of Munjoy Hill, overlooking the eastern end of Casco Bay. Here, you'll find a great, grassy slope for picnicking and rolling down, a playground, tennis courts, East End Beach, a boat launch, and the Maine Narrow Gauge Railway. Parking is available in a small lot near the boat launch and on-street along the Eastern Prom—except, of course, on July 4, when the whole area is packed with people viewing the Independence Day fireworks, which are launched from this spot.

Riverton Trolley Park
Forest Avenue (U.S. Route 302) and Riverside Street
www.ci.portland.me.us/troll.htm

Created in 1896, the Riverton Trolley Park was originally one of the premier destinations in Portland. Until 1929 the park featured not only a working trolley from Monument Square but also an amphitheater, a dance hall, and a zoo. These days, little remains of the park's magnificence, except stone pillars and the remnants of an old wall. A group called Friends of the Riverton Trolley Park maintains the trails here and organizes guided tours of the area. The park features a baseball diamond and a short loop trail (used for cross-country skiing in the winter) into the woods that connects with the Riverton Golf Course. Parking is available in the Regional Waste Services lot off Forest Avenue, which turns into

U.S. Route 302 in Riverside. To reach the park, follow the trail under the bridge or through the ball field on Riverside Street.

Western Promenade
Western Promenade between West Street and Vaughn Street

In the 19th century, city planners created the Western Promenade to allow residents to take a nice stroll and escape the cluster of development in the downtown. When it was first established, few visited it because it was too far off the beaten path. Now, the Western Prom is the highlight of the peninsula's most prestigious neighborhood, the West End. The Western Prom is little more than a walkway along the crest of Bramhall Hill, but its stunning view of Maine to the west is unmatched anywhere else in Portland. On a clear day you can see all the way to Mount Washington in New Hampshire. People come to the Western Prom to sprawl out on the grass and sunbathe, to walk their pets, to picnic, and especially to watch the sunset. Don't miss it. There's plenty of on-street parking along the promenade and in the surrounding neighborhood.

> **i** On Wednesday evenings during the summer, the city sponsors free folk concerts on the Western Prom starting at 6:00 P.M.

Southern State Parks

Bradbury Mountain State Park
528 Hallowell Road, Pownal
(207) 688–4712

Open year-round from 9:00 A.M. to sunset, Bradbury Mountain State Park is only a 20-minute drive north of Portland. Bradbury Mountain is relatively small (the summit is only 485 feet above sea level), but this 590-acre park is perfect for families. It has numerous trails, none of which are particularly difficult, leading to the summit, as well as 42 campground sites, picnic areas, and a playground. Snowshoe rentals are available in winter months. Plus, the park is only 10 minutes from Freeport and all of its outlet stores and restaurants. To get to Bradbury Mountain, take Interstate 295 North from Portland to the Freeport/Durham exit (about 16 miles from the city). Follow the sign at the base of the exit ramp to Bradbury Mountain. Entrance to the park costs $3.00 for people age 12 and older, $1.00 for children ages 5 to 12, and is free for kids under 5. Camping is also available for $10 per site, per night.

RECREATION

Adrenaline Adventures

Northern Outdoors Adventure Resort
Route 201, The Forks
(207) 663–4466, (800) 765–7238
www.northernoutdoors.com

The Northern Outdoors Adventure Resort offers family and adult wilderness adventure packages on the Kennebec, Penobscot, and Dead Rivers. White-water rafting, kayaking, rock climbing, snowmobiling, and fishing adventures are among the getaways coordinated by Northern Outdoors. Participants stay overnight in one of two sleek "lodgominiums" in either The Forks or Millinocket. Food is served in the lodgominium dining room and includes lobster and handcrafted ale from the Kennebec River Brewery. The Forks lodgo, the one closest to Portland, is a two-hour drive north, so a visit to the resort is best planned as a day trip or weekend excursion. Call for packages and rates.

Raft Maine
P.O. Box 3
Bethel, ME 04217
(800) RAFT–MEE
www.raftmaine.com

Raft Maine is an association of 13 professional white-water rafting outfitters who run trips on various rivers in Maine from October to April. Both beginner and advanced rafters can book Raft Maine trips through their toll-free number. For children, seniors, and others desiring a more serene experience, rafting on smaller rapids on the Kennebec River is an option. Those who are more daring can sign up for trips on Class IV and V rapids. All trip guides are registered white-water guides licensed by the state. Most trips start early in the morning and end mid-afternoon, so lodging at the outfitter's base facility is recommended. A variety of lodging options, including log cabins, B&Bs, motels, and campgrounds, are available at every base camp. Office staff at Raft Maine will help you plan your trip and find appropriate accommodations. Outfitter packages run from $80 to $130 per person, depending on the date and level of rapids. Most packages can be purchased with lodging included.

Skydive New England
40 Skydive Land, Lebanon
(207) 339–1520, (800) UGO–JUMP
www.ugojump.com
Located about 75 minutes by car from downtown Portland, Skydive New England offers jumps for both the beginner and the experienced adrenaline junkie. The skydive school has been in operation for more than 20 years and offers everything from tandem jumps (you and an instructor jump strapped to each other) to individual and group jumps (you're on your own, baby). Jumps range from heights of 10,000 to 14,000 feet. Tandem skydives start at $185 per person and include instruction and equipment. A variety of individual and group jumps are also available at different prices, depending on time of day, type of jump, and gear rental.

Skydive New England is also certified by the United States Parachute Association to offer skydiving classes, so you can learn to jump on your own. Prices vary according to the level of certification awarded. Call for more details.

If you want to bring home proper bragging rights, you can purchase still photos or a videotape of your jump. This way, all of your friends and family can see what sheer terror really looks like.

Archery

Nicely Equipped Archery
South Street, Gorham
(207) 839–5903
While Portland does not have any archery supply stores or groups of its own, there are a handful within reasonable driving distance of the city. One of the best is Nicely Equipped Archery in Gorham (about a 10-mile drive west of the city), which features a heated range and classes for adults and youth as well as an extensive pro shop.

Auto Racing

Beech Ridge Motor Speedway
70 Holmes Road, Scarborough
(207) 885–0111
(207) 885–5800 (24-hour race line)
www.beechridge.com
Auto racing is alive and well throughout the state, and many local racing clubs have their own elite group of racers who take the pastime very seriously. Portland's most famous track is certainly no exception. The Beech Ridge Motor Speedway bills itself as one of the top five short tracks in the United States and is one of only 80 short tracks in the country to earn NASCAR sanctioning rights. Beech Ridge works with a pool of 150 local racers during its season, from April to September. Beech Ridge has trained many national-caliber racers, including Ricky Craven and Kevin Lepage. Amateur racers can get in on the action on Thursday Thunder nights (featuring seven events open for amateurs) and during "Car Wars," the Friday-night amateur demolition derby. Beech Ridge Motor Speedway also hosts go-kart races every Friday night. Racers range in age from 8 to 50.

Baseball

Mike Bordick Summer Baseball League
512 Warren Avenue
(207) 878–2600
www.frozenropes.com
For local players ages 16 to 20, the Mike Bordick Summer Baseball League is an opportunity to

compete in baseball during the summer season away from school. The league is operated through the Maine Frozen Ropes training center in Portland, which trains amateur and professional ball players in anticipation of their upcoming seasons. You can apply as either a team or an individual. The team fee is $2,050; the individual fee is $275. The fees include uniforms, umpire fees, field rentals, and Frozen Ropes baseballs. The league has three different age divisions.

Basketball

Portland does not have a professional basketball team, so local basketball fanatics tend to closely follow the high school teams—Portland, Deering, Cheverus, and McCauley. In the past the Portland High School team has excelled, garnering a notable bit of prestige both locally and regionally. If you're interested in tossing the ball around yourself, check out any one of the outdoor basketball courts around town for a pickup game during the warmer months (Deering Oaks Park downtown and the Brackett Street courts in the West End are both popular spots) or head to the YMCA on Forest Avenue to use their indoor court. If you opt for the Y, you'll need to purchase either a gym membership or a day pass ($7.00).

Biking

Southern Maine Cycling Club
1440 Congress Street
(207) 773–1700
www.southernmainecyclingclub.org
The Southern Maine Cycling Club (SMCC) is a recreational riding club that accepts new members year-round. The prime riding months are the warmer ones (April to October), although members schedule rides throughout the year. During peak season, SMCC offers several rides a week, including road and off-road rides. The group is the largest organizer of bike races in Maine and sponsors a mountain bike race in July and a weekend of racing in August. Club dues are $20 per rider and include discounts at Gorham Bike and Ski, the store that hosts the

club. Just in town for a visit? The Southern Maine Cycling Club matches members with visitors looking for company on a ride.

Birding

Maine Audubon Society/Gilsland
Farm Sanctuary
20 Gilsland Farm Road, Falmouth
(207) 781–2330
www.maineaudubon.org
Maine, with its abundant forests and coastline, is a bird lovers' paradise. Around Portland, one of the most popular spots for bird watchers is the Gilsland Farm Sanctuary in Falmouth, a neighboring suburb. Gilsland Farm covers 65 acres of meadows, woods, and salt marshes perfect for walking, snowshoeing, and bird watching. The property is managed by the Maine Audubon Society, which keeps it open free of charge from dawn to dusk except when the property is rented for fundraisers. The main gate provides access to the Audubon store and additional parking and is open Monday through Saturday from 9:00 A.M. to 5:00 P.M., Sunday from noon to 5:00 P.M., and on all holidays except Easter, Thanksgiving, Christmas, and New Year's Day.

For more information on other bird-watching opportunities, visit www.maine birding.net. Operated by a local bird-watching enthusiast, this comprehensive Web site includes news alerts, information on the birds of Maine, and links to other local birding sites.

Billiards

These days, nearly every pub in town has at least one pool table for billiard enthusiasts. The Old Port Tavern Billiards on Fore Street and Spot Shot Billiards on St. John Street, both of which are quite popular, have several tables. If you're interested in honing your skills and committing to the sport, you might want to check out the following store.

Skillful Billiards and Barstools
58–88 Alder Street
(207) 775–3000, (800) 662–4500
www.skillfulvending.com

Skillful Billiards and Barstools has provided homes and businesses with all things billiard since 1978. Located in the Bayside neighborhood of Portland, the store features a variety of pool tables and supplies; other games, such as foosball, darts, pinball, and air hockey; and every accessory imaginable for your home game room or business.

Bingo

Bingo is alive and well in Portland. You can find games in most churches, at festivals, and at local grange halls and clubhouses. People in this neck of the woods tend to take their game very seriously—it's typical for players to arrange lucky charms around a spread of several bingo sheets. Greater Portland has two bingo halls (one in South Portland, the other in Westbrook) for both enthusiasts and dabblers. For information on games in South Portland, call John Roberts Road Bingo Hall at (207) 761–2717. For Westbrook games, call Four Seasons Bingo at (207) 797–2699.

Boating

Boating in Maine runs the gamut, including kayaking, canoeing, motorboating, and sailing. The Maine Bureau of Parks and Lands Boating Facilities Division is probably the best place to start. The division produces a free brochure listing some 400 boat launches throughout the state. Call the department at (207) 287–4952 to have a copy mailed to you or access it online at www.state.me.us/doc/parks/programs/boating. The Boating Facilities Division also places navigational markers in 24 waterways around Maine. An online list of marked lanes is available at the site listed above; you can receive the print version by calling (207) 287–4952. For boating registration and safety tips, contact the Department of Inland Fisheries and Wildlife at (207) 287–4952. If you're interested in honing your boating skills or venturing into the realm of boating for the first time, visit www.boatsafe.com, which provides information on maritime navigation and boating courses for children and adults at sites along the coast of Maine.

As you can probably imagine, boating is quite popular in Portland. You can dock your boat at several marinas in Portland and across the bay in South Portland, including DiMillo's Old Port Marina, Sunset Marina, and the Breakwater Marina. Greater Portland also has plenty of yacht clubs that run regattas and have their own marinas. While the city doesn't have a dedicated office for boating information, the Greater Portland Convention and Visitors Bureau (207–772–5800) can provide information on boating groups in the area. For tide charts, weather pages, and numerous links to all things boating and ocean related, visit www.maineharbors.com.

Bowling

Bowling in Maine looks a bit different. While we do have alleys with tenpin bowling, we also have something called candlepin bowling, which involves bowling balls that are roughly half the size of the tenpin version and are lobbed at long, thin pins. We in Maine love our candlepin bowling. If you're interested in joining a tenpin league, contact the Greater Portland Ten Pin Bowling League. The league operates out of Yankee Lanes on Riverton Street in Portland and runs a series of competitive tournaments throughout the year for men, women, and juniors. Visit the group's Web site at www.gptpba.org. If you want to find out what all the candlepin fuss is about, take a look at the Web site for the Maine Candlepin Bowling Proprietors Association at www.mainecandlepinbowling.com, where you'll find information on candlepin bowling centers in your neighborhood, a brief history of candlepin, and information on upcoming tournaments.

Boxing

Portland Boxing Club
33 Allen Avenue
(207) 761–0975
www.portlandboxingclub.org
The Portland Boxing Club is a nonprofit amateur club that offers training and practice space to boxers age 12 years and older. Dues

are $25 per month and include use of the gym, with a ring, a weight room and treadmill, and all varieties of punching bags. Members are required to purchase a mouthpiece and handwraps, which are available at the gym. New members must make an appointment for their first session to be evaluated by a coach. No contact boxing is allowed for beginners until a coach has cleared it. Portland Boxing Club is a member of the USA Boxing Association and sponsors the annual Northeastern Regional Boxing Championships, which are held in Portland.

Camping

While there aren't any places in Portland proper where you can go camping, plenty of spots are available around Greater Portland and throughout the state for you to pitch your tent. Probably the best place to start your search is the *Maine Camping Guide,* which is published annually by the Maine Campground Owners Association. The guide is available online at www.campmaine.com, or you can have a copy mailed to you free by calling the association at (207) 782–5874. Remember that many campgrounds have carry-in/carry-out trash policies. If you require amenities like running water, showers, a recreation room, or an RV hookup, be sure to check with the campground beforehand.

Climbing

Maine Rock Gym
127 Marginal Way
(207) 780–6370
www.merockgym.com
If you enjoy scaling sheer rock faces, check out the Maine Rock Gym on Portland's Marginal Way. This indoor climbing facility features over 5,000 square feet of climbing surface. The rock gym rents all necessary equipment for the climb and provides several instructional climbing clinics for beginner to advanced climbers. Outdoor climbing excursions in New Hampshire and Maine can also be booked with the Maine Rock Guides

through the gym. All first-timers at the gym must pay $25 for the introductory package, which includes basic rope-handling instruction, orientation, and a day pass. An adult day pass costs $14 after the introductory visit, a six-month membership costs $240, and a one-year membership costs $390. Outside trips are an extra charge.

Contradance

Greater Portland Community Dance Series Contradance
Falmouth Congregational Church
267 Falmouth Road, Falmouth
(207) 781–3413
The Falmouth Contradance, run by the Greater Portland Community Dance Series, has made a name for itself in regional contra circles. The dance is held on the first Saturday of every month at 8:00 P.M. at the Falmouth Congregational Church and is open to children and adults of all ages. Dancers here are known for cutting loose and having an old-fashioned good time. People stomp to the live traditional music, dancers hoot, and plenty of men wear skirts (we're not sure how this came to be). At any rate, the contradance is a reliable, wholesome good time that will work up quite a sweat. The entrance fee is usually $8.00 for adults, $6.00 for students under 21, $4.00 for kids ages 5 to 12, and free for kids under 5.

Fishing

Fishing fans must purchase an annual fishing license here in Maine before casting a line in any of the state's waters. The seasonal fishing license costs $53 and can be purchased online through the Maine Online Sportsman's Electronic System at www.informe.org/moses or by calling the Maine Department of Inland Fisheries and Wildlife at (207) 287–8000. Once you've got your license, you might want to visit www.fish-maine.com, a comprehensive Web site for the recreational fisherman that provides information on charters, guides, bait shops, and related accommodations.

Flying

Maine Aviation Flight School
Portland International Jetport
1001 Westbrook Street
(207) 780–1811, (888) 359–7600
www.maineaviation.com
The Maine Aviation Flight School offers flying lessons in its fleet of small Cessna planes. The school certifies both private and commercial pilots through a computer-based instruction program in the Cessna Pilot Center. The Pilot Shop sells a variety of pilot gear, including headsets, charts, and aviation jackets. Planes use a runway at the Portland International Jetport. Maine Aviation also sells aircraft and operates a maintenance and management service.

Football

Southern Maine has several semipro and amateur football leagues for both women and men. Perhaps the best known is the Maine Tomcats, a team for men. This team operates out of Springvale (about an hour from Portland) but plays most games in Portland. For more on the Tomcats and whether you have what it takes to join this semipro team, visit their Web site at www.mainetomcats.com. Southern Maine also has a women's semipro football team called the Maine Freeze, the state's only full-contact football team for women. The Freeze, based in Portland, is one of 40 teams nationwide that are members of the National Women's Football Association. For more on the Freeze, call (207) 650–6806 or visit www.mainefreeze.com.

Frisbee

Portland's Ultimate Frisbee league is one of the most popular leagues in the area. With hundreds of members, from beginners to advanced players, Ultimate is as social as it is athletic. Regular season games start in June. The league has coed teams and teams for men or women. There are 18 games in the summer season (two per week) and a final tournament at the end of the summer.

i Every year, the Maine Department of Inland Fisheries and Wildlife allows a handful of "free fishing" days during which residents and nonresidents can fish without a license. Call (207) 287–8000 for information.

Ultimate also hosts plenty of informal and formal gatherings, including a wild Clambake in September to wrap up the summer. Games usually start around 6:00 P.M.; check the Web site (www.portlandultimate.com) for locations. Membership dues range from $45 to $60, depending on when you sign up.

Hiking

The Maine Outdoor Adventure Club (MOAC) includes members of all ages, skill sets, and abilities. Hiking is one of MOAC's most popular activities, but the group runs all kinds of trips year-round, from kayaking to rock climbing. MOAC meets in Portland at 7:00 P.M. on the first Wednesday of every month at the Unitarian Universalist Church at 524 Allen Avenue. You can also visit the group's Web site (www.moac.org) for information on upcoming trips. Attending the monthly meetings and trying out an activity or two are free, but if you want to be more involved, it's best to join the group. Individual membership costs $15 a year, which includes an e-mail newsletter. If you want a print newsletter mailed to you, the cost of membership increases to $25.

Hunting

In order to hunt in Maine, you must obtain an annual hunting license from the Maine Department of Inland Fisheries and Wildlife. You can call them at (207) 287–8000 or buy your license online at www.informe.org/moses. Licenses vary in price depending on the nature of the game hunted. Big-game licenses cost $22 for adult residents, $88 for adult nonresidents. Children under 10 years of age are not allowed to hunt. The state limits hunting for wild birds and wild animals to the hours between 30 minutes before sunrise

Portland Trails

One of the great things about living in Portland is that it has all the amenities of city living but is also surrounded by great natural beauty, from breathtaking views of Casco Bay to lush, forested parks and saltwater marshes that are abundant with wildlife.

The city is known nationally for its green spaces and the elaborate network of scenic trails that allows residents to enjoy a morning nature walk, lunchtime jog, or afternoon bike ride within minutes of home or work. Much of this trail system and its maintenance are the result of the hard work and sweat of scores of volunteers who belong to Portland Trails, an urban conservation organization founded in 1991. The group's long-term vision is rooted in the American Park Movement, which was prevalent at the turn of the 20th century. It was during that time that Portland mayor James Phinney Baxter and renowned landscape architects Frederick Law Olmsted and John Charles Olmsted mapped out their ideas for a system of connected parkways around the city. Today, not only is Portland Trails fulfilling that vision, but its influence is also creeping beyond the city limits, with projects pending in neighboring Westbrook and Falmouth.

Portland Trails publishes a handy four-color map of the city's trails, parks, and public open spaces for $4.95. The map includes descriptions of trails with information on length, difficulty, and parking availability. It also tells you if you can fish, swim, or roller-skate in the area. The maps can be ordered from Portland Trails

Strolling along the Eastern Promenade Trail. PORTLAND TRAILS; PHOTO BY PHIL POIRIER

Crossing Stroudwater Bridge. PORTLAND TRAILS; PHOTO BY PHIL POIRIER

directly by phone (207–775–2411) or through its Web site (www.trails.org). They can also be purchased at a number of shops around town, including Coffee By Design, Books Etc., Eastern Mountain Sports, Cyclemania, Maine Running Company, and The North Face.

Here are just a few of the trails that await you on your visit to Portland.

Back Cove Trail. This 3.5-mile loop around Portland's Back Cove is probably the most popular trail in the city. You'll see Portlanders walking their dogs, jogging, biking, and strolling their kids around the trail at all times of day. After all, why trudge along on a treadmill, staring at the wall, when you can have the cove and a spectacular view of Portland's skyline as an accompaniment to your workout? The trail, a combination of pavement and stone dust, connects to the Eastern Promenade Trail at Tukey's bridge, if you feel like going farther. Plenty of parking is available at

(continued)

Preble Street Extension and Payson Park, or you can get there by Metro bus routes 2, 4, and 8.

Eastern Promenade Trail. This convenient waterfront trail, offering terrific views of Portland Harbor and Casco Bay, is another huge favorite with the locals. The 2.1-mile trail is built along an old railway corridor and parallels the Maine Narrow Gauge Railroad train tracks (see the Attractions chapter). The little train occasionally comes chugging by while you're taking your walk. Parking is available at East End Beach, or you can take Metro bus routes 1 and 8. You can also access the trail at the junction of Commercial and India Streets.

Fore River Sanctuary. This 2-mile trail off Congress Street will take you to Jewell Falls, Portland's only natural waterfall. The land surrounding the waterfall was donated by one of the founders of Portland Trails. Fore River Sanctuary is an 85-acre Maine Audubon preserve that is a great place for bird watching; you might also spot some small mammals. Pets, bikes, and ATVs are not allowed here out of deference to the wildlife. For directions, visit the Portland Trails Web site or check your Portland Trails map, or you can take Metro bus routes 4 and 5.

Peaks Island Loop. Feel like taking a ferry ride? Find your way down to Casco Bay Ferry Lines on the east end of Commercial Street and take a 20-minute ride to Peaks Island, which is part of the city of Portland—at least for now, since residents are talking secession. You can walk the perimeter road of the island, a distance of 4 miles, or rent a bike at the island's cycle shop. The ferry and the island walk offer spectacular views of Casco Bay and the Atlantic Ocean. This is also a good way to catch a glimpse of some of Casco Bay's other islands as well as of Fort Gorges, a historic island fort accessible only by private boat.

Presumpscot River Preserve. Portland's trails are beautiful, but many of them are still, obviously, located in an urban setting. For a true feeling of being in "the great outdoors," Nan Cumming, executive director of Portland Trails, recommends visiting the Presumpscot River Preserve. This 2.5-mile trail, which winds through the woods and along the river, will take you in the footsteps of the Abenaki Indians, who came here each spring to fish. The trail was only completed in the summer of 2005, so it is still little used and familiar only to true insiders. Here you might spy deer, otter, osprey, and other wildlife. Eagles are spotted regularly. To reach the trailhead, take Allen Avenue to Summit Street and then follow Summit to Curtis Road and turn right. Another right at Overset Road will bring you to a parking area marked with a Portland Trails sign. Once you reach the river, going upstream will take you to wooded areas; going downstream will lead you to Presumpscot Falls.

and 30 minutes after sunset. The exceptions are spring wild turkey, migratory game birds, raccoon, and coyote night hunting. Hunters may hunt game only during the allowable dates, listed on the department's Web site at www.state.me.us. The department also provides a handbook with information on the various types of hunting and trapping allowable in Maine, tips on hunting and taxidermy, and information on regulations such as hunting hours and hunting grounds.

Ice Hockey

Portland Ice Arena
225 Park Avenue
(207) 774–8553
www.portlandicearena.com
The Portland Ice Arena near Hadlock Field hosts several informal hockey pickup teams for adults and youth. Adult pickup games take place on Monday, Wednesday, and Friday from 1:30 to 2:30 P.M. Games cost $4.00 per person, and players must wear helmets and face masks. The recreational league is composed of 18 teams in three divisions; all players must be at least 18 years old (no high school students permitted). The Old-Timers Hockey League (for adults age 35 and older), the Casco Bay Hockey Association (for children ages 5 to 18), and the Greater Portland Women's Ice Hockey League (for women age 18 and older) all utilize the arena. For more information on these leagues, contact the ice arena or visit the Web site.

Ice Skating

Portland Ice Arena
225 Park Avenue
(207) 774–8553
www.portlandicearena.com
The ice arena holds open skating hours year-round. Public skating costs $4.00 for adults, $2.00 for children age 17 and younger, and $2.00 for seniors. Skate rentals cost $1.00. Public skating hours change from day to day and month to month but generally encompass a small block in the morning and afternoon daily. The arena also hosts "public

freestyle" skating one day a week for experienced figure skaters only. Admission to the public freestyle costs $5.00.

Karting

Maine Indoor Karting
23 Washington Avenue, Scarborough
(888) 2–GOKART
The Maine Indoor Karting (MIK) scene is not for the faint of heart. MIK bills itself as "the only indoor racing facility of its kind in the state of Maine," and the driving is of the competitive variety. Here in Maine, where stock car racing is hugely popular, that means you could get some really tough cookies out on the track. MIK offers two types of European-designed racing karts in which you can tear around the twists of this snarled course. You must show a valid driver's license and be at least 16 years old to drive one of the adult karts. If you don't have a driver's license, you must take a safety class. Kids are also allowed on the track during junior races. Children ages 8 to 15 can rent junior karts for $5.00 per quarter hour. Licensing courses for juniors and adults cost $20 apiece. Adults with valid driver's licenses can "arrive and drive" for $18. For lovers, Friday night is couples night, and at $15 for the pair per race, who could deny the romance?

Rugby

The Portland Rugby Football Club is the oldest rugby league in the state. Formed in 1969, this men's club spent five years based in Brunswick before relocating to the City by the Sea to accommodate the large number of Portland players. Today, the club plays rough with a series of games throughout the summer. The club also remains close to the game's roots by touring (and playing) in the United Kingdom. For information on practices, games, and parties, it's best to check out the club's Web site (www.portland.rugby.net), since phone contacts can change by season depending on who's playing.

Running

While you certainly don't need an organized league to get out and jog, it can't hurt to meet a few new faces and maybe race, if the spirit moves you. To this end, the Maine Track Club is a great local resource for the running enthusiast. The group has been organizing runs since 1979 and is the largest running club in the state, with branches in several towns and cities. Members of the Portland branch host group runs—one every weekday at noon, one on Sunday morning, and one on Saturday morning for gay and lesbian runners. The Maine Track Club also sponsors road races, ranging in length from 3.1 miles to 50 miles, and the Maine Marathon every fall. Membership to the club costs $25 for individuals and families and $17 for students. Membership benefits include a subscription to the newsletter, discounts on running apparel at several local stores, coaching sessions during the summer, and a membership to the Road Runners Club of America. As if you needed more reason to sign up, the Maine Track Club is a social group and regularly gets together after runs and at their monthly meetings. For more information on the group, visit their Web site at www.mainetrackclub.com.

Shooting

Falmouth Rod and Gun Club
293 Gray Road, Falmouth
(207) 797–0048
www.frandg.org
The Falmouth Rod and Gun Club serves Greater Portland's gun fans with monthly socials and shooting events. The club is affiliated with the Pine Tree State Rifle and Pistol Association, which coordinates shooting events with clubs around the state. Membership in the Pine Tree Association is separate

from membership in the local club; it costs $15 annually ($300 for life) and includes a subscription to the quarterly newsletter, eligibility to participate in Postal Competitions, and membership in the state affiliate of the National Rifle Association. For information on joining, visit www.mainerpa.org. Membership in the Falmouth Rod and Gun Club costs $125 per year plus a nonrefundable initiation fee of $75. All members must attend a "responsibility class" before being sworn in. Members have access to the clubhouse in Falmouth and the shooting ranges and competitions sponsored by the club.

Skiing

Cross-Country Skiing

Portland Ski Club
32 Pinecrest Road
(207) 879–0134
The Portland Ski Club is now in its seventh year. Run by a ski enthusiast and his wife, the club has focused mostly on establishing cross-country ski trails on the peninsula. To this end, Portland Ski is responsible for established Nordic trails at Riverside Golf Course, Deering Oaks Park, and the Western Promenade near Maine Medical Center. All trails are free to use and, of course, dependent on a good dumping of snow. The ski club is a resource for area skiers looking for trail and weather information.

Downhill Skiing

OK, it doesn't take a genius to tell you that Maine has some great downhill skiing areas. We have listed three of the area's most popular ski resorts and their contact information. None of them are in Portland proper, but you can easily drive to them.

Lost Valley, in Auburn, is located just 45 minutes from Portland. Lost Valley features 15 trails, a new snowboard terrain park (appropriate for beginners through intermediates), and night skiing. Day passes range from $21 to $33 for adults and from $19 to $30 for juniors, depending on the day. Visit www.lost

valleyski.com or call (207) 784–1561 for more information.

Shawnee Peak, in Bridgton, is the longest-running ski destination in the state. Shawnee has 40 trails (19 of which are lit for night skiing), two terrain parks, a 400-foot half-pipe, and slopes for beginner to advanced skiers. One-day lift tickets range from $34 to $45 for adults and from $23 to $31 for juniors and seniors, depending on the day. Shawnee also offers lots of discounts and daily specials, so be sure to visit their Web site (www.shawneepeak.com) or call (207–647–8444) for details.

Sunday River, near Bethel, features 128 trails across eight mountain peaks for beginner to advanced skiers, night skiing, and 18 lifts. One-day lift tickets cost $45 for adults and $35 for juniors and seniors. Lodging is available on the mountains, and there are plenty of events and activities for the whole family. For more information, visit www.sundayriver.com or call (800) 543–2SKI.

Snowmobiling

Maine Snowmobile Association
P.O. Box 80
Augusta, ME 04332
(207) 622–6983
www.mesnow.com
Maine is covered in a blanket of snow for at least three months out of the year, so it's no wonder that snowmobiling has become a popular pastime in these parts. If you're an enthusiast yourself, or looking to become one, the best place to start is the Maine Snowmobile Association (MSA) in Augusta. This organization, with some 32,000 members, maintains trails, creates new ones, provides a social outlet for snowmobilers, and produces the annual Maine Snowmobile Show the first weekend of October at the Cumberland County Civic Center in Portland. Lest you think snowmobiling is all fun and games, though, the MSA Web site also has information on trail conditions and snowmobiling accidents. Every year, Maine loses a handful of snowmobilers to trail-related acci-

dents, so be careful. To this end, the state provides a free copy of its booklet on snowmobile laws and rules. Contact the State Department of Inland Fisheries and Wildlife at (207) 287–8003 to have a free copy mailed to you.

> **i** You must be at least 14 years old to operate a snowmobile on a public road or trail in Maine.

Softball

Greater Portland Senior Men's Softball League
This seven-team league is for men age 50 and over. Currently, the league serves Portland and South Portland, but if there is enough demand in the future, the league might expand to other towns. The league was formed in 1998 and is run by the Maine Senior Games, which every year conducts a series of competitive games for seniors. For more information on joining the softball league, contact the Maine Senior Games at (207) 396–6500 or (800) 427–7411.

Spectator Sports

The Portland Sea Dogs
271 Park Avenue
(800) 936–3647
www.seadogs.com
The Portland Sea Dogs, based at Hadlock Field on Park Avenue, are our city's minor league baseball team. The Sea Dogs were formed in 1991 and are the AA affiliate of the Boston Red Sox. Tickets to games cost $8.00 for adults and $7.00 for children and can sell out fast, especially if the Dogs make it to the playoffs. Season tickets are also popular (box season passes cost $426 per person). On game days the area around Hadlock Field becomes clogged with traffic and baseball fans pouring into the stands to catch the game, enjoy a hot dog or two, and wave at Slugger, the Sea Dogs' mascot.

i The Greater Portland YMCA has a great lap pool, but unless you're a member, you'll have to buy a $7.00 day pass to use it. For free swimming, try the Riverton Community Pool at 1600 Forest Avenue. Call (207) 874–8456 for pool times.

The Portland Pirates
531 Congress Street
(207) 828–4665
(207) 775–3458 (tickets)
www.portlandpirates.com

The Portland Pirates, the local hockey team, are based at the Cumberland County Civic Center in downtown Portland. The Pirates were founded in the early 1990s and replaced the previous amateur hockey team, the Maine Mariners. The Pirates belong to the American Hockey League and are the minor league affiliates of the Mighty Ducks of Anaheim. They play home games nearly every week during the winter. If you enjoy fast-paced action with tons of cheering and yelling for blood from the audience, the Pirates' games are the place to be. Tickets range in price from $6.00 to $19.50 for adults, depending on the location of the seats. Season tickets are also available.

Swimming

New England Masters Swim Club
P.O. Box 206
Londonderry, NH 03053
(888) SWIM–NEM
www.swimnem.org

The New England Masters Swim Club (NEMSC) is the regional branch of the national Masters Swim Club, which was founded in 1970 and is part of United States Aquatic Sports. Swimmers age 19 and older are welcome to join. Members range in skill level from beginners to former Olympic athletes. NEMSC members swim in more than 100 pools in the region, half of which have organized workouts and competitions. Membership costs $35 per year and includes membership to the national organization, a subscription to *Swim* magazine, a newsletter subscription, and medical insurance for meets and organized workouts.

Tennis

Maine Tennis Association
P.O. Box 2060
West Scarborough, ME 04070-2060
(207) 883–5243
www.mtatennis.com

The Maine Tennis Association, an affiliate club of USTA/USA Tennis New England, was founded more than a quarter century ago. It currently has 1,400 members statewide and a pretty solid adult league in Greater Portland. The association sponsors not only competitive tournaments but also tennis lessons, fund-raising events, and tennis for players with handicaps. Annual membership is $40 for adults and $18 for people under 19.

NEIGHBORHOODS AND REAL ESTATE

As a boy growing up in Portland, the 19th-century poet Henry Wadsworth Longfellow fell in love with the city he called "a jewel by the sea" and returned frequently throughout his lifetime. Many visitors to Portland catch the same seaside fever that Longfellow did, returning time and again and sometimes even relocating here. This chapter gives you some basic tools to get you started on making Portland your own home-sweet-home. It describes the city's neighborhoods, notes basic real estate market trends, and lists some of the best-known real estate agencies in the area. There is also information to help you settle in.

In the past decade or so, Portland has consistently ranked among the most livable small cities in the country. Education, safety, population diversity, and other quality-of-life issues rate well here year after year. For this reason, the city's population continues to swell, with growing influences from Boston and New York City transplants. It's no wonder, then, that the real estate market here is one of the hottest in the Northeast.

In 2004 Portland led the Northeast—a region that on its own had the largest median increase in the country—in home price increases. The median price of a home in Portland jumped to $251,605 in the summer of 2006. The "jewel by the sea" is no longer the country's best-kept secret. And it's no wonder—living in Portland offers many appealing features: You'll get all four seasons in crisp, clear distinction; you'll have the culture and quirk of the downtown mixed with a deep sense of history and hometown pride; you can live in the quaint bustle of the city center or relax in one of its popular sleepy suburbs; you can even settle down on one of five islands in Casco Bay, known for their tight-knit, safe communities.

As you begin to regard Portland with an eye for commitment, be sure to check out this chapter's brief rundown of the city's neighborhoods, each of which has its own distinctive history and character. In the end, though, nothing can make up for careful research and a solid gut feeling. Welcome to Portland. Why don't you put up your feet and stay awhile?

NEIGHBORHOODS
Old Port/Downtown

Stretching roughly from State Street to India Street and from the bay to Cumberland Avenue, the downtown and Old Port neighborhoods sit on what was the original site of George Cleeve and Richard Tucker's first settlement back in 1633 (see the History chapter). The Portland downtown is where the old and the new collide. It is home to some of the oldest architecture in Portland as well as most of the city's retail stores, cultural outlets, and nighttime haunts. Because of the high premium on commercial property in the downtown, most of the housing options here are in the form of apartments. And because many of the buildings date back to the massive rebuilding effort after the Great Fire in 1866, most of the apartments here are small Victorian-era digs; and rents are high due to the hip location. Average rates run from $600 to over $1,000 for a one-bedroom apartment. The neighborhood tends to be populated by

> **i** Fore Street and Wharf Street, where most of the area bars and clubs are located, can be especially rowdy and noisy on weekend nights. If you are a light sleeper, avoid hanging your hat near this part of the downtown.

young singles who enjoy the bustle of these busy streets.

North

Back Cove

The Back Cove refers to the area bracketed by Baxter Boulevard, Washington Avenue, Canco Road, and Forest Avenue. This neighborhood has it all, from quiet seaside homes along the ocean inlet called Back Bay to homes and apartment buildings lining the busiest streets in the city. The Back Bay is one of the most popular walking and jogging paths in the city and is busy year-round with runners, kids on bikes, and families. The residential areas of Back Cove nearest the Back Bay are quiet, with wide streets and stately homes. If you're looking for a more urban feel, try renting an apartment along Washington Avenue or Forest Avenue in the neighborhood.

Bayside

The Bayside neighborhood straddles the industrial and commercial areas of downtown Portland. Bordered by four busy roads (Franklin Arterial, Forest Avenue, Marginal Way, and Congress Street), Bayside is currently the focus of an urban renewal effort by the city after decades of industrial development and poor management made the area one of the most impoverished in the city. Today, Bayside residents include families, urban homesteaders, the elderly and disabled, and students. One-third of the neighborhood is residential; the remainder is still commercial and industrial. Due to the relative dearth of residential housing in the neighborhood, few houses are available for purchase, although the area beyond Franklin Arterial, known as East Bayside, has more houses and apartment buildings for sale. Bayside is home to many of the city's social service agencies, including Goodwill, the Salvation Army, and the Preble Street Resource Center homeless shelter and soup kitchen.

Deering

In February 1899 the city of Portland annexed Deering, which had previously been an independent town. Today, Deering is a haven for families and is home to many of the city's best schools. Schools here include Longfellow Elementary School; Catherine McCauley and Cheverus High Schools, the area's parochial giants; and Deering High School, which is one of four public high schools in Portland (the others are Portland Arts and Technology on Allen Avenue, Casco Bay High School on Allen Avenue, and Portland High on Congress Street). The Deering neighborhood, which is divided geographically into North Deering and East Deering, is known for its quiet streets and spacious family-size homes. Along Stevens Avenue, the central artery of the Deering neighborhood, you'll find many of the area's schools, hangouts, and churches. Much of Deering is about a 10-minute drive from the downtown (walking is somewhat prohibitive from this distance), and the city center is accessible without being in your backyard.

> **i** If you're in Deering, be sure to try a sandwich at Pat's Meat Market on Stevens Avenue. This grocery store and deli is consistently rated one of the city's best in area newspaper polls.

East

Munjoy Hill

Munjoy Hill—named for its first settler, George Munjoy—spent roughly the first two centuries of its existence as a grazing ground for cattle. The area has also been romantically referred to on some period maps as "Mount Joy." Today, the Hill, as it is known to natives, is a densely populated neighborhood known for its affordable rents and generations-old working-class communities. It covers the area roughly from India Street at the eastern edge of the Old Port up to the Eastern Promenade, whose view of Casco Bay is just as stunning as its western counterpart's vista. Most buildings on the Hill are multifamily units. The neighborhood has become something of a hot spot lately for families and young singles alike, who flock here for its funky, unpretentious personality and its proximity to the downtown. The Hill has long been the city's best-kept real estate secret, although national magazine coverage and a healthy amount of bragging have made finding that gem of a deal a bit more challenging. Nonetheless, you can still find apartments and homes renting or selling well below market.

South

Islands of Casco Bay

Of the more than 365 Calendar Islands in Casco Bay, five are inhabitable parts of the Portland municipality: Little Diamond, Great Diamond, Peaks, Cliff, and Cushing Islands (Long Island is independent, and Cheabeague Island is part of the nearby town of Cumberland). If you have the tenacity, the schedule flexibility, and the independent spirit that seem to define all Portland island residents, you might be suited for living on one of our Casco Bay islands. Island residents, especially those who stick around all year, tend to form tight-knit communities. Many of the islands play host to artists who have chosen to escape city life on the mainland. Some of the islands have their own grammar schools, often out of one small house, and life here is simple. Peaks Island, which is closest to the mainland, is the most popular in part because the ferry stops here frequently (the Casco Bay Ferry stops shuttling to all other islands around 5:00 P.M., while the Peaks shuttle continues on until nearly midnight). Recently, water taxis have started to run residents across the bay, but their routes are not yet frequent enough to alleviate what is perhaps the biggest drawback to island living—getting to the mainland and back.

If you do decide that you can handle the commute, be aware that renting or buying a house here is the rule. There are very few apartments for rent on the islands, and many of the residents tend to be families, retirees, or extended-stay vacationers. The population at any of these spots tends to be small during the winter months (the most popular residen-

In 2003 Portland residents formed the Greater Portland Neighborhoods Coalition to facilitate citizen participation in the city's various neighborhoods. Nearly every neighborhood in Portland has its own volunteer neighborhood association, which works to organize social events, advocate for the neighborhood, and otherwise maintain a sense of community. Visit www.livinginportland .org for information on your local chapter.

tial island, Peaks, boasts a winter population of only 1,000), but the island communities swell to three to five times their cold-weather numbers during the summer months, when homes are rented to out-of-towners for the warm season. Homes on the islands range in price from $150,000 to more than $3 million.

Stroudwater

Located along the Stroudwater River near the southern end of outer Congress Street, the Stroudwater neighborhood is host to some of the oldest homes in the city, including the former home of George Tate (see the Attractions chapter for more information). Stroudwater spent its early years as a vibrant hamlet that used its rivers to power mast mills for the Royal Navy. Today, Stroudwater is a sleepy little neighborhood sandwiched between the bustle of outer Congress Street and Brighton Avenue. Here, you'll find the Portland International Jetport across the street from the Elks Lodge. Churches exist side by side with strip malls. Many of the homes here are single-family houses that are tucked away from the busy streets in quiet blocks. Homes in Stroudwater enjoy a sense of suburban solitude with the convenience of city living.

West

Parkside

Parkside enjoys the distinction of being the most densely populated and ethnically diverse neighborhood in all of northern New England. The neighborhood borders the largest park in Portland, Deering Oaks Park, and stretches all the way west to St. John Street, south up the hill to Congress Street, and east to Forest Avenue. Residents enjoy the convenience of a short walk downtown as well as the option of lounging in the park, just a stone's throw away. While some of the homes here, like the stately brick houses on Deering Street, rival the grandeur of those on the West End, parts of Parkside have developed a reputation for noisiness—Grant Street, Mellon Street, and Park Avenue being the most notable—and neighbors hanging out on porches and gangs of children crowding corners are not uncommon. Much of the property here dates back to the early 20th century. Rents in Parkside tend to be much cheaper than for other, traditionally quieter neighborhoods in Portland.

The West End

As you wander the streets of this posh neighborhood, chances are you'll never guess that some people once thought that developing the area was a waste of taxpayers' money. In Portland's early colonial days, staying close to the Neck (what we now know as the Old Port and downtown) was considered essential to avoid attacks by aggressive Native Americans. Only a few daring souls braved the wilderness to erect their homes on the wild western hill during these early years. More than a century later, development was still slow to reach the West End. In 1836, when the walkway called the Western Promenade was laid out by the city for citizens' recreation, many townspeople decried the development as a waste because no one would want to trek that far out of town for a nice walk. But nowadays Portlanders gather every evening at the Western Prom to enjoy the city's best view of the sunset.

Today, the West End is one of the most esteemed, and crowded, neighborhoods in town. The area is renowned for its Victorian-era architecture, much of which was built after the Great Fire of 1866. The West End, which roughly includes every home on State Street west to the Promenade, is famous for its stately mansions, impeccably clean streets, and expensive property. The serene, friendly atmosphere of the West End comes at a predictable price—apartment rents in the lavish section of the neighborhood along the Promenade tend to run at least $100 above the city average. And if you'd like to snag the deed to your own West End home, be ready to plunk down between $150,000 and upwards of $1 million.

LIFE OUTSIDE OF PORT CITY

As a newcomer to the area, you might opt to live outside of the city in one of the neighboring towns or cities. Maybe you want more space, or a different school system, or more peace and quiet. Here's a quick thumbnail sketch of some of Portland's most popular suburbs, along with median single-family home prices, according to 2004 local real estate figures. You'll notice that housing costs are more expensive in many of Portland's suburbs in than in the city itself. Suburban living in southern Maine is still at a premium.

Westbrook

Located to the west of Portland, Westbrook was for decades known primarily as a mill town. The Sappi paper mill on Main Street still processes paper but in the past few years has significantly cut back on output, causing the town, which previously relied heavily on the mill for employment, to seek to reinvent itself. These days, Westbrook is an up-and-coming working-class town that is home to artists, new families, and rooted Mainers alike. The town's population is just under 17,000 people, according to the 2000 U.S. Census; half the population is married, and one quarter of residents have children under 18 years old living in the home. Although you're only a 10-minute drive from downtown Portland, you can still find a good deal on a house due to Westbrook's relatively new hot-spot status—the median home price is $205,000.

South Portland

The city directly south of Portland is some-times thought of as two cities. The mall area, which is the largest retail, commercial, and office complex in northern New England, sprawls over much of the western part of South Portland. The rest of the city is largely residential. Here, you're within minutes of the downtown, but you don't have to deal with the noise or the population density of the peninsula. In recent years South Portland has become more and more popular among Port-land's young families. Because of the proxim-ity to both the city and the ocean, houses here certainly aren't cheap, but many families are wooed by the promise of a larger back-yard, a safe place for their children to wander, and quality urban schools. The median price for a single-family home in South Portland is relatively low for the area—$203,000.

Cape Elizabeth

The Cape, as it's known here, lies south of Portland and has a reputation for being one of the chicest suburbs in Greater Portland. Once a farming community, Cape Elizabeth is now home to retirees, families, and singles who live in neat, beautiful country homes. While South Portland manages to be both metropol-itan and quaint, the Cape has abandoned the metro vibe for the soothing pace of country living. Here, you'll find beaches and farms sell-ing strawberries next to country clubs and golf courses. It is one of the most expensive places to live in the state, but a lot of people think it's worth it. The median price in 2004 for a single-family home was $355,000.

Falmouth

Located north of Portland, Falmouth is an affluent suburb with rolling country roads and a modest main street with enough large stores and diverse offerings to keep residents from schlepping into the city whenever they need to go shopping. Falmouth, like South Port-land and the Cape, is sprawling and doesn't have much of a walkable downtown, but it

does have stately homes with plenty of land and neighborhoods where people know each other by their first name. The schools here are good, as they are in much of Greater Portland, and the Falmouth Country Club is one of the most prestigious in the area. Homes here rank among the most expensive in the state. Many people who look for homes here also search in nearby Cumberland and Yarmouth, which in both affordability and tone are similar to Falmouth. In 2004 the median price here for a single-family home was $399,000.

Scarborough

The fastest-growing city in the state, Scarbor-ough is currently wrestling with the chal-lenges of being too popular. Hot with families looking for great schools and space off the peninsula, Scarborough has exploded in pop-ulation and development over the past few years. Needless to say, popularity has driven up the price of homes, but Scarborough is fighting to retain its affordability by encourag-ing cluster housing and affordable rents and home prices. Scarborough's downtown is strewn along Route 1 and is navigable by car but not really appealing for a leisurely Sunday walk. Plans are under way to cluster retail development in order to re-create an old-fashioned downtown, but so far, the city has had trouble making this dream a reality. The median price in 2004 for a single-family home was $315,000, according to local real estate figures.

REAL ESTATE

Housing prices in each of Portland's various neighborhoods can run the gamut. As a thumbnail rule, however, homes along the Western and Eastern Proms and those in the affluent suburbs of Falmouth, Cape Elizabeth, Cumberland, and Yarmouth are the most expensive in the area. For example, the median home price in Cumberland County, where Portland and its suburbs are located, is $229,000, according to a 2004 report by the Maine Real Estate Information System. But the median home price in Falmouth, one of Portland's most popular suburbs, is $320,000. And plenty of homes in Falmouth and the other suburbs sell well above that mark, with some going for more than $1 million. Bargain hunters can still find nice homes with great acreage in the city's distant suburbs, especially those a half-hour to an hour commute out, such as Gorham, Windham, and Buxton.

The type of housing in Portland also varies broadly, from old brick and wood-frame homes dating back to the 19th century to modern high-rise apartment complexes and condominiums. Because property in the neighborhoods and suburbs of Greater Portland tends to be so diverse, you may find it helpful to consult a local real estate agent to find the dream home that best suits your aesthetics and your budget. Fortunately, help is not hard to find—the real estate sector in Greater Portland is extensive and crowded. We have compiled a brief list of some of the most established Realtors in the city. This list, while by no means exhaustive, will give you a solid introduction to some of our largest agencies as you begin your search. Happy house hunting!

Realtors

Century 21
72 Auburn Street
(207) 741–2727
www.century21fcr.com
This local Century 21 office is one of five in the area. The Auburn Street branch focuses on single-family residential homes throughout Greater Portland. A team of 16 Realtors will help you evaluate the market and make your selection. Century 21 also offers free valuation analysis and employs an in-house builder to help design new homes.

Fishman Realty Group
2 Cotton Street
(207) 775–6561
www.fishmanrealty.com
The Fishman Realty Group, owned by Alan Fishman, opened its doors in 1987. Today, the small staff of five Realtors (including Alan's son Mark) works from an office in the heart of the downtown and is best known for its commercial real estate sales. Along with commercial property sale and rental, Fishman Realty also offers residential sales and rentals, property management, and vacation rentals.

Greater Portland Keller Williams Realty
49 Dartmouth Street
(207) 879–9800
www.kwmaine.com
Founded in 1983, Keller Williams Realty International added the Portland office to its roster of 240 offices in 2003. The Portland office, which employs 132 agents and is locally owned, not only handles real estate purchases and rentals but also provides educational seminars for real estate agents and

Real Estate Resources

There are several resources to help you with your realty needs. The Web site of the Maine Association of Realtors, www.mainerealtors .com, offers information on Realtors, commercial properties, and homes for rent or for sale.

The Portland Board of Realtors is a private, nonprofit industry association with over 700 member Realtors. The group works primarily with real estate agents, but if you visit their Web site (www .portlandboardofrealtors.com), you can search listings and contact a member Realtor.

MaineToday.com, the Web site of the Blethen Maine Newspapers, features an excellent section on real estate in Maine, including articles on market trends, real estate listings, and resources for finding a Realtor. For more information, visit www.mainetoday.com and click on "Real Estate."

those interested in launching a career in real estate. Keller Williams does not deal in rentals. Visit the Portland Keller Williams Web site for tips on moving as well as virtual tours of many of their available properties.

Port Island Realty
14 Welch Street
(207) 766–5966, (207) 775–7253
www.portisland.com
Owned by Kirk Goodhue, this small agency of six Realtors specializes in real estate on the Casco Bay islands. The agency covers all of the islands reachable by the Casco Bay Ferry as well as Cushing Island. Port Island Realty has been in operation for more than 20 years and facilitates the rental and sale of homes and cottages on islands such as Peaks, Great Diamond, Little Diamond, and Cliff.

RE/MAX By the Bay
970 Baxter Boulevard
(207) 773–2345, (800) 707–7214
www.homesinmaine.com
One of three area franchise branches of the international real estate giant RE/MAX, RE/MAX By the Bay features more than 50 agents who specialize in property in the Greater Portland and Cumberland County areas. RE/MAX By the Bay, like the company's two other franchise offices in Westbrook and Yarmouth, focuses solely on residential property. The office does not handle rentals. RE/MAX By the Bay also specializes in new construction and land purchasing. Of the three RE/MAXoffices in Greater Portland, By the Bay is the largest, and the agency claims that the average agent has more than 15 years of experience. For the past three years, RE/MAX By the Bay has sold more homes than any other Greater Portland agency.

Town and Shore Associates
1 Union Wharf
(207) 773–0262
www.townandshore.com
Town and Shore Associates, employing a staff of 13 Realtors and often representing homes priced at $400,000 or more, has marketed

high-end listings in the Greater Portland area for more than 20 years. It may be no surprise, then, that Town and Shore is the local Sotheby's International Realty and RELO premier real estate representative. In addition to realty service, Town and Shore also offers relocation assistance. Their comprehensive Web site includes a property search database as well as suggestions for seasonal activities in the Greater Portland area.

RELOCATION INFORMATION

Be careful. If you come to Portland for a visit, the city is likely to seduce you into a longer stay—like, maybe, a lifetime. If you're one of those people "from away" who have been entranced by the quality of life in this seaside community and want to call it home, you'll find some quick references in this section that will help you settle in.

For more information, see "Moving to Maine" at www.maine.gov/portal/family/moving.html and check out the "Moving to Maine" guide on the *Maine Today* Web site at http://realestate.mainetoday.com/moving.html.

Utilities
Electricity
Central Maine Power
83 Edison Drive
Augusta
(800) 750–4000
www.cmpco.com

Gas
Northern Utilities
1075 Forest Avenue
(800) 677–5052
www.northernutilities.com

Water
Portland Water District
P.O. Box 3553
225 Douglass Street
Portland, ME 04104-3553
(207) 761–8310
www.pwd.org

Oil Heat

If your new home is heated with oil, there are many companies in the area that can provide you with the fuel you will need to stay warm during your first Maine winter. To compare prices and services, go to www.maineoil.com.

Useful Telephone Numbers in Maine

Emergency 911
Directory Assistance 411

Alcoholics Anonymous
(207) 774–4335

Animal Refuge League
(207) 854–9771

Better Business Bureau
(207) 878–2715

Bureau of Veterans Services
(207) 878–2683

Child Abuse or Neglect Reports
(800) 452–1999

Community Counseling Center
(207) 874–1030

Crisis Intervention Hotline
(207) 774–4357

Department of Environmental Protection
(207) 882–6300

Family Crisis Services
(207) 874–1973

Legal Services for the Elderly Hotline
(800) 750–5353

Local Offices of Maine's U.S. Congressional Delegation:
  Sen. Olympia Snowe, (207) 874–0883
  Sen. Susan Collins, (207) 780–3575
  Rep. Thomas Allen, (207) 774–5019

Rep. Michael Michaud, (207) 942–6935 (Bangor)

Maine Department of Health and Human Services Mental Health Crisis 24-Hour Hotline
(888) 568–1112

Pine Tree Legal Assistance
(207) 774–8211

Poison Control Center
(800) 222–1222

Portland Chamber of Commerce
(207) 772–2811

Portland Coalition for the Psychiatrically Labeled
(207) 772–2208

Sexual Assault Crisis and Support
(800) 871–7741

Sexual Assault Response Services of Maine
(207) 774–3613

Suicide Prevention 24-Hour Hotline
(207) 774–4357

Telephone and Internet Service Providers

Verizon
45 Forest Avenue
(800) 870–9999
www.verizon.com

AT&T
(800) 222–0300

Time Warner Cable of Maine
118 Johnson Road
(207) 253–2584

Pine Tree Networks
92 Oak Street
(207) 699–2300, (866) 900–7463
www.pinetreenetworks.com

Great Works Internet
8 Pomerleau Street
Biddeford
(207) 286–8686, (866) 494–2020
www.gwi.net

Fairpoint Communications
(800) 400–5568
www.fairpoint.com

Northern Lights Internet Services
(207) 761–0257
www.nlis.net

Motor Vehicle and Licensing Information

Motor Vehicle Registration

If you're registering your car for the first time, the first thing you need to do is visit City Hall to pay the motor vehicle excise tax. The excise tax is a yearly fee that comes due every time you register or re-register a vehicle, and the money stays with the city. The amount you pay varies from year to year, depending on the age and value of your car. The excise tax rate ranges from $4.00 to $24.00 per thousand dollars of value. To pay the tax, go to the Treasury Division in Room 102 in City Hall (207–874–8490). The hours are 8:00 A.M. until 4:30 P.M. Monday through Friday. On Thursday the office is open until 7:00 P.M.

Once you've paid your excise tax, then go to the Bureau of Motor Vehicles to complete your new registration. Bring along proof of insurance, the bill of sale for the vehicle, and the title if the model year is 1984 or newer.

Bureau of Motor Vehicles offices are located at 125 Presumpscot Street (207–822–6400) and at 704 Maine Mall Road, South Portland (207–822–0730), in the Maine Mall next to Macy's.

Once you've registered the first time, you can renew in subsequent years using the state's online "Rapid Renewal" service: www.informe.org/bmv/rapid-renewal.

Driver's License

If you have a valid, out-of-state driver's license, you can use it for 30 days after moving to Maine. When you're ready for your new license, go to one of the Bureau of Motor Vehicles offices to turn in your old license and complete a vision screening.

Voter Registration

In Maine you can register to vote anytime, even on election day. Registration can be completed at City Hall, at any Bureau of Motor Vehicles branch office, or at most state and federal social service agencies. Be sure to bring some form of photo identification, such as a driver's license, along with something that shows a current address, such as a checkbook or bill.

You can also mail in your registration to City Hall or the secretary of state's office in Augusta, but you'll still need to send in proof of identity (for example, a photocopy of your driver's license) and something with your current address. Questions can be answered at (207) 874–8677.

Trash Disposal and Recycling

Drive around Portland neighborhoods and you'll see a lot of blue bins sitting on the curb, right next to trash bags made out of light blue plastic. Those are the cornerstones of the city's mandatory curbside recycling program. Residents often grumble about the price of the trash bags, which can be bought at any grocery store, but the damage to your wallet does ensure that you recycle as much of your trash as possible. The blue bins can be purchased for several dollars each at the city's Department of Public Works.

The recycling program takes newspapers and magazines, food boxes, cardboard, glass, aluminum, letters, bulk mail, and a majority of household plastics. For a tutorial on how to separate your trash, visit http://publicworks.portlandmaine.gov/waste.asp or direct your questions to the recycling hotline at (207) 756–8189.

Portland also offers curbside leaf collection in October and November. Leaves should be bagged in the designated biodegradable yard waste bags sold in local retail outlets and placed on the curb on your trash collection day.

In the spring, the city has a "bulky item" pick-up program that allows residents to get rid of large items without having to haul them to the dump themselves. Acceptable items include old mattresses, air conditioners, washers, dryers, and furniture. The dates for the program are announced each year. Each single-family household is allowed to place up to six large items curbside for pick-up. To see a list of items that are allowed, visit www.portlandmaine.gov/public works/heavy.asp.

The hotline for the bulky waste program is the same as the recycling hotline: (207) 756–8189.

If you have trash or yard waste that you need to dispose of yourself, you should take it to the Riverside Recycling facility at 910 Riverside Drive (207–797–6200). The city issues electronic punch cards to eligible residents who want to use the facility. You can apply for a card online at http://recycling.portland maine.gov/riversidedefault.htm or call (207) 756–8189 and a staff member will help you over the phone. There are also numerous businesses listed in the yellow pages that you can pay to haul away your unwanted trash and other items for you.

Post Offices

Portland Post Office
125 Forest Avenue
(800) ASK–USPS

Downtown Station
400 Congress Street
(800) ASK–USPS

Station A
622 Congress Street
(207) 871–8437

Jet Video
199 Pleasant Avenue
(207) 773–9968

Rite Aid
701 Forest Avenue
(207) 871–8437

Library

Portland Public Library
Main Branch
5 Monument Square
(207) 871–1700
The Portland library was founded in 1867 and includes both a main branch in downtown Portland and five neighborhood locations. Most of the neighborhood locations are in or near schools. Hours are Monday, Wednesday, and Friday from 9:00 A.M. until 6:00 P.M., Tuesday and Thursday from noon until 9:00 P.M., and Saturday 9:00 A.M. until 5:00 P.M.

HEALTH CARE

It's no wonder that Portland—with its location two hours north of Boston and with the largest population of any city in the state—is the center of Maine's health care sector. The city has the largest hospital in the state, Maine Medical Center, as well as an array of traditional and holistic medical practitioners who treat everything from advanced-stage cancer to the common cold. The breadth of health options available in Greater Portland attracts patients from all over Maine who are seeking high-quality health care.

This chapter highlights some of the major players on the local health care stage, including the area's two major hospitals (Maine Medical Center and Mercy Hospital), therapeutic recovery programs, holistic health care providers, birthing centers, community counseling centers, support services for a range of disabilities, and the state's major insurance providers. Many of the health care practitioners listed in this chapter accept major health insurance, but you should always confirm the method of payment prior to your visit.

This chapter is an introduction to health care providers and services in Maine, but, due to space limitations, it is necessarily brief. Please note that we do not endorse any of the insurers or health care practitioners listed in this chapter and the care they may or may not provide.

WELLNESS

Acupuncture and Chinese Herbal Center
4 Sheffield Street
(207) 772–5368
Renchi Zhang, MD (China), L.Ac., L.MT, relies on more than 30 years of experience in both Western and Chinese medicine. The Acupuncture and Chinese Herbal Center opened in 1995 and provides care using acupuncture, Chinese herbal medicine, Tui-Na massage, and Asian medicine counseling. Zhang worked in his native China as an orthopedic surgeon for 20 years before studying Asian medicine in Germany and the United States. Because of his background in orthopedics, Zhang specializes in the treatment of musculoskeletal injuries and disorders like arthritis and TMJ. Zhang accepts some insurance but encourages you to call ahead to verify coverage.

Coastal Naturopathic Center
281 Veranda Street
(207) 772–4447
www.coastalnaturalhealth.com
Dr. Richard Maurer, a naturopathic practitioner, and his wife, Alexandra Maurer, a licensed acupuncturist, have run this successful holistic health center in Portland since 1994. Maurer is a member of the American Association of Naturopathic Physicians and is trained in naturopathic medicine and the Bowen Technique—the practice of gentle muscle manipulation that was developed more than 50 years ago in Australia. Maurer uses the Bowen Technique to treat a variety of ailments, including asthma, fibromyalgia, and hip and back pain. The Maurers claim to be able to treat a lengthy list of ailments with their alternative approach, including attention deficit/hyperactivity disorder, Alzheimer's disease, Crohn's disease, and high cholesterol.

Coastal Women's Healthcare
96 Campus Drive, Scarborough
(207) 885–8400
Coastal Women's Healthcare (CWH) is a private office with 10 staff physicians specializing in OB/GYN and related care for women. Staff at CWH, which was formed in 1995 when

two long-standing local OB/GYN practices merged, treat high-risk pregnancy and infertility, in addition to offering routine obstetrical care and gynecological services. All of the staff physicians are also OB/GYN surgeons. Lab, ultrasound, mammography, and bone-density testing are available on-site. Most major health insurance is accepted.

Freeport Integrated Health Center
174 South Freeport Road, Freeport
(207) 865–1183

Dr. James Hendricks, a chiropractor as well as a nutrition therapist, has run this small office specializing in sports-related injury for more than five years. An in-house massage therapist is also available.

Goulding Chiropractic
96 India Street
(207) 775–6782

For more than 15 years, Goulding Chiropractic, located in the Old Port, has helped relieve patients' back pain. The two resident chiropractors, Dr. Michael Goulding and Dr. Garry Bracken, specialize in low-impact chiropractic. Most health insurance is accepted.

Institute of Feng Shui and Geopathology
P.O. Box 838
Portland, ME 04104
(207) 772–7888
www.instituteoffengshui.com

Werner Brandmaier, the owner and chief consultant of the Institute of Feng Shui and Geopathology, enjoyed a long career as an engineer in Austria before quitting more than a decade ago in order to study feng shui. Since then, Brandmaier has apprenticed with several international feng shui masters from China, Europe, and the United States. The institute integrates feng shui (the Eastern tradition that relates the placement of objects to a person's personal energy) and the Western tradition of geopathology (which considers the influence of the earth and underground water currents on human beings) and offers feng shui and geopathology consultations for

private and commercial clients. To become especially keyed in to your environment, you can also buy any number of hard-to-find feng shui and geopathology items (like dowsing rods and power discs) at the institute's online store.

Maine Whole Health Center
4 Milk Street
(207) 828–5645
www.mainewholehealth.com

Cynthia Garner, RN, HNC, LMT; Devra Krassner, ND; and Alan Weiner, DO, CCN, make up the Maine Whole Health Center in Portland's Old Port. These three independent holistic practitioners see patients separately or as part of an integrated holistic health care plan. Maine Whole Health offers more than 20 methods of treatment, or "modalities," including allergy medicine, detoxification, chelation therapy, stress management, intravenous nutrition, and chronic pain therapy. Dr. Weiner provides a unique alternative-therapy service for cancer patients, and Garner, a nurse with close to 30 years' experience in both the mainstream and alternative health worlds, helps patients design an integrated wellness regimen called a "Mind-Body Healing Program."

To Life Chiropractic
190 Route 1, Falmouth
(207) 781–8008

To Life Chiropractic, based in Falmouth, features two chiropractors: Dr. Paul Perreault and Dr. Greg Golliday. The office was founded in 2003 and made a quick name for itself both for the quality of its chiropractic care and for its emphasis on holistic health. For example, staff massage therapists and physical trainers work out of an expanded classroom in the chiropractic office to enhance treatment. Trainers offer breathing and relaxation classes as well as movement and flexibility workshops using the Yamuna body rolling technique. In line with its commitment to overall health, To Life Chiropractic also houses the Total Wellness Center. The center is run by Jill Dewitt, who is certified by the Wellness Alliance Program in New Jersey. Dewitt evaluates stress levels and how they interact with the patient's overall health. Chiropractic and some services at To Life Chiropractic are covered by most health insurance providers. Call the office for more details.

True North Health Center
Foreside Place, 202 Route 1, Falmouth
(207) 781–4488
www.truenorthhealthcenter.org
True North is the brainchild of three nurses who formerly held morning meditation sessions for patients and practitioners at Mercy Hospital in Portland. In 1997 the three women struck out on their own and created True North, an independent health center that focuses on integrated, holistic health care. True North provides a range of services, from OB/GYN treatment to massage and polarity therapy. New patients are encouraged to conduct a free 15-minute intake evaluation with one of the center's advanced practice nurses to develop a well-rounded course of holistic care. True North employs more than a dozen practitioners, who specialize in everything from comprehensive health care for women and men to acupuncture, shamanic healing, and holistic psychiatry. True North also has a store that sells books on holistic health, nutritional supplements, and health care products.

Women to Women
3 Marina Road, Yarmouth
(207) 846–6163, (800) 340–5382
www.womentowomen.com
Located in a quiet suburb of Portland, Women to Women has provided revolutionary health care to women for more than 20 years. The health care clinic was founded by Christiane Northrup, MD; Marcelle Pick, OB/GYN NP; Mary Ellen Fenn, MD; and Annie Rafter, NP. It bills itself as one of the first clinics in the world dedicated to health care for women, by women.

Health practitioners at Women to Women focus on the causes, rather than the symptoms, of illness and stress natural and preventive health care. Clinic staff specialize in hormonal imbalance, premature aging, degenerative and autoimmune diseases, nutrition and digestion, breast health, and depression. The clinic prides itself on helping a woman's body regain the power to heal itself. The Women to Women clinic has developed a natural alternative to hormone replacement therapy called the Women to Women's Personal Program.

HOSPITALS

Maine Medical Center
22 Bramhall Street
(207) 662–0111
www.mmc.org
Maine Medical Center (MMC), the state's premier hospital, is located in the center of Portland's West End neighborhood. First opened in 1875 under the name Maine General Hospital, MMC underwent a $46 million expansion in 1984. Today, the MMC complex now covers more than 1 million square feet and holds 606 licensed beds, making it the largest hospital in northern New England. MMC is a nonprofit, private corporation that spans three campuses in the West End and Deering neighborhoods of Portland and in Scarborough. It includes the Barbara Bush Children's Hospital, honored in 2003 by *Child Magazine* as one of the top 25 children's hospitals in the country, and the Maine Heart Center, a nonprofit organization partnered with five southern Maine hospitals to provide superior cardiac care. As the flagship hospital for the Maine Heart Center, MMC was named one of the

i Maine Health, a Portland-based consortium of Maine hospitals that includes Maine Medical Center, offers continuing "Community Health Education" seminars at classrooms in Scarborough and throughout the state. Topics covered recently include pediatric first aid and breast cancer awareness. For information on upcoming workshops, call Maine Health at (207) 775–7001.

100 best cardiovascular programs in the country in 2003 by Solucient, a nationwide health care resource company.

MMC offers excellent inpatient and outpatient health care. The hospital runs close to three dozen health clinics in and around Portland and offers an ever-growing list of outpatient services at the main hospital on Bramhall Street, including day surgery, lab testing, and cardiac catheterization. MMC is affiliated with the New England Rehabilitation Hospital on Brighton Avenue, the largest rehabilitation center in the state (see this hospital's listing under "Rehabilitation Centers"). The hospital runs the MMC Diabetes Center, the AIDS consultation service, and the Center for Lipids and Cardiovascular Health. It also places a strong emphasis on research and teaching and provides programs in undergraduate through postgraduate medical education. Maine Medical Center offers the area's only hospital-based Integrative Medicine Program, which includes massage therapy and osteopathic manipulation.

Mercy Hospital
144 State Street
(207) 879–3000, (800) 293–6583
www.mercyhospital.com
Affiliated with the Sisters of Mercy convent on State Street in Portland, Mercy Hospital provides thorough inpatient and outpatient health care with a focus on Christian spirituality. The hospital's mission statement, as detailed on its Web site, sums up what distinguishes this smaller of Portland's two hospitals: "Mercy Hospital carries out the healing work of Christ by providing clinically excellent, compassionate health care for all, with special concern for the poor and disadvantaged." Founded in 1918 during a flu epidemic, Mercy began as Queen's Hospital and was originally located in a 25-bed facility on the corner of Congress and State Streets. Today, Mercy Hospital occupies a sprawling brick building along State and Spring Streets and is known for its compassionate caregiving and a sense of social responsibility. Mercy

i The Maine Bureau of Health Web site, www.mainepublichealth.gov, lists more than 100 state-affiliated health care resources and groups.

Hospital's mascot is life-size stuffed animal called the Mercy Bear.

Mercy offers primary care, surgical services, cancer care, and obstetrical care, among other services. The Mercy Family also runs several affiliate agencies, such as the Portland Free Clinic, the Recovery Center (for former substance abusers), and Gary's House, an inexpensive bed-and-breakfast for relatives of patients receiving hospital care in Portland.

In keeping with its goal to serve all members of the population, regardless of income, Mercy makes a special effort to help patients manage billing and access useful health programs in the greater community.

REHABILITATION CENTERS

While both Mercy Hospital and Maine Medical Center offer acute rehabilitation for patients in the days immediately following a debilitating event, a number of agencies in and around Portland focus solely on long-term rehabilitation. The organizations listed here span a range of services, from physical and occupational rehabilitation to recovery programs for alcohol and drug abuse.

Bayside Neurorehabilitation Services
26 Portland Street
(207) 761–8402, (800) 341–4516
Bayside Neurorehabilitation Services, run by Goodwill Industries of Northern New England, bills itself as the most comprehensive acquired-brain-injury rehabilitation facility in Portland. Located in new facilities on Portland Street in the Bayside neighborhood, Bayside offers specialized day treatment programs that include speech therapy, physical therapy, peer support, and psychiatry. Bayside focuses on improving independence for patients with brain injury and therefore conducts many programs in the community. Bayside also runs a

separate residential facility for brain-injured clients. The center accepts all major private and state health insurance.

Crossroads for Women
114 Main Street, Windham
(207) 892–2192

Located in a town about a half-hour drive from Portland, Crossroads for Women is one of the area's only addiction recovery houses strictly for women in the Greater Portland area. The house can accommodate up to 14 women. Children of residents who are under the age of 10 are also allowed to stay at Crossroads. Crossroads offers support services for anorexia/bulimia, cocaine addiction, heroin addiction, parenting, and drug relapse. The house also runs a special program for alcohol dependency. Group and family therapy forms the core of the treatment. Self-pay and some public assistance payments are accepted.

Day One
P.O. Box 231
Cape Elizabeth, ME 04107
(207) 874–1045
www.day-one.org

Day One was founded more than three decades ago to address the underserved community of juvenile drug and alcohol addicts. Today, Day One is a respected resource statewide for children and families struggling with juvenile substance abuse. Day One offers a variety of rehabilitation, prevention, and aftercare programs for adolescents and teens in both outpatient and residential care formats. Home-based family counseling is also provided. Day One's adolescent substance abuse treatment program includes outreach to children in the juvenile justice system. Day One also works to increase aware-

ness about juvenile substance abuse through community outreach and education efforts.

Mercy Hospital Recovery Center
40 Park Road, Westbrook
(207) 879–3600

Operated by Mercy Hospital in Portland (see Mercy's listing in the "Hospitals" section), the Recovery Center is the largest substance abuse treatment center in the state and offers both inpatient and outpatient care. The center's physicians, therapists, skilled nurses, and psychiatrists work with patients to evaluate and treat drug addiction at their outpatient clinic in the neighboring town of Westbrook. Detoxification treatment and medical management of withdrawal are stressed here. The center accepts most insurance and Medicaid.

New England Rehabilitation Hospital of Portland
335 Brighton Avenue
(207) 775–4000
www.nerhp.com

New England Rehabilitation Hospital (NERH) on Brighton Avenue is the largest provider of acute rehabilitation services in the state. NERH is co-owned by Maine Medical Center and HealthSouth Rehabilitation, the largest rehab provider in Maine. At NERH, patients who suffer from mental and physical disabilities as a result of stroke, amputation, head injuries, or other trauma receive a range of services from physical, occupation, and speech therapists. The 100-bed facility accepts all kinds of private and state insurance and receives many of its patients on referral from a doctor, hospital, or nursing home. The facility is accredited by the Joint Commission on Accreditation of Healthcare Organizations. NERH also offers an outpatient clinic to treat patients suffering from trauma such as spinal cord injury and stroke.

Orthopedic & Sports Physical Therapy Clinic
1601 Congress Street
(207) 774–5710

The Orthopedic & Sports Physical Therapy

Clinic has occupied its location on Congress Street for more than a decade, and owner Brett Eberle, a doctor of physical therapy, has practiced for more than 20 years. Eberle and two other physical therapists at the clinic treat patients for a range of orthopedic problems, including lower back pain, fractures, sprains, and injuries related to car accidents or sports. The clinic accepts most major health insurance. Because the clinic is owned entirely by the practicing physical therapists, they claim that this eliminates any potentially restrictive oversight from a physician unfamiliar with physical therapy.

Salvation Army Adult Rehabilitation Center
88 Preble Street
(207) 774–7818

The nationwide network of Salvation Army Adult Rehabilitation Centers (ARCs) emphasizes the empowerment of people struggling with challenges to their mental, physical, and spiritual health. The Portland ARC is a residential facility catering exclusively to men. Group therapy and individual counseling for drug and alcohol addiction and problems related to homelessness form the core of the rehab center's offerings. The Portland ARC also hosts Narcotics Anonymous and Alcoholics Anonymous meetings that are open to both women and men.

SPECIAL SERVICES

Ballard House
131 Spring Street
(207) 773–3938
www.ballardhouse.org

Ballard House provides homelike suites for natural childbirth in accordance with guidelines set by the National Association of Childbearing Centers. The house was named in honor of Martha Ballard, an 18th-century midwife who attended more than 800 births in central Maine. At Ballard House, expectant mothers and their families receive support from a range of qualified staff, including certified midwives, nurse practitioners, doulas,

i The Maine AIDS Hotline provides anonymous test-site referrals, information, and counseling for callers interested in learning more about HIV and AIDS. The hotline number for in-state callers is (800) 851–2437.

massage therapists, and a lactation consultant. Ballard House also sponsors classes and seminars on childbirth and parenting. It accepts some health insurance and negotiates payment plans as needed.

Ballard House operates in conjunction with BirthPartners, a nurse-midwifery office located across the street.

Community Counseling Center
343 Forest Avenue
(207) 874–1030
www.commcc.org

The Community Counseling Center (CCC) in Portland is part of the nonprofit Community Counseling of Maine, Inc., which offers therapy and support services for children, families, and the elderly and disabled. CCC specializes in brief treatment therapy but also offers marriage, family, and couples counseling. The center takes both Medicaid and Medicare as well as most third-party insurance and managed care payments. A sliding scale is available for private pay.

Iris Network Serving the Blind
189 Park Avenue
(207) 774–2162
www.mcbvi.org

Every seven minutes, someone in the United States loses the ability to see. The Iris Network works to help blind Mainers achieve independence through its chain of eight locations throughout the state, each offering rehabilitation, support, and advocacy resources for the blind. The Iris Network was founded in 1905 under the name Maine Institution for the Blind. Early supporters of the Iris Network include Helen Keller, who raised $1,000 to help launch the center, and Civil War hero Joshua Chamberlain, who served on the board. Today, the Iris Network is the premier resource for Maine's blind population and has helped thousands of people adjust to the loss of vision. The rehabilitation center run by the network includes a comprehensive training program and day residence aimed at helping the blind learn to live and work independently.

Maine Center on Deafness
68 Bishop Street, Suite 3
(207) 797–7656 (TTY & V)
(800) 639–3884 (TTY & V)
www.mainecenterondeafness.org

The Maine Center on Deafness (MCD) is a nonprofit organization dedicated to providing resources to and advocating for the state's deaf and hard-of-hearing population. MCD provides a number of services, including a Maine TTY directory, health education and referrals, workshops and classes, and social events. One of the most popular services provided by MCD is the Telecommunications Equipment Program, which supplies free or reduced-cost telephone equipment to Mainers with hearing, speech, or physical disabilities that interfere with their ability to use a regular phone. MCD also sponsors peer support groups in Portland, Augusta, and Bangor as well as Camp Sign-A-Watha, a five-day summer retreat for hearing-imparied children.

Multiple Sclerosis Society of Maine
77 Preble Street
(207) 761–5815, (800) FIGHT–MS
www.msmaine.org

The Maine chapter of the National Multiple Sclerosis Society helps families and individuals struggling with MS find appropriate

i You can contact the local Alcoholics Anonymous chapter by phone at (800) 737–6237 or through their Web site at www.aamaine.org. For information on southern Maine's Narcotics Anonymous group, call (800) 974–0062 or visit www.namaine.org.

resources in the community. The local chapter also hosts a series of peer support groups and community events that help raise local awareness of the disease.

Planned Parenthood of Northern New England
970 Forest Avenue
(207) 797–8881, (800) 230–7526
www.ppne.org

Planned Parenthood of Northern New England (PPNNE) is the largest advocate and provider of reproductive health care and sexuality education in the region. Part of the national nonprofit Planned Parenthood, PPNNE serves nearly 60,000 patients a year at its 26 health centers throughout Maine, New Hampshire, and Vermont. The Portland center offers an array of health services for women, including annual OB/GYN exams, emergency contraception, STD and HIV/AIDS testing and counseling, abortion services, birth control prescriptions, and cervical and breast cancer screenings. PPNNE also advocates for reproductive and health rights for women and provides education to family planning professionals. PPNNE accepts many types of health insurance and also charges on a sliding scale for private-pay patients with limited income.

Portland Community Free Clinic
103 India Street
(207) 874–8982

The Portland Community Free Clinic serves adults with limited income and those without insurance or a primary physician. The clinic is staffed by more than 200 volunteer physicians, nurses, and other medical workers and is run by a partnership between Mercy Hospital and Portland's Public Health Division and the Health and Human Services Department. Many of the volunteer medical staff at the clinic are specialists who run their own private practice elsewhere in the city; thus, an unusually wide range of treatment is available here, including cardiology, dermatology, dentistry, gynecology, gastroenterology, urology, and plastic surgery. The clinic also runs a needle exchange program and provides STD testing and counseling.

Due to the often specialized nature of treatment provided at the clinic, patients are not seen on a walk-in basis. Patients must call ahead to schedule an appointment. The clinic is open Monday through Thursday evenings from 5:00 to 9:00 P.M. Calls are accepted Monday through Thursday from 8:00 A.M. to 5:00 P.M.

HEALTH MAINTENANCE ORGANIZATIONS

The health insurance companies listed below offer a wide range of health insurance packages for Maine residents. We have included the area's biggest players, along with 2005 statistics provided by the state on the number of individuals covered on all fully insured health insurance or HMO plans, a brief description of the plans offered in Maine, and contact information for each.

Dirigo Health

In February 2005 Maine governor John Baldacci's progressive health care plan, Dirigo Health, came into being. The plan, which the governor hopes will assist the state's 130,000 uninsured residents, is one of the few state-sponsored health care plans in the country, and policy makers nationwide are watching it as a possible model. Under Dirigo, small businesses and the self-employed can receive health care insurance with Anthem Blue Cross/Blue Shield at a reduced rate. For more information on Dirigo Health, call (800) 541–4251 or visit www.dirigohealth.maine.gov.

Aetna Health, Inc.
151 Farmington Avenue
Hartford, CT 06156
(800) 323–9930
www.aetna.com
Aetna is one of the nation's largest providers of health care, dental, group life, disability, and long-term care insurance. The company has branches in all 50 states and reported revenue of $25.1 billion in 2006. In Maine, Aetna is second only to Anthem Blue Cross/Blue Shield in the number of locals covered under its insurance umbrella. In 2005 the state reported that 45,609 Mainers were covered under Aetna health insurance or HMO plans. The company offers HMO and point-of-service plans for individuals and small or large groups.

Anthem Blue Cross/Blue Shield of Maine
2 Gannett Drive, South Portland
(207) 822–8282, (800) 527–7706
www.anthem.com
Anthem Blue Cross/Blue Shield is the largest health care provider in the state, covering more than 257,000 Mainers under individual, small group, and large group HMOs; point-of-service plans; Medicare supplements; and nonmanaged care plans. Maine is one of nine states nationwide that have local Anthem offices. Nationally, the company has received the highest performance rating from the National Committee on Quality Assurance. In 2005 Anthem also became the provider for the statewide Dirigo Health Insurance Plan, which was created by Maine governor John Baldacci to help small businesses and individuals in the state afford quality health care.

Cigna Healthcare of Maine, Inc.
2 Stonewood Drive, Freeport
(800) 244–6224
www.cigna.com
Nationwide, Cigna Healthcare covers millions of individuals under a variety of health insurance plans. In Maine, Cigna provides coverage for almost 24,000 residents under

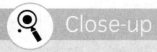

Close-up

Maine Medical Center Healing Garden

Just outside the entrance to the Maine Medical Center's children's cancer unit sits a special garden that its creators hope will help heal the body as well as the mind. The Maine Medical Center Healing Garden was completed in June 2004, the result of volunteer efforts from local horticulturists, a landscaper with a background in environmental energy, and an experienced local feng shui practitioner. This small garden in the center of Scarborough functions as a quiet retreat from the stress and pace of the world outside.

Susan Babb, a horticulturist at O'Donal's Nursery in Gorham, says she became convinced that Portland could benefit from a healing garden when she attended a lecture at Harvard University in 2001 on the centuries-old tradition. "A healing garden is a collection of plants on a landscape designed to provide anyone using the space with healing power," says Babb. "The concept has been around since the Middle Ages, when the square in center of the hospital was a garden for herbs raised to treat patients."

The garden, which is roughly 130 feet long and 40 feet wide, features hundreds of plants known for their medicinal or calming influence, including daffodils, tulips, chrysanthemums, and evergreen trees. Ted Carter, president of the Carter Design Group in Portland, volunteered his experience as a landscape designer and energy specialist to design the garden landscape. Carter used curvilinear design, open space, and a still pool in the garden's center to help create a soothing environment for spiritual, mental, and physical renewal. Local feng shui master Werner Brandmaier acted as a consultant during the garden's construction to help create a relaxing design.

The Healing Garden is open to the public 24 hours a day, year-round. Carter says the best time to view the soft colors of the flowers in the garden is during the summer months from mid-June to mid-September, although he stresses that the garden's healing properties are potent in any season.

"Most people look forward to spending time there," Carter says. "People look forward to sitting there. It's very tranquil."

HMO and point-of-service plans to large groups. Cigna received a rating of excellent from the National Committee on Quality Assurance in 2003.

Harvard Pilgrim Healthcare
48 Free Street
(888) 333–4742
www.harvardpilgrim.org
Harvard Pilgrim is the oldest nonprofit health care insurance provider in New England. The 30-year-old company, which is based in Massachusetts, provides health insurance to residents of Massachusetts and Maine. Harvard Pilgrim has received a rating of excellent from the National Committee on Quality Assurance. The company provides HMO and point-of-service plans to small and large groups and HMO plans for individuals. Harvard Pilgrim covers more than 12,000 Mainers.

Patriot Mutual
14 Maine Street, Brunswick
(800) 491–7336
www.patriotmutual.com
Patriot Mutual has been providing dental
health insurance statewide since 1985, with
plans for individuals and companies. In 2002
Patriot began offering property and casualty
insurance to clients in Maine, New Hampshire,
and Vermont. As of 2005, more than 25,500
Mainers were enrolled in one of Patriot
Mutual's dental insurance plans. Employers
need have only two or more eligible employees to qualify for the insurance, which is also
available to individuals.

RESOURCES AND REFERRALS

**City of Portland Health and
Human Services Department**
389 Congress Street, Room 304
(207) 874–8784
www.ci.portland.me.us/hhs/hhs.asp
The city of Portland offers a handful of free
programs, including Maternal and Child
Health home visiting, Perinatal Smoking Sur-
veillance, and Lead Poisoning Prevention education. Health promotion aimed at providing
information about chronic diseases and low-
cost health care for the city's poor forms the
crux of the Public Health Division's programs.
The city also runs school-based health clinics
at six Student Health Centers in schools
throughout the city.

i Food Addicts Recovery Anonymous
is a national nonprofit support network for people struggling with compul-
sive eating. The Portland chapter was
formed in 1998 and currently holds three
meetings a week. For more information,
visit the group's Web site at www.food
addicts.org.

Maine Health Information Center
16 Association Drive, Manchester
(207) 623–2555
www.mhic.org
This independent nonprofit has worked since
1976 to provide Maine and northern New
England with access to reliable information
about health care providers. The Maine
Health Information Center (MHIC) was originally incorporated to provide data on the
health care industry to providers, employers,
and the state. Today, the MHIC continues to
perform this function, primarily serving as a
resource for policy makers, but patients
interested in researching available care can
also make good use of the MHIC Web site,
which includes links to MaineCare (the
state's health program for children, the elderly and disabled, and low-income residents)
and the Maine Health Management Coalition
(a network between the state and area businesses that provides information on local
doctors and hospitals).

CHILD CARE AND EDUCATION

CHILD CARE

As dual wage-earning families become increasingly more common, reliable child care in turn becomes more and more crucial. Fortunately, Portland (and Maine as a whole) has a network of committed, professional child care providers who make quality child care a priority. It's not surprising, then, that Maine was cited as the best state in the nation to raise a child in 1999 by the Children's Rights Council, an advocacy group based in Washington, D.C. Here in Portland, several reliable referral services offer excellent resources for choosing quality child care and advocating effectively for our children and schools, and independent support services exist to assist parents at every step in their child's development—from infants to adults. At the state level, the Maine Department of Health and Human Services (DHHS) keeps close tabs on child care providers and maintains a public list of those with violations.

For families looking for child care, the DHHS Office of Child Care and Head Start is a great resource. The department's Web site (www.state.me.us/dhs/infoparents.htm) lists child care centers, summer programs, in-home care, and programs for teens. Their publication "Steps to Choosing Childcare" gives important tips on finding the right child care provider. The department also offers other publications, including various government reports on the state of child care in Maine; tips on financial aid for child care; and information on parents' rights and responsibilities.

The DHHS Office of Child Care and Head Start funds eight resource development centers (RDCs) throughout the state that provide in-depth coverage of child care providers by region. Portland's local RDC is the Scarborough-based agency Child Care Connections, which is described in detail under "Referral Services."

This section does not attempt to list all of the child care arrangements available, nor does it recommend individual providers. Instead, we have tried to supply resources for evaluating individual providers, the means to advocate for your child, and information on support groups for you and your family. This list of resources should put you on the right track to finding healthy, nurturing child care in one of the best places in the country to raise children.

Referral Services

Child Care Connections
136 Route 1, Scarborough
(207) 396–6566, (888) 917–1100
www.childcaremaine.org
One of Maine's network of eight child care resource development centers, Child Care Connections (CCC) provides parents with child care referrals and information on choosing a quality child care provider and also offers a child care subsidy program to income-eligible families. CCC was established in 1984 to service Cumberland County and is funded in part by the Maine Department of Health and Human Services. Today, the private/public partnership provides services to child care providers, employers, and parents.

i To receive a free copy of "Choosing Quality Child Care in Maine," call the Maine Department of Health and Human Services Office of Child Care and Head Start at (207) 287–5060. You can also find information about child care at www.maine.gov/dhhs/occhs/infoparents.htm.

Parenting Classes in Portland

Kids First Center
222 St. John Street
(207) 761–2709
www.kidsfirstcenter.org
Specializing in divorce and separation support.

Maine Medical Center—Family
Practice Center
272 Congress Street
(207) 842–7345

YWCA—The Parenting Place
87 Spring Street
(207) 874–1130, ext. 3063

While CCC refrains from recommending any particular provider, the agency does offer a number of comprehensive contacts for parents shopping around for the right place for their children. Trained referral staff will help you locate providers in your area who meet your needs, will give you child care checklists to take along with you during visits to prospective programs, and will provide information on how to find and hire in-home caregivers. The referral staff can also help you determine if your family is eligible for child care subsidies offered by the agency. Ask for a copy of their free booklet, which lists dozens of local and national parenting and child care resources.

For providers, CCC offers a number of resources, including training programs and workshops, a lending library, information on state licensing and regulations, and information on starting and running a day-care facility. CCC also helps businesses establish child care policies.

Cultural Care Au Pair
1 Memorial Drive
Cambridge MA 02142
(800) 333–6056
www.efaupair.org
Cultural Care Au Pair is a part of EF Education, which offers language education and cultural exchange to young people from more than 30 countries. Cultural Care Au Pair provides families with carefully screened men and women between the ages of 18 and 26 who work as live-in nannies during a yearlong cultural exchange program. The live-in au pairs work up to 45 hours a week, no more than 10 hours a day, providing child care in exchange for room and board. The average cost to the host family is roughly $260 per week, regardless of the number of children requiring care. Contact the above home office number for the regional coordinator for southern Maine.

National Association for the
Education of Young Children
1509 16th Street, NW
Washington, DC 20036
(800) 424–2460
www.naeyc.org
Child care providers register with the nonprofit National Association for the Education of Young Children (NAEYC) voluntarily and must meet a strict set of guidelines to receive accreditation. Contact NAEYC via phone or snail mail or visit their Web site to receive a list of the Portland child care providers they accredit. NAEYC also offers a slew of other resources for families and providers and advocates for quality child care. Their Web site provides links to articles on parenting and child development and the latest on federal and local legislative trends related to children.

i To find out if a child care provider has ever been charged with child abuse or neglect, call the Maine Department of Health and Human Services Day Care Licensing Department at (800) 452–1926.

Special Care

Early Childhood and Family Services
Governor Baxter School for the Deaf
Mackworth Island, Falmouth
(207) 781–6337
Early Childhood and Family Services (ECFS) is part of the statewide Educational Services Department, with offices in Portland, Bangor, and Aroostook. ECFS provides support and education on deafness for families with deaf or hearing-impaired infants, toddlers, and preschool children. Along with several support resources, the agency offers home visits and day-care/preschool observations for children up to age five who have hearing loss. The Portland ECFS office, located at the Governor Baxter School for the Deaf on Mackworth Island, also sponsors the Parent-Infant-Toddler Program—a twice-weekly playgroup facilitated by therapists for hearing-impaired children three years old and younger.

Hear ME Now!
Yarmouth Hall, Suite 201
19 Yarmouth Drive at Pineland Farms, New Gloucester
(207) 688–4544
This preschool and auditory/oral learning center is designed to meet the needs of deaf and hard-of-hearing children. Hear ME Now! provides children with individual attention in a language-rich preschool environment that includes group activities and daily individual and group therapy. The preschool is located in classrooms designed to minimize background noise and reverberation.

The Spurwink School
Therapeutic School
899 Riverside Street
(207) 283–3846
www.spurwinkschool.org
The Spurwink School runs five therapeutic preschool classrooms in Cumberland County for children ages three to five with developmental disabilities, behavioral disorders, or autism/pervasive development disorders (PDDs). The child-to-staff ratio in the Portland preschool is 1:1, and children learn from a multidisciplinary team that includes occupational therapists and speech therapists. The school emphasizes those skills that are most important for independent functioning and tailors a learning program according to each child's specific needs. Typical programs include developing communication, social, and pre-academic skills.

The preschool offers primarily center-based services, but parents may also request services in the home.

i Learning to adjust to the pitter-patter of more than one pair of little feet? Try calling the Greater Portland Mothers of Multiples Club, a support group for moms of twins and higher-order multiples. The group meets the first Wednesday of every month. For more information, call Kate at (207) 828–4948.

EDUCATION

Portland Public Schools is the state's largest school district, serving 7,200 students. Facilities range from a one-room schoolhouse built in 1895 on Cliff Island to a state-of-the-art elementary school in downtown Portland.

Portland High School, located on the peninsula in downtown Portland, was the third public high school to be established in the United States. It counts among its graduates John Ford, the well-known movie director, and Admiral Robert Peary, the explorer credited with discovering the North Pole.

Portland teachers recently ratified a new contract that turns 40 years of tradition on its head. Believed to be the first of its kind in Maine, the new contract stipulates that teachers will receive pay increases based on performance in the classroom and their professional achievements rather than years of experience alone.

Maine is not very diverse, but Portland's status as a refugee resettlement community has given it the most diverse student population in the state. Students at Portland High

School, for example, come from 30 different countries and speak 50 languages.

For more information on each school, visit www.portlandschools.org.

Elementary Schools

Cliff Island
P.O. Box 7
Cliff Island, 04109
(207) 766–2885

East End Community School
195 North Street
(207) 874–8228

Fred P. Hall
23 Orono Road
(207) 874–8205

Harrison Lyseth
175 Auburn Street
(207) 874–8215
Howard C. Reiche
166 Brackett Street
(207) 874–8175

Longfellow School
432 Stevens Avenue
(207) 874–8195

Marada Adams Community School
48 Moody Street
(207) 874–8228

Nathan Clifford
180 Falmouth Street
(207) 874–8180

Peaks Island
4 Church Street
Peaks Island
(207) 766–2528

Presumpscot Elementary
69 Presumpscot Street
(207) 874–8220

Riverton School
1600 Forest Avenue
(207) 874–8210

Middle Schools

King Middle School
92 Deering Avenue
(207) 874–8140

Lincoln Middle School
522 Stevens Avenue
(207) 874–8145

Lyman Moore Middle School
171 Auburn Street
(207) 874–8150

High Schools

Casco Bay High School
196 Allen Avenue
(207) 874–8160

Deering High School
370 Stevens Avenue
(207) 874–8260

Portland Arts and Technology
196 Allen Avenue
(207) 874–8165

Portland High School
284 Cumberland Avenue
(207) 874–8250

Higher Education

After graduation from high school, Portland students have lots of options for continuing their education. The University of Southern Maine, part of the statewide University of Maine system, is located in the heart of Portland and has satellite campuses in Gorham and Lewiston. Located just across the street from USM's Portland campus is the state's only law school, one of the smallest in the nation. The University of Maine School of Law is an administrative unit of USM.

Portland also has a well-regarded art

school, the Maine College of Art, located right in Portland's downtown arts district. And students who are looking for vocational training need go no farther than across the bridge to the Southern Maine Community College in South Portland. Located right on Casco Bay, SMCC boasts probably one of the most scenic community college campuses in the country. There's also Andover College, which offers associate's degrees in a variety of subjects, including business.

Students willing to commute a short distance have access to many excellent centers of higher education, including the private Bowdoin College, just a 30-minute drive away in the town of Brunswick. Bates College in Lewiston is about 40 minutes away. The University of New England in Biddeford, about a half-hour away, is the home of Maine's only medical school—a college of osteopathic medicine—and a brand new college of pharmacy.

Andover College
901 Washington Avenue
(800) 639–3110
www.andovercollege.com

Maine College of Art
97 Spring Street
(207) 775–3052
www.meca.edu

Southern Maine Community College
2 Fort Road
South Portland
(207) 741–5500 (general information)
www.smccme.edu

University of Maine School of Law
246 Deering Avenue
(207) 780–4355
http://mainelaw.maine.edu/

University of New England
11 Hills Beach Road
Biddeford
(207) 283–0171
www.une.edu

University of Southern Maine
P.O. Box 9300
Portland, 04104-9300
(207) 780–4141, (800) 800–4USM
www.usm.maine.edu

PART-DAY AND AFTER-SCHOOL PROGRAMS

Many school districts in the Greater Portland area offer before-school and after-school child care programs for school-age students. In Portland, programs are offered through the city's Parks and Recreation Department. Often, the before-school program includes breakfast. Before-school and after-school programs are most often located at the child's school and include games, sports, and study time. Various churches and synagogues in the city also offer after-school child care.

The local YMCA offers a before- and after-school program at its headquarters on Forest Avenue in downtown Portland, as well as discounted gym membership for teens and arts classes for children. The Y also runs day-care programs for children ages six months to four years. Call the Portland YMCA's child care program at (207) 874–1111 for more information.

Parent and Family magazine, the local publication for parents, is another great resource for families. The magazine, available at any local library, lists several playgroups in every edition.

SUPPORT ORGANIZATIONS

Autism Society of Maine
72B Main Street, Winthrop
(800) 273–5200
www.asmonline.org
The Autism Society of Maine advocates for quality services for people with autism and their families. The society offers a toll-free information line; a lending library; a newsletter; educational materials; workshops for parents, educators, and providers; a family retreat weekend; and a summer camp for autistic children.

The Center for Grieving Children
49 York Street
(207) 775–5216
www.cgcmaine.org

The Center for Grieving Children (CGC) was founded in 1987 by former minister Bill Hemmons following the death of his sister. In the wake of his sister's passing, Hemmons tried to find help and support for her young daughter, Erin. Through his experience supporting Erin, Hemmons realized how profoundly unsettling death can be in the lives of the young. To help others like Erin, Hemmons founded CGC as a free resource for families and children struggling with the loss of a loved one.

Today, CGC offers a number of support services for children and families. The peer-support groups forming the core of CGC's programs are clustered according to developmental stage, from four years old (the Little's Group) all the way up to adult. In recent years, the center has added Tender Living Care, a program that provides peer support for families with a member experiencing a life-threatening illness, and the Multicultural Program, which helps newly immigrated children process the loss of their native homes. CGC has a small paid staff and a roster of more than 100 active and part-time volunteers. Volunteers undergo intensive training before being placed as peer-support group facilitators. CGC also occasionally provides grief support off-site for those unable to come to Portland, as well as community outreach for schools, businesses, and organizations experiencing loss. All services are free.

Maine Children's Alliance
303 State Street, Augusta
(207) 623–1868
www.mainechildrensalliance.org

The Maine Children's Alliance is a coalition of individuals and organizations that advocates for state policies to improve the lives of children, youth, and families. Started in 1994, the Maine Children's Alliance currently has a staff of seven based in Augusta. Individual membership to the alliance costs $25 a year. Members participate in statewide surveys, receive support from the alliance for grassroots community action for children, and receive periodic updates about Maine's children and issues affecting them. The Maine Children's Alliance also sponsors the popular Champions for Children/Giraffe Awards, which every year identifies local individuals and organizations that "stick their neck out for kids."

Mainely Parents
188 State Street, Suite 400
(207) 842–2984
(800) 249–5506 (talk line)
www.mainelyparents.org

Mainely Parents is a statewide network of grassroots support groups for parents and families. The local chapter, with offices on State Street in Portland, offers parental support groups with names like "Parents of Teens" and "Dads Only," as well as parenting courses. A statewide toll-free talk line is available for parents in crisis or for those just looking for extra support. The help line, which is available Monday through Friday from 9:00 A.M. to 4:00 P.M., assists parents with challenges ranging from a teething child to a runaway teen. Mainely Parents also distributes a quarterly newsletter, *Maine Parent Express*, which focuses on preventing child abuse and neglect and offers parenting tips. The current edition of the newsletter and back issues from that year are available on their Web site.

Office of Multilingual and Multicultural Programs—Portland Schools
150 Ocean Avenue
(207) 874–8135
www.multilingual.portlandschools.org

Portland's population includes hundreds of recently immigrated children, so the city's schools have made a concerted effort to help students from other countries feel comfortable in the classroom. The Office of Multilingual and Multicultural Programs, funded by the city, offers training for English-as-a-Second-Language teachers affiliated with the

Portland public schools and is in charge of the intake and assessment for multilingual students entering the city's school system. The office also offers parent outreach programs to help keep multilingual families informed about and involved with their child's education. The offices on Ocean Avenue house their Multilingual Resource Library, with books for adults and children in eight languages, foreign-language videos, ESL activity books, maps, and more.

MEDIA

In our own travels, we've found that the surest way to feel like a native is to pick up the local paper and give it a nice, leisurely read over a morning cup of coffee at the local cafe. Here in Portland, you won't have any problem finding great media resources. In fact, your biggest challenge might be to decide which newspaper, television news show, or radio station to spend your time on.

Recent population growth in the city and its suburbs and an increasingly diverse readership make Greater Portland a prime target for media entrepreneurs looking to find their own lucrative niche. And for the first time in her history, Portland's media outlets, which had for most of the 20th century been locally owned, are now largely owned by out-of-state companies. Despite the growing influence of national and regional media companies, some of Portland's media outlets have bucked the national trend and continue to be owned and operated by locals. The greatest example of local ownership is in Portland's suburban weekly newspapers, whose number has mushroomed in the past two years from one weekly per suburb to three or four in some areas. And all of Portland's weeklies, from the *Portland Phoenix* (a funky alternative weekly owned by the *Boston Phoenix*, in Massachusetts) to the suburban *Portland Forecaster* or the *Current Weekly*, compete in some way with the mother of local print media—the *Portland Press Herald*.

Our local daily, the *Portland Press Herald*, remains the top provider of statewide news despite its 1998 sale to the Washington-based Seattle Times Company. Since the *Press Herald* was founded by Guy Gannett in 1921, the paper has undergone numerous editorial and cosmetic changes, from offering an evening edition to publishing a biweekly

for retirees. Today, it is largely regarded as the best daily print resource for southern Maine news.

A healthy mix of locally owned weekly newspapers also serves the city and its suburbs, including the *Current Weekly* (covering Scarborough, South Portland, Cape Elizabeth, Westbrook, Gorham, Windham, and Standish) and the *Forecaster* (three separate editions serving Portland and the suburbs, including Falmouth, South Portland, and Cape Elizabeth).

On television, you can get your daily news fix on one of three local stations: WCSH Channel 6 (offering the longest-running and most popular local broadcast), WGME Channel 13, and WMTW Channel 8. These stations offer several broadcasts throughout the day of breaking news and human-interest stories covering southern Maine, the state, and beyond.

The top-rated radio stations in the city are owned by three companies: Saga Communications of Detroit, Michigan; Citadel Communication of Las Vegas, Nevada; and Harron Capital of Pennsylvania. Recently, Nassau Broadcasting of New Jersey joined the fray, purchasing frequencies 104.7 FM, 106.7 FM, and 107.5 FM.

Portland is also home to an award-winning community radio powerhouse—WMPG. Broadcast from a white house on the University of Southern Maine campus in Portland, WMPG is sponsored by listener donations, local businesses, and the student body of the University of Southern Maine. More than 100 volunteers vie for slots in the 24-hour broadcasting schedule. You can listen to anything from a debate on local and national policy to music as varied as zydeco, Harlem Renaissance jazz, and Eastern European techno broadcast by a Polish deejay speaking entirely in his native tongue. Tune in for information on WMPG's frequent free parties, which are often worth a visit.

Needless to say, here in Portland, news about life in our community and beyond is not hard to come by. The toughest part is figuring out which publication or broadcast to spend time on. This chapter lists the major media outlets and tells you where to find them. You'll feel like a native in no time.

DAILY NEWSPAPERS

Portland Press Herald
390 Congress Street
(207) 791–6650
www.pressherald.com
This section actually should be titled "Daily Newspaper" in the singular because the *Portland Press Herald* is really the only daily publication in town. As one local suburban weekly editor summed it up: "The *Portland Press Herald* remains the 800-pound gorilla of local newspapers."

And this gorilla has been around longer than any other news outlet in the state. In 1921 Maine publishing guru Guy Gannett purchased the *Portland Daily Press* and the *Portland Herald* and combined the two publications under the name *Portland Press Herald*. The following year, construction began on the seven-story building at the corner of Exchange, Federal, and Market Streets that to this day houses the 50-plus staff members working at the *Press Herald*.

Guy Gannett had an eye for news, as they say, and also a good handle on business. Besides his ownership of the daily *Waterville Morning Sentinel* to the north and the *Kennebec Journal* to the south, Gannett purchased a radio station and named it after himself—WGAN—and in 1954 the Gannett Company, then run by his daughter Jean, purchased its first television station. The station was also named WGAN but in 1983 was renamed WGME-TV (see the "Television Stations" section for more on WGME). Neither WGME nor

For an instant link to the goings-on in southern and central Maine, visit www.mainetoday.com. Run by the Blethen Maine Newspapers division of the Seattle Times Company, this Web site includes online versions of three of the largest dailies in the state—the *Portland Press Herald*, the *Kennebec Journal*, and the *Morning Sentinel*.

WGAN is currently owned by the *Portland Press Herald*.

Since the early 20th century, Guy Gannett and the company he created have tried various incarnations of print news on the Portland audience. Along with the *Portland Press Herald*'s daily editions, the Gannett Publishing Company printed a late-afternoon edition called the *Evening Express* from 1925 to 1991 and a short-lived biweekly for the retirement population, which ran from 1985 to 1987. Finally, after nearly a decade of Gannett news in Maine, the granddaughter of Guy Gannett sold the *Portland Press Herald* and two other Maine dailies (the *Central Maine Morning Sentinel* and the *Kennebec Journal*) to the Seattle Times Company.

Today, the newspaper is published seven times a week under Editor-in-Chief Jeannine Guttmann and is partnered with WMTW television news. The Sunday edition contains extra sections such as "Maine/New England," "The Outdoors," and "Insight." For those interested in local op-ed writing, Bill Nemitz's regular column is a must-read. The *Press Herald* can be found in any major gathering place and in dozens of vending machines around Greater Portland.

ALTERNATIVE WEEKLY NEWSPAPERS

Portland Phoenix
482 Congress Street
(207) 773–8900
www.portlandphoenix.com
The *Portland Phoenix* fills the void left by the demise of the locally owned *Maine Times* and

Casco Bay Weekly and is the state's largest weekly newspaper. It's also free and can be found all over town and as far north as Augusta. The *Portland Phoenix* is a subsidiary of the Phoenix Media/Communications Group based in Boston, which also owns FNX radio, an alternative music station in Portland.

Until 2002 the *Portland Phoenix* was dealing with some pretty heady competition from the decades-old homegrown alternative weekly, the *Casco Bay Weekly*. But after years of financial struggle, *CBW* closed up shop in 2004, leaving the *Phoenix* as the only alternative weekly in town.

Since its launch in 1999, the *Portland Phoenix* has thrived and now boasts a circulation of about 44,000. The paper offers a distinctive voice apart from the *Portland Press Herald* and is often looked to as the local source for music and entertainment happenings in the city. The *Portland Phoenix*, like its parent paper in Boston, also tempers in-depth coverage of what's hot and what's not with hard-news features and quirky human-interest stories that can't be found anywhere else. And because of the *Portland Phoenix*'s connection to Boston, it often includes articles on national political topics siphoned from the Boston bureau.

You can find the *Portland Phoenix* pretty much anywhere—in any major gathering place (coffee shops, bars, libraries, bookstores) or in bright-red vending machines scattered up and down Congress Street and throughout the downtown. A must-read for those seeking a good time in Portland.

MAJOR SUBURBAN WEEKLIES

Current and American Journal
27 Gorham Road, Scarborough
(207) 883–3533
www.keepmecurrent.com

The *Current*, published by Scarborough resident Lee Hews Casler, is one of the area's newest weeklies. Since launching in 2001, the *Current* has expanded from its original

coverage of the suburbs of Scarborough and Cape Elizabeth to include South Portland. In 2003 Casler purchased the *American Journal,* a weekly covering Westbrook, Gorham, Windham, and Standish. Today, the newspapers have a combined circulation of roughly 13,500 in and around the city.

The *Current*'s staff is small, with a handful of reporters and three editors, divided between two offices in Westbrook and Scarborough. The coverage tends to focus on issues important to the community as a whole, such as school events, city council meetings, and senior news. The *Current*'s sports section has its own editor and is one of the best among community papers. Its dozens of color photos of local high school sports stars regularly receive rave reviews from parents. You can pick up the *Current* in stores in its coverage area or by calling the number listed.

The Forecaster
8 Fundy Road, Falmouth
(207) 781–3661
www.theforecaster.net

The Forecaster, which originally covered the northern suburbs of Falmouth and Yarmouth, expanded in 2003 to cover South Portland, Cape Elizabeth, and Scarborough. In 2004 it added a Portland edition. The three *Forecaster* incarnations are all weekly newspapers focusing on news and human-interest stories in the various communities in their coverage area. The Portland edition usually includes several news stories on city politics that are hard to find anywhere else. *The Forecaster* is free and can be picked up most anywhere, including in vending machines in downtown Portland. For a complete list of the distribution sites, visit their Web site.

Mainebiz
30 Milk Street
(207) 761–8379, (800) BIZNEWS
www.Mainebiz.biz

Mainebiz is an award-winning newspaper focusing on business issues throughout the state. Founded in 1994, it was purchased in 1999 by Massachusetts-based Worcester Publishing Ltd., which expanded the coverage, changed the editorial staff, and revamped the design and tone of the publication. The newspaper has won several awards for the quality of its writing and reporting. *Mainebiz* is published twice a month by a five-person editorial staff with offices in the heart of Portland's Old Port. The staff is comprised of former general-interest journalists who try to make this business newspaper as accessible as possible for everyone from entrepreneurs checking out their industry's news to the average reader looking for an interesting feature article. *Mainebiz* is mailed directly to Maine businesses and subscribers but can also be found at a few locations, including the JavaNet coffee shop on Exchange Street and the Portland Public Library.

MAGAZINES

Port City Life Magazine
53 Exchange Street
(207) 774-3775
www.portcitylife.com
Port City Life is Portland's youngest magazine. Started in 1999 by former owner Carolyn Cianchette, the magazine was purchased by a former freelance writer, Laurie Hyndman, in 2002. The magazine, currently published six times a year, focuses on lifestyle and recreation in and around the city. The "Beyond 295" section offers great suggestions on day trips in southern Maine. You can pick up a copy at any bookstore and at most coffee shops.

Portland Monthly Magazine
722 Congress Street
(207) 775-4339
www.portlandmonthly.com
Portland Monthly Magazine is the city's most established local glossy. Published by local poet Colin Sargeant, the magazine has been highlighting the city's famous people, favorite activities, and issues of interest since 1985. The magazine also includes a monthly fiction

installment and interviews with famous Mainers or part-time Mainers (past interviews have included Liv Tyler, Mel Gibson, and Steven King). *Portland Monthly Magazine* is a great resource for anyone looking to uncover local experiences or stories that normally only residents are privy to.

TELEVISION STATIONS

WCSH 6
1 Congress Square
(207) 828-6666
www.wcsh6.com
WCSH 6 has been broadcasting television programming for its affiliate NBC for more than 50 years from its central location in downtown Portland. The channel also consistently broadcasts the most-watched local 6:00 P.M. news show (as well as other shows at 5:00 P.M. and 5:30 P.M.) plus noon shows and early-morning installments. WCSH is also the only station of the three listed in this section to offer its own local news magazine show. Called *207* after Maine's area code, the show explores local news stories in-depth and covers local culture, with special segments such as cooking classes and interior design tips. The show airs every evening. Also, *Bill Green's Maine*, which airs every Saturday night, follows reporter Bill Green during his outdoor adventures in the state.

WGME 13
1335 Washington Avenue
(207) 797-1313
www.wgme.com
Owned by the Sinclair Media Group, WGME 13 is the local CBS affiliate and broadcasts news several times daily from its offices on Washington Avenue. The *Daybreak* show (5:00 to 7:00 A.M.) includes a recap of the previous night's news and any breaking news as well as lighter spots on cooking and health. A noon show, three evening news broadcasts (at 5:00 P.M., 5:30 P.M., and 6:00 P.M.), and an 11:00 P.M. roundup of the day's news finish out the broadcast news offerings.

WMTW 8
477 Congress Street
(207) 775–1800
www.wmtw.com
WMTW is the local ABC affiliate. The news team broadcasts local news at 5:00 A.M., noon, 6:00 P.M., and 11:00 P.M. Local Time Warner Channel 9 also rebroadcasts WMTW news every day around the clock. WMTW has an arrangement with the *Portland Press Herald* to share news and weather reports.

RADIO STATIONS

News and Talk

WGAN 560 AM
www.wgan.com

WLOB 1310 AM

WMEA 90.1 FM
Maine Public Radio
www.mainepublicradio.org

WZAN 970 AM
www.970wzan.com

Sports

WJAE 1440 AM

WJJB 900 AM

Rock

WBLM 102.9 FM
www.wblm.com

WCLZ 98.9 FM ("The Point")
www.989wclz.com

WCYY 94.3 FM
www.wcyy.com

WFNK ("Frank") 107.5 FM

WHXR 106.7 and 104.7 FM ("The Bone")

Contemporary/Soft Rock

WBOR 91.1 FM
WJBQ 97.9 FM

i **Blunt Radio**, an award-winning debate show for teens, airs weekly on WMPG. The Blunt program provides free radio deejay training for Portland-area teens and young inmates in the area juvenile prison. Visit www.bluntradio.org for more information.

www.wjbq.com

WMEK 99.9 FM ("Kiss")

WMGX 93.1 FM ("The Coast")
www.wmgx.com

WRED 95.9 FM

Oldies

WYAR 88.3 FM

WYNZ 100.9 FM
www.wynz.com

Country

WPOR 101.9 FM
www.wpor.com

Classical

WBQW 106.3 FM

Jazz

WBCI 1490 FM
www.wbci.net

Christian

WMSJ 89.3 FM
www.wmsj.org

Community Radio

WMPG 90.9 FM/104.1 FM
www.wmpg.org

INDEX

Y

Z

ABOUT THE AUTHORS

Sara Donnelly, a Portland native, works as a journalist and a writer. The former staff writer for the city's alternative weekly, the *Portland Phoenix*, Sara is currently the senior writer for *Mainebiz* newspaper. She has also written for the *Boston Phoenix* and *Down East Magazine*. Two of Sara's favorite things about Portland are its proximity to the ocean (beautiful) and its unusually bountiful collection of ice-cream shops (yummy). Sara is willing to bet you $10 you'll love Portland. And if you don't love it, Sara thinks it's because you're feeling cranky. Have some ice cream—it'll cheer you up.

Meredith Goad is a native of Memphis, Tennessee, and has also lived in Colorado, Missouri, and Maryland. She moved to Portland 17 years ago, fell in love with the city, and decided to stay. She is an award-winning reporter for the *Portland Press Herald/Maine Sunday Telegram,* where she began her career as a science writer and covered the environmental beat. Recently she moved to the features department, where she writes for the Sunday features sections and produces a weekly food and dining column called "Soup to Nuts."

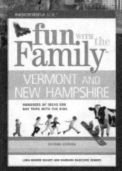

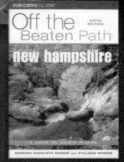